The Goldsboro Broken Arrow

– Second Edition

The B-52 Crash of January 24, 1961, and Its Potential as a Tipping Point for Nuclear War

BY JOEL DOBSON

Copyright © 2013 Joel Dobson.

All rights reserved. No part of this book may be reproduced, stored, or transmitted by any means—whether auditory, graphic, mechanical, or electronic—without written permission of both publisher and author, except in the case of brief excerpts used in critical articles and reviews. Unauthorized reproduction of any part of this work is illegal and is punishable by law.

ISBN: 978-1-4834-0132-4 (sc)
ISBN: 978-1-4834-0131-7 (e)

Because of the dynamic nature of the Internet, any web addresses or links contained in this book may have changed since publication and may no longer be valid. The views expressed in this work are solely those of the author and do not necessarily reflect the views of the publisher, and the publisher hereby disclaims any responsibility for them.

Any people depicted in stock imagery provided by Thinkstock are models, and such images are being used for illustrative purposes only.
Certain stock imagery © Thinkstock.

Lulu Publishing Services rev. date: 06/20/2013

I know not with which weapons World War III will be fought, but World War IV will be fought with sticks and stones.

Albert Einstein

Now I am become Death, the Destroyer of Worlds.

From the *Bhagavad Gītā*

As quoted by J. Robert Oppenheimer at the Trinity Site.

Everybody grab a throttle and run forward.

Takeoff announcement made by unknown B-52 pilot

DEDICATION

This book is dedicated to Adam Columbus Mattocks, a man ahead of his time. He was a professional United States Air Force officer, a skilled pilot, a black man in the South in the 1960s. He was a member of Strategic Air Command in a difficult time when his country needed him. He was willing to go into harm's way, and was on *the point of the spear*. But most of all, he was a gentle, Christian man, whose only thoughts during his time of crisis were of his family and of his Maker.

CONTENTS

LIST OF ILLUSTRATIONS xi

FOREWORD xv

AUTHOR'S PREFACE xvii

PROLOGUE AND NOTES ON SECOND EDITION xxi

PART I: PRE-FLIGHT 1

Chapter 1. The Crew and Their Plane 3

Chapter 2. The Mission 57

Chapter 3. The Bail Out 121

Chapter 4. The Crash Site 137

Chapter 5. The Chance of Nuclear Detonation 181

Chapter 6. The Cause of the Crash... 211

Part II. AFTERMATH... 221

Chapter 7. The Tension of Command.. 223

Chapter 8. The Worst Case 231

Chapter 9. After Goldsboro 259

PART III. DE-BRIEF 283

Chapter 10. Comparison With Chernobyl and Fukushima 285

AFTERWORD By Wilton W. Strickland, Lt. Col, USAF, (Retired) 307

Appendix A Crew Members Information 309

Appendix B "This Is What It Was Like," Major Tulloch's Narrative, written 1961 311

Appendix C Findings of Official Accident Board [With descriptive notes] 323

Appendix D Table of Component Behavior, Fusing and Firing System 327

Appendix E List of Known Broken Arrows (Declassified as of 1980) 329

Appendix F BOMB LOCATIONS AT FARO: 333

Appendix G Where Did The Keep 19 Crew Members Land? 337

Appendix H. HAND WRITTEN "RANDOM NOTES AT GOLDSBORO," BY Scolman and Smith 343

Appendix I. The First Ten Years of Broken Arrows. 345

Appendix J. Presidential Memo on "FURTHERANCE" 365

ACKNOWLEDGMENTS 367

NOTES AND SOURCES 375

BIBLIOGRAPHY 415

ABOUT THE AUTHOR 425

LIST OF ILLUSTRATIONS

B-52 Alert Scramble

The BUFF

Major Walter Tulloch, Aircraft Commander

Captain Dick Rardin, Co-Pilot

Lieutenant Bill Wilson, Electronic Warfare Officer

Sergeant Frank Barnish, Gunner

Major Gene Shelton, Radar Navigator

Captain Paul Brown, Navigator

Lieutenant Adam Mattocks, Third Pilot

Major Eugene Richards

Crew Positions

Major Richards' Station

The Bomb Switch: the DCU/9A

B-52s on 'bust-out,' minimal interval takeoff

Wing Spoilers

B-52 Approach to Landing

"Christmas Tree" Alert Ramp

Chrome Dome Southern Routes

B-47 Alert*

Bail Out Routes

Ejection Seat Trigger

"Night Scene Over Faro: The Crash of Keep Nineteen"

Scott and Betty Tulloch, on Their Wedding Day

Crash Site, Air Force Fire Fighters

Bomb Number One

First Lieutenant Jack ReVelle, 1960

ReVelle during Flight Training

Debris Field, Faro, North Carolina

Retrieval of Parachute Pack, Bomb Two

EOD Team from Wright-Patterson AFB

Wing Removal

Crash Scene, Then and Now

Theoretical Impact of MK-39, on Manhattan

Schematic of MK-39 Type Weapon

SAC Command Post*

Bomb Detector Alarm

General Curtis LeMay*

General Thomas Power*

The Three Graves

Plaque on Faro Fire Station

Jack ReVelle Returns to Bomb Site One

Nahunta Swamp Bridge and Site Easement

Crew Landing Estimates, After Bailout

EOD Team, Seymour Johnson, with Jack ReVelle

*These materials are reproduced from www.nsarchive.org with the permission of the National Security Archive.

FOREWORD

Dr. Roy Heidicker, Wing Historian, 4th Fighter Wing

In 2005 I arrived in Goldsboro, North Carolina, at Seymour Johnson Air Force Base. I soon discovered that as an Air Force Historian I had struck gold in the 4th Fighter Wing. Their heritage, from the Eagle Squadrons through today, is unsurpassed in the history of the United States Air Force.

I also discovered that even though I was the Wing and not the base historian, I would be asked a lot of questions about the history of Seymour Johnson. One particular question kept coming up again and again. Many people wanted me to tell them all about the crash of the B-52 bomber in 1961 that involved two nuclear bombs. But the questions were often phrased in such a way that I soon realized the person asking knew a lot about the crash but they wanted me to answer the questions, "What really happened?" and "Why won't the Air Force tell people that a live nuclear bomb is buried in Faro, North Carolina?"

I found a Web site that dealt with the crash so I was able to answer questions in a more informed manner. But I also realized that my answers to *the bomb* questions never really satisfied the person asking the question. This was the case for several years. Although I didn't intend it, some people probably looked at me as being part of the great B-52 crash conspiracy. Then in 2011 something wonderful happened. It was the fiftieth anniversary of the crash and a reunion of people involved in the crash met in Faro, North Carolina. As the wing historian I was invited to attend this event. Joel Dobson, who was finishing a book about the crash, put together the event. I spoke with Joel and enjoyed his presentation at the reunion. Joel, a former officer in the Strategic Air Command, has now written the go-to source for questions regarding the Goldsboro B-52 crash in 1961.

He has gone through the records, interviewed the participants, and grilled the experts. This fine book is the last word on this event. There are no stones left unturned because Joel Dobson has turned them all. In addition to answering all the questions, Joel's book is a great story well told about brave Americans dealing with an unbelievable crisis. The Goldsboro Broken Arrow could have been the greatest man-made disaster in the history of North America. Instead it is an edge of your seat tale about close calls and disaster averted. Everyone in eastern North Carolina owes a debt of gratitude to Joel Dobson for finally revealing "what really happened," and "Why won't the Air Force tell people that a live nuclear bomb is buried in Faro, North Carolina?" But seriously, the most grateful person is me. From now on when people want to grill me about the crash I will direct them to this fine book.

AUTHOR'S PREFACE

I first got interested in this story when my son told me about the *lost bomb* of Goldsboro, a nuclear bomb supposedly buried somewhere near Goldsboro, North Carolina. I had been an Air Force lieutenant in Strategic Air Command (SAC) back in the 1960s but I had never heard of this 1961 B-52 accident. A Broken Arrow is an accident or incident involving a nuclear weapon with the potential for detonation. The closest I had ever even been to a Broken Arrow was the time I almost triggered an alert when I was the Officer Of the Day on the SAC base where I was stationed, but luckily it never reached the point of alert. I was on duty at the OOD desk and had received a call from the tower that "an aircraft was burning on the flight line." We had the Convair B-58 Hustler bombers, the first operational supersonic jet bombers capable of Mach Two, and they could very well be loaded for alert duty. If one was burning it would probably have nuclear weapons aboard, and I would be the lucky one to kick off an unstoppable telephone alert for the base. As I was pondering the written procedures for a Broken Arrow, a second call reported that it was only a transient Marine Corps fighter jet that had landed for refueling and the landing gear had collapsed. In fact, it was still sliding down the runway emitting sparks during the phone calls. No harm, no foul. The Broken Arrow recall alert was not necessary.

We have lived in North Carolina for thirty years now, and I figured it would be interesting to check out this *Goldsboro lost bomb*. Little did I realize what I was getting into.

That 1961 accident of a B-52 at Goldsboro, and the lessons learned from it, is the subject of this book. Two thermonuclear bombs fell from the plane as it disintegrated in mid-air, and I look at just how close we came to a major disaster, a nuclear detonation on United States soil, hundreds of times larger than that of Hiroshima. The book also looks at the known Broken Arrow accidents in the ten years before Goldsboro, as well as non-aircraft nuclear accidents such as Chernobyl and Fukushima, and the inherent dangers that lie within. I was not involved with this Broken Arrow, just someone who was in SAC in the 1960's and who wants to pass on to my grandchildren what happened then, and what could have happened, because I believe that Nature has a simple rule: The Lesson will be repeated until it is learned.

One statement made by the Stockholm Peace Research Institute Yearbook of 1977: "... *Goldsboro could have been the largest man-made disaster in history...* " caught my attention, and has been the source of controversy for several years now. While it is not my intent to resolve that controversy, at least we should know about it and consider its results.

I found that the 3.8 megaton yield of either bomb would exceed that of all munitions (outside of testing) ever detonated in the history of the world: by TNT, gunpowder, conventional bombs, and the Hiroshima and Nagasaki blasts, combined. It was big enough to have a kill zone of seventeen miles according to the man who deactivated it. And part of one of those two bombs still is buried at Faro, in a field twelve miles north of Goldsboro.

This book is about the men of that flight, *Keep 19*, how that mission developed through the complex process that was Strategic Air Command, and what the consequences were. It also contains the stories of the last surviving member of the crew, Adam Mattocks, who was one of the pilots, as well as the man who deactivated both bombs, Jack ReVelle. The people of Faro, North Carolina, have their own stories to tell about how they dealt with the fire that rained down on them that night in January 1961. Interviews with individuals are noted in the text, as well as personal experiences. My intent is to make this an interesting read about something important that happened in my lifetime.

In over sixty years of flying, the B-52 has been modified many times. So has much of the information published in periodicals about the Goldsboro Broken Arrow of 1961. It is impossible to cover all aspects of the event, just as it is to cover all the variations of the aircraft. There may be inaccuracies, gaps, and inconsistencies, just as there are in fifty-year old memories. I want to show what the aircraft was like in 1961 along with the weapons and their safety features: what we thought then and now—a half-century later.

The timing of this book is both fortunate and unfortunate. It is fortunate in that so many previously classified pieces of information are now declassified and obtainable. It is unfortunate in that so many of the people involved in the event are now getting along in years. It is time to write their stories down.

The far-reaching story is about how we as a nation arrived at that place in time when we were ready and willing to sacrifice everything based on what we thought to be right. We are now finding out that during a short period of time in 1961, we were very vulnerable to nuclear war, not from an attack, but by accident. How to measure that vulnerability is still going on, but we should at least recognize that there was in fact, a chance that the perfect storm of accidental nuclear war existed.

The Strategic Air Command does not exist anymore, but the B-52 still flies. There remains a remnant of that time still in the ground at Faro. We have learned a lot of things since 1961, but we are still running up against the consequences of decisions. We still have to deal with the results of Chernobyl and now its twin sister, Fukushima.

This is the story of how that one accident happened in 1961, how the bomb site was located, and how people involved in an event fifty years ago got together fifty years later at the exact place where it all happened. It also reflects on how close we came to an accidental nuclear detonation, and, by the conditions in place at that time, to accidental nuclear war.

Joel Dobson
2013

> In memory of my good friend, Tom Jankiewicz
>
> 1963 - 2013

PROLOGUE AND NOTES ON SECOND EDITION

As the history of the Cold War is now being written for future generations, most military and political scholars will agree that the Cuban Missile Crisis of October 1962 was one of the most dangerous moments in history. The United States and the Soviet Union had built enough megatonage to destroy each other many times over. We had the machines and procedures for nuclear war, and the greatest fear was that the restraining voice of human logic might not be heard in the rush to mutual destruction. The best teachable moment during the Cuban Crisis, if there was such a thing, was the fact that the crisis occurred mostly in the open. The eyes of the world were upon the daily events of the Naval blockade as they were unfolding near Cuba. President John F. Kennedy and Premier Nikita Khrushchev made speeches carried by the world press. The Commander of the Strategic Air Command, General Thomas Power, broadcast his instructions to his forces in the clear, wanting the Soviets to understand. But as dangerous as that crisis was, we should also remember that there was an equally dangerous possibility of such a holocaust erupting, not as an willful event, but by shear accident.

If accidental nuclear war ever did erupt, it would have occurred at a time when several conditions would be in place: a rapid and massive build-up of nuclear weapons systems, a communication system with unanticipated weaknesses, and a readiness by a single commander with the authority, the willingness, and the means of execution of nuclear war. If all those conditions were in place, all that would be required would be a spark... an event that could be the tipping point for nuclear war.

It now becomes more apparent that such a possibility did exist just over fifty years ago. The degree of that possibility is debatable, but due to the seriousness of the possible outcome, the subject deserves consideration. And that is the reason for this second edition. For a short period of time, the conditions for a perfect storm of accidental nuclear war came together near Goldsboro, North Carolina, on January 24, 1961. It happened more than a year before the Cuban Crisis, and the weaknesses of that time would be recognized and repaired, but this event did happen. Many more documents concerning this weakness have now been made available through the Freedom Of Information Act, some very recently. That tipping point, and the stories of even more people who were involved in the 1961 Goldsboro Broken Arrow, needed to be recorded.

On that moonlit night, a B-52 bomber disintegrated in midair twelve miles north of Goldsboro, and its two huge bombs spilled out. They were three-ton MK-39 thermonuclear bombs. A giant one-hundred-foot-wide foot retardation parachute opened on the first one and it caught upright in a group of three trees, the nose just hitting the ground. The parachute on the second bomb failed to open due to the violence of the exploding airplane, and that bomb, traveling over seven hundred miles per hour, buried itself in a farm field. The radioactive core of that bomb is still there, about 180 feet below ground level, at the farming community of Faro, North Carolina.

PART I: PRE-FLIGHT

Chapter 1. The Crew and Their Plane

The short swarthy guy from Boston had been taking the good-natured ribbing from his fellow crew members all week as the Presidential inauguration drew closer. Since the dashing young Jack Kennedy with the beautiful wife won the election two months ago, anybody on base from Massachusetts was the target of at least some casual comment, usually in the Irish brogue of the Kennedy clan. Frank didn't tell anyone, but being from the same state was about as close as he was to the Kennedys. Frank was much closer in many ways to the outgoing president, Dwight D. Eisenhower. After all, they soldiered together in World War II. Frank served, howbeit at a very great distance, under General Eisenhower as an Army Air Corps sergeant, flying out of England. He was shot down over Germany and bailed out of his B-24 bomber on the ill-fated Kassel Mission when he was the turret gunner on the bomber *Our Gal*. It was shot out of the sky along with twenty-four other aircraft in just three minutes on September 27, 1944. He was nineteen-years-old then, and became a prisoner of war in central Germany.

After the war, Frank left the Army Air Corps and became an auto mechanic, but it was a tough go, with a new wife to support. So when the new US Air Force was created and was building up, it needed experienced gunners to join the Strategic Air Command.

Frank thought about it long and hard, but decided that sounded like a good deal, so he reenlisted. Americans were growing very afraid during the 1950s, there was this national fear that Soviet bombers and missiles would come swarming in over the North Pole at any time and blow us all away.

They were all afraid of these new threats from the Russians, the 'bomber gap,' and later the 'missile gap.' Now they were told the Russians could attack America and level entire cities with ICBMs in fifteen minutes. We didn't know it, but the National Security Council, just six months before had written a Top Secret study predicting that Soviet missiles would constitute a "great threat" to United States cities by the end of 1960, and that we should change our policy from "launch on attack," to one of "launch on warning." Hit them before they hit us. The council was very concerned that the White House and Defense authorities would not have adequate time for making decisions to put Strategic Air Command bombers in the air, not only to prevent their destruction on the ground but also to launch an attack. "By 1961 (the Soviet ICBM force) will present an extremely dangerous threat to SAC bomber bases, unhardened ICBM sites and command installations." A new warning system, the highly classified Ballistic Missile Early Warning System (BMEWs) was in the works but would not be available for several years. Until then, the network called NUDETS, a nation-wide nuclear detection system including seismic devices, radiation detectors, optical instruments, and the secret Bomb Alarm System, created by Western Electric and then being deployed, could give information on nuclear detonations. But that as not a warning system, it only worked after the detonations occurred.

Frank was Francis R. E. Barnish, thirty-five, from Greenfield, Massachusetts, and he was the gunner, a Technical Sergeant in the US Air Force, and the only enlisted man on Readiness Crew R-10. They flew the Boeing B-52 Stratofortress, the eight-engine jet bomber nicknamed the BUFF, (an acronym politely translated to "Big Ugly Fat Fellow"). His crew was part of the 4241st Strategic Wing at Seymour Johnson Air Force Base, Goldsboro, North Carolina. The base was one of many "satellite bases," spread out to disperse the bomber force in the event of a Soviet attack. This was SAC, the Strategic Air Command. It was pronounced *Sack,* never *S-A-C.* The headquarters were at Offutt Air Force Base, Omaha, Nebraska, and it operated as a specified command under the direct operational control of the Joint Chiefs of Staff, with the Air Force as executive agent. Few other air commands in the US military had ever been set up that way, and it showed the power of SAC that was built into it's command structure.

Frank was the only enlisted man aboard his B-52 and one of a rare breed—the flying sergeant. He liked the job and he liked to fly, but he didn't care much for the part called "standing alert." He didn't like the tension of being in the concrete alert facility for several days and nights straight, just waiting for the jarring Klaxon horn to sound. It was like being in jail, an underground jail at that. But a sudden breakout from that jail would mean either an Operational Readiness Inspection, or something much worse: the nation might actually be going to war. So far every time the horn had gone off it was for a no-notice exercise. It was the stress in waiting for the horn that was the worse. He liked to fly, but not this waiting around. Even the long twenty-four-hour flight that was coming up meant he would be out of the molehole and back in the B-52. Frank was looking forward to climbing aboard the big bomber and flying the following Monday.

The alert facility was called the 'molehole' because the bottom half of the concrete two-story building containing the living quarters was below ground level. The upwards-sloping exit ramps resembled mole runs. When the horn went off, the crews would run up those ramps to ground level, jump into their blue station wagons or four-door pickup trucks, and peel out to the aircraft. The two pilots would climb into the aircraft first through the lower hatch and begin engine start-up. The SAC quick alert response was the first line of defense during the 1960s when the Soviet Union presented the greatest threat to the Free World.

The crews at Seymour Johnson "stood alert" about one week out of three, depending on the needs of the Air Force. The first few days on alert were always very busy. On the first day the crew would show up at 7:45 a.m., get the weather briefing at 0800, and then go out in their assigned alert vehicle to set up their gear in the airplane. It was said those trucks and station wagons had a short vehicle life. During an alert, they were only driven a few hundred yards-and very hard at that. In this business, seconds really did matter.

B-52 SCRAMBLE. B-52 Alert crews dash to their aircraft during a 'no-notice exercise. Photo courtesy USAF.

The airplanes were always ready to go and well guarded twenty-four hours a day. There was a temporary sign posted in front of each that said "Cocked," meaning they were loaded with nuclear weapons. And no one was allowed to enter the area of a cocked B-52 without authorization. And never alone. No one person was ever in a cocked bomber by himself—individual crewmen had to be listed by name on the authorization manifest for a specific aircraft. The new crew would switch baggage with the old crew, stowing their gear and briefcases in the airplane in the process called the *bag drag*. Each crew member's baggage included a RON kit, in the event crewmen had to *remain over night* someplace. Crew members were never sure where they would wind up if for any reason the plane had to divert. And if they had to divert it could be any place on earth, so they always carried their arctic gear.

If necessary, the new pilots would meet with the crew chief at the nose of the aircraft to discuss the current condition of the machine. The crew chief was always experienced and proud of "his bird." The flight crew was just borrowing it for a while, and they had better bring it back in one piece. When that aircraft was first put on ground alert, the pilots and crew chief would do the pre-flight walk-around inspection, examining everything, looking for leaks and anything unusual. The crew chief and the pilots did not want to find any problem that the maintenance crew overlooked, but if there was, this was the time to find it. No maintenance guy wanted to be the one who missed something that took a B-52 off alert. The airplane might sit there for weeks without being fired up, but it was always ready to go. If it was only a crew change, and not a change out of aircraft, the preflight would be thorough, but abbreviated.

As part of his pre-flight inspection, Frank went into the upper deck with the gun specialist and checked out the controls. Even though the guns were over a hundred feet away in the tail, Frank's station was in the front section of the airplane, a situation that suited Frank just fine. He had already examined the four guns back in the tail. Soon, the two navigators would set up and climb a stepladder to peer into the bombs up in the bomb bay, while the Electronic Warfare officer would be back at the aft section containing his specialized ECM antennas and other electronic countermeasure gadgets.

After pre-flight inspection on this first day, it was back to the alert facility for the daily 0800 weather briefing, breakfast, and then briefings followed by more briefings. The two navigators would go off to the Wing target vault, for DITR study. That was Defense Intelligence Target Reconnaissance. They would look at aerial photos of their targets. Frank didn't know how good those spy cameras were, but sometimes the navigators would discuss the scores at Russian soccer games. The photos were taken by U-2 aircraft that crisscrossed Russia at incredibly high altitudes for numerous missions by the CIA. When the U-2 was being developed, one of the selling points to President Eisenhower came in May 1957. Photos from 70,000 feet over Ike's Gettysburg farm were shown to him. "This is close to incredible," he said, when he saw his own cows feeding at a trough. The Commander In Chief of SAC, General Curtis LeMay was not so impressed with the U-2 as an aircraft. He said it didn't have any guns or even a full landing gear. Somebody had to run along side and grab a wingtip after touchdown and taxiing in. He called the U-2 a "pile of bullshit."

But there was also a new system in the works, the CORONA spy satellites, to send back three-dimensional pictures of the Soviet Union from 100 miles up with amazing resolution. Their existence would not be acknowledged for another fifty years.

SAC tried to make the alert facility as comfortable as possible. It was air conditioned and central heated, and had a theater that doubled as a briefing room; a library, a combination TV/game/lounge, and a mess hall. There was a pool table and card tables and study rooms. Outside, there was a separate fenced area with a swimming pool and picnic area for family gatherings in warm months. It was standardized for crew quarters: 18,000 square feet, enough for 70 men. The real flying action happened between pulling alert duty.

That would mean long hard days of 'gear-up' time, some of it as full twenty-four hour missions, exhausting, but at least it was different from sitting in that concrete molehole, studying.

Frank's six-man crew had reached the end of their four days of alert and had just finished the mission briefing for the next day's flight. Now he would go home for one night, then go out and fly for twenty-four hours. And after that he would have an actual day off.

They would be flying a large convoluted loop around the US East Coast on a so-called training mission. SAC Commander-In-Chief General Thomas Power had just met his announced goal of having one third of SAC bombers on ground alert by the end of 1960. Now they were in 1961 and the pressure was on to comply with even more alerts. By the end of next month, February, there would be a number of armed bombers in the air at all times, twenty-four hours a day. The program itself was called airborne alert, and the specific long-range route itself was called Chrome Dome. It would involve flying over Greenland, Canada, and around the Mediterranean. Crews from Seymour Johnson flew the Southern, or Mediterranean Chrome Dome route. This week's mission was a 'profile' mission to prove that Crew R-10 was able and ready to fly an exact duplicate of that route in matching time and distance. It would be one of the most important training missions crew R-10 would ever made. It would show them as qualified for Chrome Dome.

Operation Chrome Dome would continue for another seven years, always ready to carry the fire to the Russians. The fire that Crew R-10 would carry on Monday morning was in the form of two MK-39 thermonuclear weapons—hydrogen bombs. Combined, these two fully armed special weapons had the destructive power five hundred times that of the Hiroshima bomb, used seventeen years before. One airplane: two bombs, five hundred Hiroshimas.

THE AIRPLANE

The B-52 was, and still is, a prime workhorse of the United States Air Force bomber fleet. It has served in many engagements—the Cold War, Vietnam, Iraq, Afghanistan—even involved in space programs for NASA by hauling X-15s to the edge of space. It is highly effective when used for such missions as ocean surveillance and can assist the Navy in anti-ship and mine-laying operations. Two B-52s, in two hours, can monitor 140,000 square miles of ocean surface. The B-52 could fly at 50,000 feet, at Mach 0.86, about 650 miles per hour, and carry up to 70,000 pounds of bombs—and do it all day and all night in a perpetual giant loop. At the end of the assigned SAC tour, a BUFF would be replaced by another BUFF, followed by another, and another. Based on longevity alone, it is probably the most successful and versatile military aircraft ever designed. Compared to the prop driven B-29 Superfortress, we think of the B-52 jet Stratofortress as relatively modern, but some people may find it curious that the B-29 is only ten years older than the B-52. The B-29 first flew in 1942, the B-52's first flight was on April 15, 1952. That is now more than a half-century ago, and the B-52 will probably still fly for decades more. Today's B-52 is frequently twice as old as the airmen who service it. Lieutenant Chuck Lutter, a B-52 pilot, recently said in an interview about the Air Force, "It may not be your father's Air Force, but it could be his airplane. In my case, it is." His father flew in the exact same B-52 aircraft in Vietnam: the same 'tail number.' And at the 5th Bomb Wing at Minot Air Force Base in North Dakota, one of the pilots is a third generation B-52 commander; both his father and grandfather flew the B-52.

The last B-52 made, an H-model, was delivered to the Air Force in October 1962. The B-52s that are still flying are stationed at Barksdale Air Force Base, Louisiana, and Minot Air Force Base, North Dakota, and are expected to fly for another forty years.

It is not at all a graceful aircraft on the ground. It is huge. When a group of fat, gray B-52s move at maximum taxi speed from the alert pad to the active runway, they lumber from side to side because of their heaviness and width. Due to their enormous size, it appears that they move very slowly and awkwardly. This is called the *elephant walk*. After a soaking rain, jets of water will shoot up from the expansion joints of the concrete taxiways as the heavy bombers pass by.

For the B-52 to be as big as it is, the crew members sit in a relatively small portion: the front, or *sharp end*. Depending on the model, the aircraft is 160 feet long and the wingspan is about 180 feet across. It weighs close to a half million pounds at takeoff—488,000 pounds.

The Two Hundred Ton Boeing B-52 Stratofortress- The BUFF. Which stood for Big Ugly Fat (Fellow),..... or something like that.

Photo courtesy USAF.

It was always ready in the 1960s, refueled in midair, always ready for thermonuclear war. There were between six and thirteen B-52s in the air at any time during this period. At the height of the Cold War, the Strategic Air Command flew the B-52s an incredible 47,168 hours for the month of October 1962. Airborne alert operated at highest strength during the Cuban Missile Crisis with approximately sixty-five bombers in the air and "target effective" at any given time. When SAC was at its peak, it had 2,921 bombers and tankers, and 15,468 nuclear bombs, aimed at 3,729 targets, with the equivalent megatonnage of 13 Hiroshima's per target. The Soviets, by contrast, had 1,060 bombs at that time. This was a far cry from 1945, at the end of World War II, when the United States was the sole nuclear power, but without a single operational nuclear weapon. We had just used both of them on Japan.

It had already been determined that the Soviets would have the ability to launch intercontinental ballistic missiles (ICBMs) against

America in a surprise attack that would result in massive destruction. It was also determined the US would only have fifteen minutes of advance warning. That made it essential to have the ability to launch the bomber fleet within that fifteen minute time period to both act as an armed deterrent and to save a portion of the fleet—to get aircraft safely away from SAC bases that were sure to be targets. The bombers would have to be completely ready to go, fueled up, weapons aboard, fully trained crews standing ready. The ground alert was born in 1957 and it would continue for decades, augmented by the airborne alert. It would be enormously expensive, both in treasure and manpower. It would require an initial investment of an estimated capital outlay of 8.5 billion dollars, bigger than the largest industrial corporation in the world at that time: Standard Oil of New Jersey. The amount of force necessary to retaliate was calculated to be a minimum of one third of its 550 bombers and 350 tankers. That is what it would take in 1961, to be able to survive to fight the nuclear fight.

The fifteen-minute launch window for a SAC wing was in reality much shorter. A typical wing at that time was made up of forty-five bombers and thirty tankers. To get one-third off the ground within fifteen minutes meant that the first of the fifteen bombers and ten tankers would have to be *wheels up* in about seven minutes. That was the goal set by SAC at the time Crew R-10 was being readied to fly. Seven minutes from watching a movie in the alert shack to wheels up.

Every man on a SAC bomber crew in the 1960s was aware of something that very few modern warriors ever had to face. If they went off to war—the war they were trained to fight—there was a very good chance it would be their families, not them, that would pay the ultimate price. If the worst-case scenario came and they had to launch a nuclear strike against the Soviet Union, they knew their families would be at extreme risk. They might return safely from their mission to find out their families were the casualties of a nuclear counterstrike.

The Men

The pilot of Alert Crew R-10 was Air Force Major Walter Scott Tulloch, forty-six, of San Diego, California. On the day Pearl Harbor was attacked, he was a twenty-six year old clerk with a high school education and a private pilot's license. Three days later he was enlisted in the Army Air Corps as an aviation cadet. Six months after that, he earned his Army Air Corps pilot wings, a very fast track. In World War II, he flew thirty-one combat missions from the Northern Mariana Islands over Japan in B-29s. By 1961 he was a senior, or command pilot in the Strategic Air Command, had logged almost six thousand flying hours, and had been a pilot for nineteen years. He was at the pinnacle of what SAC wanted: a highly trained, professional bomber pilot. He had flown every heavy bomber the Air Force had in inventory at that time, from B-17s, to B-29s, to B-36s, to the B-52.

His co-pilot, flying *right seat* was Captain Richard Rardin, thirty-three years old, from San Antonio, Texas. He enlisted as a private as soon as he was eighteen years old, in his home state of Ohio. After four years of enlisted service, he was commissioned in 1950, and he became a pilot in 1952. He had been a fighter pilot and test pilot, and had survived three flameouts in test aircraft. Captain Rardin was also a World War II veteran, a tall, gray-haired thirty-year old. He didn't talk much about the war. The way he saw it, his job, with that of his boss Major Tulloch, was to keep them out of the rocks.

Major Walter Scott Tulloch, Aircraft Commander of

"Keep Nineteen."

Photo courtesy of Betty Tulloch

(Left) Captain Dick Rardin, The Co-pilot of "Keep 19" in 1961.

(Right). A much older Lt. Colonel Dick Rardin, photo probably in the 1980s.

Both photos, courtesy USAF.

The electronic warfare officer, or EW, was First Lieutenant Bill Wilson, age twenty-seven, of Somerville, New Jersey. He sat ten feet behind the co-pilot, facing aft; his job was to identify and use various countermeasures against incoming missiles, whether they were guided by radar, optically, or infrared. His profession was new to flying. Pilots and navigators have always been pilots and navigators, and gunners have always been gunners. But when the Air Force first started the Electronic Countermeasures Program the other crew members didn't even know what to call them: EWOs, EWs, ECMs? Inside the airplane, they soon would be answering to "E-Dub." They even spoke their own language, which sounded like gibberish when they congregated together at the Officer's Club. They wore the wings of the navigator rating, and sat in the far dark corner of the B-52 upper deck facing backwards, surrounded by their black boxes. Up until the G-model B-52 they sat back there by themselves. The EW's specialty group of veterans would later be known as the Old Crows, as in wise old birds. Bill Wilson's job was to defend his aircraft by jamming, decoying, and confusing enemy missiles or radar, for the EW's fight was a war with invisible electronic impulses.

To Lieutenant Wilson's right sat the gunner. He fought with very traditional bullets: .50 caliber shells. Technical Sergeant Frank Barnish occupied the fourth ejection seat on the top deck, also facing aft, where he watched radar and TV monitors. He used the screens to remotely control his four .50 caliber machine guns back in the tail, capable of firing twenty-four hundred rounds a minute. They were fired in short bursts, otherwise, the gun barrels would melt. While they were being fired, the speed of the B-52 would actually increase about five knots.

Lieutenant Bill Wilson, Electronic Warfare Officer (EWO), 1961. Photo courtesy USAF.

(Left) Sergeant Frank Barnish, photo at 1961. Photo courtesy USAF.

(Right) Sergeant Frank Barnish, taken early in WW II, probably around 1943.

Courtesy Jerry Barnish.

BUFF gunners on the G-Model said that they had a good deal because previous models of the B-52 had the tail gunner physically located back in the tail, just like some World War II bombers. Just getting into that cramped office way back in the earlier models was different from the rest of the crew. The tail gunner usually did not climb into the aircraft at the belly hatch like everyone else, if he wanted to avoid a very long crawl through the bomb bay dragging his parachute and other gear. Instead, he used a ground maintenance stand and entered through a hatch up high on the side of the rear fuselage, under the right horizontal stabilizer. If the ground stand was not available, he could crawl in through the aft wheel well. Also, the tail gunners were isolated on the other B-52 models. Being way out back, away from the wing, made for a very rough ride during turbulence. But the worse thing was that if a bail out command came, the section containing the entire big gun assembly would be dropped—cut completely loose from the airplane—right there in front of the gunner. He would then release his seat belt and "step out," actually take a tumbling dive through this new opening. If he was above 14,000 feet, his parachute would automatically open. Below that, it would be up to him to hand-deploy his parachute.

The relocation of the gunner from the tail section to a much safer ejection seat behind the pilot greatly improved the morale of the gunners of the G-model B-52. It even had his cup warmer and small oven. In addition to his own job, the gunner picked up the additional duties as de-facto cook, waiter, and aide-de-camp for the rest of the crew, but Sergeant Barnish was happy to have his ejection seat up front. Sergeant Frank Barnish was the only man on the airplane who had been a Prisoner Of War in WWII.

These two fellow crewmen, 'E-Dub' and 'Guns,' the only ones who rode around the world backward, formed a very small fraternity of two. Some EWs and gunners had a shoulder patch showing a gruff bulldog firing a machine gun alongside a crafty-looking black bird. The other men frequently kidded them, asking if the shoulder patch was on backward just because of their weird seating arrangement in the aircraft.

There were two more ejection seats, both on the lower deck. Major Eugene Shelton was forty-one-years-old, from San Antonio, Texas, and as the radar navigator (RN), he sat in the left seat downstairs facing forward. Major Shelton had a wife named Rusty and they had three sons and a daughter. The other seat was for the navigator (NAV), Captain Paul Brown, thirty-seven-years-old, of Beardstown, Illinois. He had survived two crashes in World War II. These were men who had answered the call back in the "brown shoe" days, when it was the Army Air Corps. They were side-by-side down on the lower deck in what was called 'The Black Hole.' It was an area of muted light, only a few feet from back to front, about nine feet wide, and not enough room to stand up. No windows. While they were down in the hole, they could not tell if it was day or night.

Only the two pilots on the upper deck could see outside the aircraft.

(Left): Major Gene Shelton, Radar Navigator, ca. 1961. Photo courtesy USAF.

(Right): Gene Shelton as a younger man, probably around 1943. Photo courtesy Shelton Family.

Captain Paul Brown, Navigator. The photo is dated 6 Feb, 1961, two weeks after the crash.. Photo courtesy USAF

The Extras

During that mission in 1961, using the Instructor Pilot seat behind and between the pilot and co-pilot, sat First Lieutenant Adam Mattocks. He was the only African-American of Crew R-10, and for that matter, the entire squadron. He was there as a fully qualified pilot—the third pilot. The third pilot in the B-52 was an essential member for these long missions; primarily because of the physical limits of the human body. Aerial refueling gave the B-52 a range limited by crew endurance, but twenty-four hours was also the limit of something else: oil. The bearings of the J-57 engines required constant lubrication, and they took a total of 55 gallons each. The Boeing Airplane Company had not figured out a way to get additional oil to the engines while flying. That became the limiting factor: twenty-four hours, and the physical goal of the crew was built around it. The job of flying the B-52 for that long was physically exhausting. Consequently, the need for the third pilot.

Mattocks' seat was not an ejection seat, but it was right behind and between the two pilots. The seat position was called the IP, for Instructor Pilot. The position was originally designed for the instructor for the pilots, a seat for the grading officer while he guided them through training, and rated their efficiency and professionalism. Now, with this new requirement for twenty-four hours of flying, it was the seat of the new relief pilot. Mattock's job was to assist where needed on the gauges and controls, frequencies and checklists, and to fly the airplane whenever either the pilot or co-pilot needed a break. He would then take over and whomever he replaced could stretch out for a few minutes on a pad that could be unrolled on the floor right behind the IP seat in this airplane. Other models of B-52 would get an upgrade to a narrow bunk.

Lieutenant Mattocks was the youngest man on board. He was twenty-seven-years-old and from nearby Maysville, North Carolina. He first trained as a F-86 fighter pilot and was assigned to a squadron in Arizona. He loved being a jet fighter pilot, but his entire fighter squadron had been reassigned to SAC to fill much-needed bomber pilot vacancies. That process was known as being 'SAC-umcised,' and was certainly not a well-liked policy by the fighter pilots, moving from the single seat 'fast burners' to flying a 'bus.' General LeMay didn't help relations between fighter pilots and bomber pilots when he said, "Flying fighters is fun. Flying bombers is important."

Adam had assignments and flight schools in Georgia, Maine, Arizona, and North Carolina. When he was transferred from the F-86 to the B-52, he asked for the Seymour Johnson assignment to be near his kinfolk. He was a native of Onslow County, North Carolina, and was the youngest of seven children, and the first in his family to go to college. His father talked to the rest of his brothers and sisters, and together they worked hard to send Adam to North Carolina A&T University in Greensboro. Adam knew his future wife Anne in college, but he couldn't date much because he was studying so hard. He studied pre-med, he wanted to be a doctor. He was commissioned an Air Force second lieutenant through ROTC and went off to Florida for flight training. Other young black officers told him they doubted that the Air Force would allow a black man to fly jets.

There were times when Adam Mattocks was the only African-American officer on base, and this was during the 1960s, so he did experience discrimination in some assignments. One time he and Anne had saved to buy a nice car, a 1958 white Cadillac, and one of the other officers made a crack about how he was able to afford it. "I don't spend all my money at the Officer's Club bar," was the reply. Adam always paid his club dues; he just didn't feel like eating there frequently.

Adam believed a nearby high-ranking officer somehow overheard his comment about the Officer's Club and misinterpreted it—as if Adam didn't support the Club. That's the only reason he could figure out for getting only a *satisfactory* on his next efficiency report. For SAC flight-rated officers, getting a much higher *outstanding* or *exceptional* rating was expected. Getting the lower *satisfactory* mark was a real downgrade in the world of SAC-speak. Adam tried to find a way to quietly contest the evaluation, and needed someone to guide him. He asked Major Scott Tulloch, who got him assigned as the extra pilot for his crew, and gave him up-close-and-personal flight training. More importantly, he was a friend with the gold leaves of a major, a field-grade officer. The *satisfactory* in Adam's performance rating soon climbed back to the top of the Officer Efficiency Reports.

Reassignment to different bases around the country meant a sudden relocation move by aircraft for Adam, but could be a slow car or bus trip for Anne and the kids. Traveling alone cross-country with children was especially difficult, according to Anne. Sometime she would have to carry food for three or four days in case she couldn't find a restaurant to let them eat; to sleep in the car if she couldn't not find a hotel to let them stay. Somehow, someone always watched over her and the children. Once, they had to sleep in the car beside a riverbank, and a policeman told them he would check on them during the night and watch out for them. Another time, traveling by bus to catch up with a new Air Force assignment, a child became sick, and needed juice and medicine. A pharmacist turned her away. When the driver of the bus inquired, she told him of her concerns, and the next thing she knew the driver brought her the needed medicine. Over the years, Anne kept a book of the people all over the country who took her and the children in for an overnight stay, or sometimes much longer. She has stayed in touch with many of them throughout the years. She still visits with a lady who is over eighty years of age. When they moved to Arizona, for Adam's assignment there, she lived with a black cowboy and his Indian wife. She wondered why it would take the base commander to have to order people to treat her family appropriately, especially since they were all there serving their country.

(Left). Adam Mattocks as a very young student pilot. He was in training as an F-86 fighter pilot, one of the few black flight officers in the Air Force at that time.

Photo courtesy of Mattocks family.

(Right): 1st Lt. Adam Mattocks, 1961, as published in the Raleigh Observer.
Photo courtesy USAF.

Major Eugene Richards, 1961. He was a 'ride-along'. Photo courtesy USAF.

Major Eugene Richards was forty-two-years-old from Toccoa, Georgia. His seat in the aircraft also was not an ejection seat, but his was on the lower deck. He held a staff position at wing headquarters, and was the wing electronic warfare officer responsible for all EW training. After the aircraft would take-off, he would climb the ladder to the upper deck and work with the EW in the back of the plane on procedures and training.

As a wing staff officer, he was not required to fly as a crew member on a regular basis, but as a rated flying officer, he was required to stay current and fly each month. That's the reason he was flying that day, "to help the defense team smooth out their operation," according to Major Tulloch's later comments, but it was also to qualify for his monthly flight pay of one hundred dollars. Major Richards had to accomplish and record his flight time before the end of the month and this day was the twenty-third. He was one of the most popular officers in Wing and very qualified. He and his wife, Sue, owned a motel, the El Rancho, on the Wilson Highway just north of Goldsboro. That's also where they lived. As a major, he was eligible for base housing, but elected to live at the motel that was his place of business when off duty. He would be approaching retirement age soon, and it was not uncommon for SAC officers and sergeants to make local business investments; they had to plan for that retirement.

These two men, Lieutenant Mattocks and Major Richards, were the two *extras*, on this flight: people without ejection seats. Mattocks was the required third pilot, and Richards was known as a 'ride-along.'

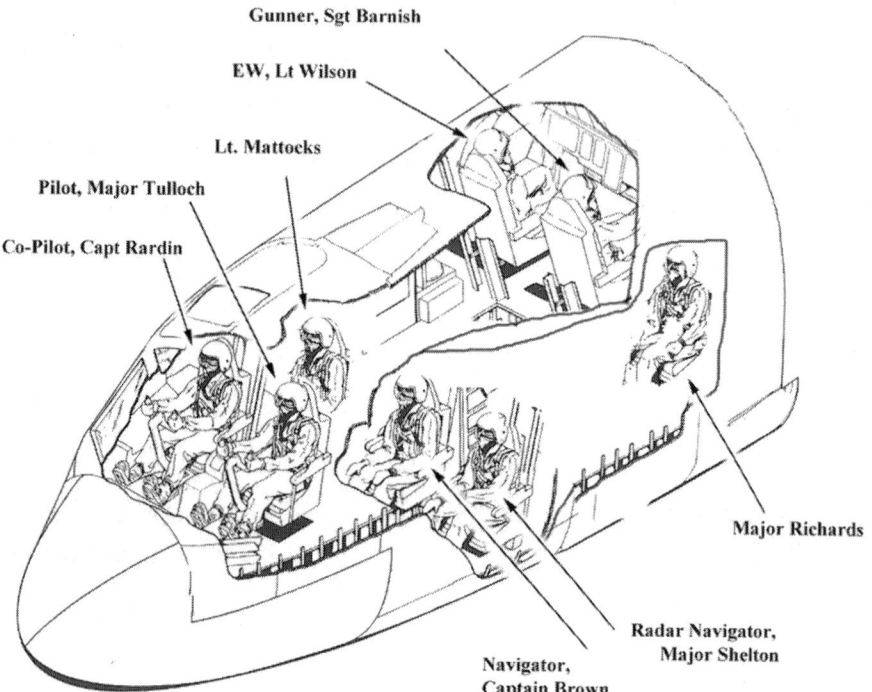

Crew positions of Keep 19. Five crewmen on the upper deck, three on the lower deck. Illustration by author.

If there was such a thing as seating preference on a B-52, Major Richards had the least desirable, the equivalent of steerage. In a cramped spot at the back of *The Hole* on the lower deck his seat was an uncomfortable, nonadjustable fold-away panel with a seat belt and plug-in jack for the interphone. This seat station was officially known as the *IN,* for Instructor Navigator. The backrest was a thin cushion attached to the access door of a pressurized bulkhead. Behind that door was the cavernous forward wheel well, containing four huge landing tires, with the complex landing gear. And behind that was a huge area: the bomb bay, and then the aft wheel well. An orange colored medal grid called the *egg crate* lay under his feet—it was a movable grating that protected the fold-up stairway mechanism of the crew access hatch. That was the hinged hatch in the bottom of the aircraft that served as the main access portal through which all crew members entered. It was also the point where anyone coming on board first noticed the unique personality of that particular aircraft—the smell. It was the point where any spilt liquid usually ended up, at the lowest point of this section. There was always something being spilt: coffee, bodily emissions, food crumbs, lubricants, cigarette ashes—the ground crews tried to keep the airplane clean, but there was only so many locations that could be reached. It was said that at least a fighter aircraft got inverted every now and then and shook out everything that was stuck somewhere. The older the BUFF, the more varied the smells, everything from burn wiring to burnt coffee.

Major Richards did not have much of a view from his seat tucked away in his alcove, he could only see the back of the two navigators' ejection seats. To his right and left sides were equipment bulkheads with masses of wiring, and in front of him to the right was the ladder to the upper deck. That's where the chemical toilet was located, just at the top of the ladder, along with a cloth privacy screen. To his left on the lower level was the crew urinal canister. Some ride-alongs who were assigned to this location on the lower deck referred to it as the men's room.

But the position on the lower deck was only Major Richards' seat during take-offs and landings. His 'working office' was upstairs, identified as the *ID Position*, for Instructor, Defense. It was where he worked with the EW on defense training. His office seat was the top of a box labeled "Ditching Hammocks." That box was secured to the side of the chemical toilet.

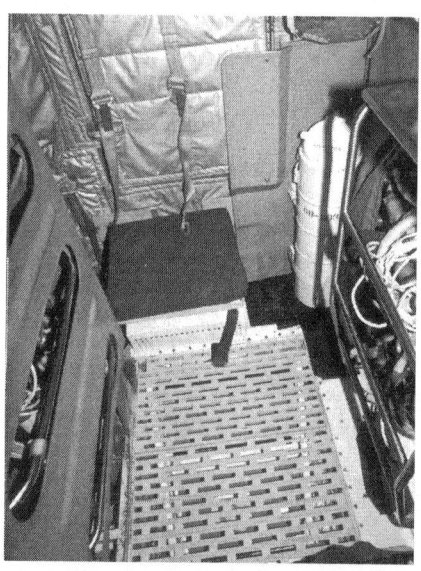

Major Richards' seat was the "Navigator Instructor's position." This view is on the lower deck at the crew entrance hatch, looking aft. The seat's backrest was the access door to the forward wheel well. Beyond the wheel well was the bomb bay.

Courtesy USAF.

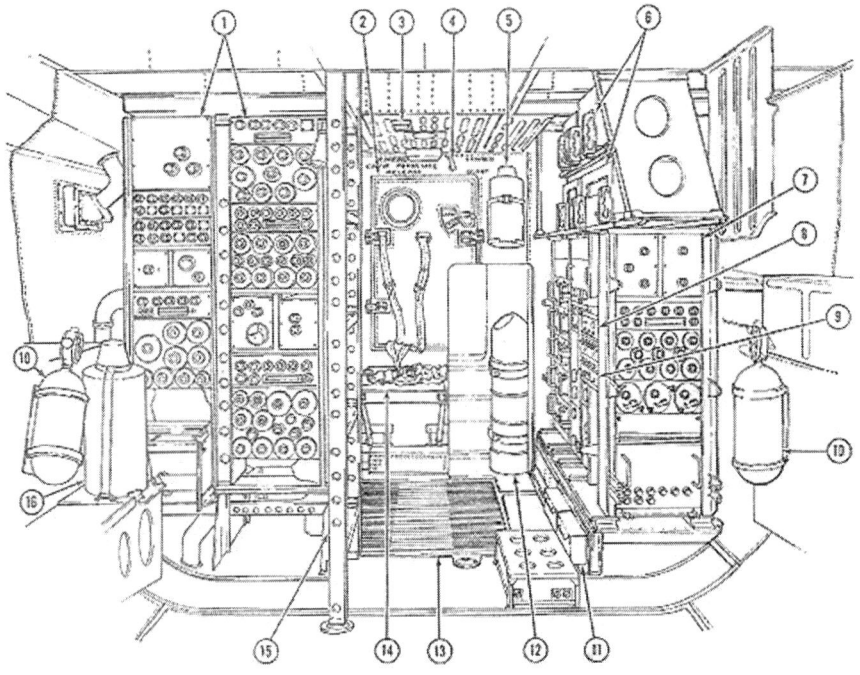

Drawing from the aircraft's 'Dash One' manual, showing Navigator's Instructor position (IN). The seat is Item 14. Other Items:15 is the ladder to upper deck, Item 12 is the Crew Urinal. Item 2 is the access door back to the wheel well.

Illustration courtesy USAF.

All the officers on Crew R-10 held Reserve officer commissions, as compared to Regular commissions. The number of Air Force Regular commissions was limited by Congress. Regular commissions were highly desirable and guaranteed to graduates of the Air Force Academy, top graduates of ROTC classes, certain other military academy graduates transferring to the Air Force, and sometimes directly by Congress itself. The remaining Regular commissions were few and hard to get. Since 1961 was a time of urgent need for more officers in Strategic Air Command, the fastest way to get them was through the Officer Training Program, as Reserve commissions by using recent college graduates. There was no difference in the Regular or Reserve officer's pay, rank, or uniform insignia. You could not tell them apart from Reserves. But the Regular officers somehow knew who the other Regular officers were on base. For an officer who wanted to make a career of the Air Force, it was a mark of distinction to be awarded a Regular commission.

One of the additional duties of the author was handling the Regular commission applications on base. I recall trying to explain to a B-58 aircraft commander, a major, who had just returned from an extended flight over far corners of the world, just why his application for Regular had been turned down by the Pentagon due to a very slight high-frequency hearing loss in one ear. He was certainly qualified to fly, that was what he did just about every day. His hearing was fine for the flight physical, it was just that little bit extra needed for a Regular commission. He was standing before my desk in his sweat-stained and rumpled flight suit, complete with large pistol under his arm, and in a bit of a bother. He had been trying to 'make Regular' for some time, and he wanted it for his promotional possibilities.

"Do you mean to tell me, Lieutenant, that my hearing is good enough to fly B-58s and haul nukes, but I am NOT good enough to make REGULAR? Somebody besides YOU, Lieutenant, is going to have to explain that to me!"

There are methods of official redress available for any officer when they feel the need for correction of an error. One method is to go over everybody's head and write to his Congressman. On base that is called a congressional inquiry, even though it's not—technically it's just a letter *requesting* a congressional inquiry. But it causes much concern and consternation by many people in many offices on base, beginning with the aggrieved officer's commander and going right on up the chain of command. This officer's inquiry skipped right over the Congressional level, right past the Senatorial level, up to a letter requesting a Presidential inquiry. No one on base had ever seen that before. It is unknown how it was resolved.

Secrets Box

Thermonuclear bombs were known as special weapons, and in order for one to be released, a complex series of steps had to occur, all in exactly the right order. An eight-letter Go Code was received on a discrete radio frequency and copied with grease pencils on plastic-covered forms, independently by three people: the EW, the navigator, and the radar navigator, and then decoded. All three had to agree. The first four letters of the code referred to a page in a code book, and the second four letters on that page had to match the color code and characters of execution tickets kept in a heavy, double-locked safe. The 'Secrets Box' had been signed out, carried aboard, and locked down by two armed officers. When the Emergency War Order message called for it, the aircraft commander and the navigator each unlocked and removed his personal combination lock and took the highly classified strike orders out of the box and distributed them to the various crew members.

There would be many more tasks to do before the arming of the bomb: navigate, avoid detection, find the target, etc. On the final bomb run the radar navigator could even fly the aircraft if necessary by using the autopilot at his station on the lower deck. When to release, when to open and close the bomb bay doors, were all actions based on the data he carefully entered before and during the flight. The bombing checklist also included other details to be read off and complied with, such as: the pilots closing their thermal curtains to prevent flash blindness; going to combat cabin pressurization, in case the hull was breached; reminding the crew to set their personal locator beacon lanyards to activate and start sending impulses in case their parachute was engaged—this may not apply on all missions—sometimes you didn't want people to know where your were if you had to eject; and a number of other items, such as seals to break, and circuits to engage. On older models, there was even a reminder to cover the optical bombsight, to block the blinding light from a nuclear blast. When the Hiroshima bomb had been released from the Enola Gay, the bombardier decided to ignore the warnings and watch it go off. At the last second, he thought better of it, and jerked his head back. A terrific beam of light, "like a laser," blasted up through the bombsight and against the airplane ceiling. He said later that if he had kept watching, he would have lost an eye.

The thermal, or flash curtains were very important. They were used to seal off, to 'button up' the cockpit from outside light. There was at least one incidence during a live bomb test in the Pacific where a gap in the thermal curtain allowed the nuclear flash to actually ignite a paper chart that had been left on the co-pilot's instrument panel. Flash curtains were used immediately after a maximum effort takeoff, where nuclear attack by the Soviets was considered a distinct possibility at any moment. "When we were 'busting out' we would have 12-15 second spacing between bombers. We'd get airborne, fan out, pull down our thermal curtains and button up the bomber," said Colonel Jim Maker, SAC BUFF pilot.

Bomb Drop

Each officer involved in the release of a nuclear weapon had a book that told him exactly how to do it: a classified notebook signed out to him personally. It contained a section on yellow paper labeled *Weapon Preparation For Release*. It would be referred to only when all the codes matched and preliminary formalities had been satisfied, and they were official executing the war plan, or SIOP.

First, the radar navigator on the lower deck would ask the electronic warfare officer, situated on the upper deck, "Pull and stow the special weapons manual lock handle." The EW would reach down to a slightly raised petal beside his right foot, break a copper safety wire securing a D-handle on the end of a cable, rotate the handle out of its detent and pull. That would physically remove a locking pin from the bomb's mounting rack back in the bomb bay. The EW would then stow the cable to prevent its accidental return to the locked position.

The RN would then ask the pilot to "Place the bomb readiness switch to READY." That was when the pilot would turn to his left, to a panel marked "Munitions Consent," and he would "consent" by breaking a copper safety wire on a red plastic guard, lift it, and move the switch to READY. That would send 28 volts of DC electrical current downstairs to a panel at the Radar Navigator's left hand. The pilot did not, contrary to some novels and movies, have the ability to either arm or drop the bombs. He consented, but did not arm or release the bomb. No one person could perform that task alone.

It was the Radar Navigator downstairs who completed the next task: arming the bomb. That might be completed many miles away from the target, as long as they were not over friendly territory. It was not one person, but the actions of these three officers who would perform those incredible steps that would, for only the third time in history, open Pandora's Box on Planet Earth ... to drop a nuclear bomb on an enemy.

The exclusive reason for the B-52 as the major deterrent to nuclear war lay at Major Shelton's left hand: the Weapons Monitor and Control Panel, one for each of the two nuclear bombs. Major Shelton's job as radar navigator was somewhat of a misnomer because this officer did much more than navigate by radar—he is the bombardier—responsible for the arming, aiming, and releasing of the weapons or bombs. A better name would probably be radar navigator/bombardier since he performed jobs that were three separate crew positions on the earlier bombers. The panel, the DCU/9A, is only about five inches by eight inches in physical size, but its potency was enormous. On the flat metal panel was a round wafer switch held in the SAFE position with a knobbed pin sealed by a breakable copper wire. It is very difficult and awkward to actuate, designed that way for a very good purpose. It takes both hands: break the safety wire, unscrew the knobbed release pin with your right hand, and pull it straight out toward you for a fraction of an inch. It is the only control device—out of about three hundred devices spread over eighty separate panels—that requires both hands to operate. While holding the release pin out with the right hand, the RN would probably take a deep breath, maybe say a prayer, and turn the round wafer part with his left hand to either GRND for ground burst, or AIR for air burst. That would send a 28-volt DC electrical current to the MC-772 ARM/SAFE Switch, located inside the back end of the selected thermonuclear bomb hanging in the bomb bay, causing it to rotate to the appropriate ARMED position.

Each bomb was carefully examined on every preflight inspection. A retired radar navigator once told me, "On your preflight, you could look through a little window in the bomb to inspect the Arm/Safe Switch and see either a green S (for SAFE) or a red A (for ARM). If you saw the red A, somebody had really screwed up, and this would be a good time to get excited."

The final switch the Radar Navigator engages to drop a nuclear weapon: the DCU/9A. Photo courtesy USAF.

Nothing would happen immediately. The aircraft would continue to fly it's assigned heading, maintaining altitude, all based on the mission as planned. The pilots are still flying the plane, guided by the navigators. While waiting for release, the Radar/Navigator would continue his duty, to monitor, refining the cross-hairs, watching over his minions. He had in his power the ability to stop the process entirely by yanking a handle to pull out the Release Circuits Disconnect, a large electrical plug as big as two fists. That would unplug everything. Or he could override the system entirely and manually drop the weapon by pulling an overhead D-ring, the special weapons release cable.

The computers would decide when the moment was right. At the last instant, when to flip open the bomb bay doors and release the weapon, all in one motion. As the computer reached its inevitable conclusion, as everyone knew it would, the bomb bay doors would open and stainless steel pins would withdraw and release the U-2 hook on the big bicycle chain holding up the weapon.

The armed bomb would drop.

It had three parachutes, packed in series. The first was a six-foot drogue chute. It was pulled out of the rear end of the bomb by a fixed nylon static line attached to the bomb rack in the aircraft. After a set time, the drogue chute would then automatically release from the bomb and take along with it a cloth bag. That bag surrounded the second parachute: the twenty-eight foot stabilizing ribbon parachute. The reason the ribbon parachute was not opened immediately upon bomb drop was that it might be too close to the airplane. An eleven-foot long weapon with a twenty-eight foot parachute on the back end opening up right below the bomb bay was considered just too close to the airplane. The ribbon configuration was to absorb the shock of a high-speed opening.

After slowing the bomb to the proper speed, the ribbon parachute would be released automatically. This in turn would pull out the third chute: the big retardation parachute, a one-hundred-foot-wide, ivory-colored monster, believed to be the biggest parachute in use at that time. That size was necessary to support the 6,750-pound weight of the bomb. The bomb was eleven feet long, and thirty-five inches wide at the middle, forty-four inches at the tail section. It was designed in three configurations: air burst, ground contact, and laydown. The laydown modification was to allow for a quick getaway for a high speed, low-level bomb drop, and it was just that—it would lay on the ground for a designated length of time, and then detonate.

The bombs at Goldsboro were Mod 2, set for ground contact.

Human Reliability

These three officers, the pilot, the electronic warfare officer, and the radar navigator, are located in three different areas of the aircraft, areas that are the most physically distant from each other: two were on the upper deck, one on the lower. Each would have to perform a physical task in the planned, deliberate, and exact sequence to release a nuclear weapon. That was the intent of SAC's Human Reliability Program. That program would ensure that no single person, at any time, would be alone with a nuclear weapon, and that every member of the team was equally familiar with the task at hand to know when proper procedures were followed. The policy required the conscious decision of more than one knowledgeable crew member, men in that plane, at that time, to physically set the circuitry to start the process of an armed weapon drop. That effectively removed the possibility of a rogue crewman taking over a SAC aircraft and dropping the bomb single-handedly.

The SAC Human Reliability Program used psychological evaluations to insure that every person who had access to nuclear weapons could be trusted. The SAC missile programs, such as the Titan and Minuteman, would be under the same policy. The two missile launch officers in the underground launch command had different keys to be inserted in different switches, located physically apart, and turned at the same instant. In some units, the keys of the missile commander and the deputy commander were on big metal rings worn around their necks. At the change of their twenty-four hour tour of duty, a short procedure was held in the underground silo signifying the transfer of control of the missile. It involved the old and new crews facing each other, a countdown, and the simultaneous flipping of the big key rings from the out-going two officers' necks to the on-coming crew. Another part of the Human Reliability Program was the arming of the missile launch officers with sidearms. It was rumored, hopefully in jest, that the pistols were not just for intruders breaking into the underground missile silo. If the other guy started acting crazy and you thought he was trying somehow to launch a missile by himself, shoot him.

A major complaint from BUFF crews was about the comfort level of the ejection seats, or rather, the lack of comfort. Many marveled at how it was possible to spend millions of dollars to perfect an ejection seat that is adjustable six ways and still is not quite able to make it to a bearable sitting position. You could not adjust the seat too frequently because you had to let the electric seat motors rest to avoid overheating. You could not bring a seat cushion from home (although some did), because "the chance of vertebral injury during ejection is increased considerably by sitting on too thick a compressible mass." You just had to sit there, for twenty-four hours or so, on those chute straps that were part of the complex system that would "save your sorry butt during an ejection." The seats of the G model were eventually redesigned with the intent to lessen the fatigue of the 24-hours missions. Success of the redesign got mixed reviews.

For the B-52 to be as big as it is, the amount of room for the occupants is extremely small. For other than the pilots, it is comparable to taking a very long trip in a very small car, a small car without windows. Another way is to visualize sitting in front of a computer screen for twenty-four hours, which is inside an aluminum aircraft cargo container, the kind that holds passenger luggage. Now load it in a cargo aircraft and fly it to Spain and back, all the while tilting, shaking, dropping, and climbing. It was not quite as bad as the way one of the early Gemini astronauts described the two person orbital space flight: "Both of you put on space suits, then get in a Volkswagen. One of you carries a television set on your lap for eight days. That's it."

There were other expressions of opinion. In the center of each steering yoke for the pilot and co-pilot was a circle with a stylized *Boeing B-52*. At the bottom of the black yoke was printed, in white, *STRATOFORTRESS*. At least one joker, with too much time on autopilot, scratched out seven of those letters, and changed the second *O* to an *A*, thus christening his airplane *RAT FART*.

Sometime before a scheduled combat crew flight, a briefing would be held at Base Operations for the basic stuff: time of takeoff, air refueling time and place, any training details, and landing time. The navigator would then spend hours on his job: weather forecasting, winds aloft, altitudes, headings, turn points, and how to avoid restricted airspaces. The navigator was convinced that the mission was not planned sufficiently until the weight of the paperwork equaled to or exceeded the weight of the weapons carried.

The day before the flight, there would be 'the big brief.' Joint mission planning was the point where the entire crew discussed in detail the upcoming flight. The co-pilot was sometimes in charge of this meeting, not the pilot, because the co-pilot was the "right hand man," and "commander-in-training." And this session usually lasted a full day and every crew member had an input. Everyone, including any additional crew members and instructors who would be on the airplane, would discuss their required duties and expectations. The aircraft commander, who had overall responsibility for the sortie, would close out the meeting with a quick summary of the mission and a few words of encouragement, a pep talk. If the entire crew had worked well together in the past, he would remind them of that. If not, he would remind them of that also. He would cover any common sense rules of safety, such as never saying the word "bailout" at any time; he alone would be the only person on that aircraft to say that word. And if he ever said it, do it.

From the days of sailing ships, navigation has always relied on accurate time keeping. If you want to get from here to there, you had better have a good clock. The job of keeping the time in the B-52 fell to the navigator. Not only did he maintain the official government chronometers of the aircraft, he would also carry at least one stopwatch and two personal watches, each with the ability to stop and reset the second hand. Lieutenant Colonel Wilton Strickland, who was the chief of radar navigation standardization on many flights, told the story where he was flying as the certification officer for a new navigator. He approached the officer at the crew briefing. The lieutenant was pretty tense and sweating a bit. He needed to relax to do his job smoothly. Colonel Strickland asked him if his watches had been checked against the command post's official Zulu clock.

"Yes sir!" said the lieutenant, practically shouting. He was facing the Wing Standardization Officer, the guy who could send him into some other line of work.

"Well, let's compare it to MY watch," said Colonel Strickland.

They stood facing each other with their wristwatches held before them.

"Sir, at my mark it is sixteen minutes, thirty seconds. MARK!" He correctly went by minutes and seconds past the hour, not the hour itself.

The colonel looked stern. "Well, lieutenant, MY watch has Mickey's little hand on the eight, and his big hand is......"

The entire group in the briefing room loosened up.

Years later in the Vietnam era this sense of humor was considered essential. At every SAC installation was a sign with the SAC emblem: a mailed fist holding lightning bolts and an olive branch with the phrase, "Peace Is Our Profession." Someone would usually add: "War Is Just Our Hobby."

The official phrase came about by accident. A painter, who was supposed to put the original legend "Maintaining Peace Is Our Profession" on a recruiting billboard, found that he did not have enough room for all the words, so he eliminated the only word he could: 'maintaining.' The revised phrase became the new official phrase.

In spite of all the discomfort and stress of flying the B-52, there was still the thrill of the hunt and the need for speed that all pilots know. Here is the way a former pilot with the Strategic Air Command described it to historian Doug Keeney: "After takeoff, we'd go get gas and then we'd fly to out first waypoint, our PCTAP—the Positive Control Turn Around Point. If we were executed, that is, if we were told to proceed, we'd go as far as the H-Hour Control Line. If we got the proper codes, at our Start Descent point, we'd push over the nose.

At our Terrain Avoidance Point we'd be flying low level inbound to our target, maybe two hours out, as low to the ground as our sortie required. We were already low level. The Soviet fighters couldn't see us down low. When we got to our Initial Point, which was where we'd start the bomb run, we'd go another four, five minutes then pop the bomb bay doors at ten seconds, pull the nose up at five seconds, release our weapon, then push it over and get back down. We're going 390 knots with our hair on fire."

SAC created special routes across the US countryside for this low-level training. They were called Oil Burner routes, and were sometimes hundred of miles long. The name came from the streams of black smoke pouring out of the B-52 as it flew at near treetop level.

I experienced one of these Oil Burner exercises, from the ground level. I was using the small airport at Post, Texas in 1977, flying a small plane, working on my instrument rating. I had finished off with some touch-and-go landings, and had put the plane away. I was driving home and decided to stop and enjoy the West Texas sunset with a cold 'Texas longneck.' It was utterly quiet except for the birds, and miles away from civilization. The fading light was incredible, a perfect evening along the rolling hills of west Texas below the Caprock of the high plains.

A low rumble shook the ground. I turned around to find the source, when suddenly, from out of nowhere, the biggest, loudest, meanest looking airplane in the world rose out of the low hills just to the north, navigation lights on, black smoke pouring out, and screamed right over my head: or rather, my butt, because I had hit the deck. The ground was shaking, dust was flying, and small stones levitated. The noise was incredible. The BUFF looked like it was flying about fifty feet off the ground. It had to be at least two hundred feet or so, but it sure looked, felt, and smelled like fifty or less.

I later checked the NOTAMs, Notices To Airmen, and found that I was near the exit end of an Oil Burner route that began in Oklahoma.

There are several phrases for describing flying speed, such as "going 390 knots with our hair on fire." Another is, "Taking off like God's ape, late for work." I have no idea where that phrase came from.

The B-52 on takeoff is quite impressive. As an additive to the fuel, some models, including the G, could use up to ten thousand pounds of water, depending on gross weight and temperature, in the first two minutes of takeoff. This water injection would give a boost of around 15 percent in takeoff power by blowing water into the rear section of the engines. The water would cool the engine fins, letting them spin faster without coming apart, and give mass to the thrust. It would also contribute to dense black smoke spewing out, as almost four times the amount of water as fuel was pouring into the engines en masse. The water had to be completely used up on takeoff, or else it would have to be dumped before reaching altitude where it would freeze. At the beginning of a takeoff roll, a B-52 could actually be over the allowed maximum takeoff weight, but as it rolled faster and faster down the runway, it would use up 5,000 to 10,000 pounds of fuel as well as 10,000 pounds of water, and was suddenly down to takeoff weight. The BUFF actually lifted off with the nose in a slight downward angle, which defied imagination. In fact, just watching a BUFF somehow get off the ground was always amazing to me.

MITO is SAC-speak for the Minimum Interval Take Off, where the bombers are launched down the runway in fifteen-second intervals, usually as part of an Operational Readiness Inspection, or ORI. The crews call it 'busting out.' On a hot day, where the exhaust temperature from the engines is added to an already hot runway, things can really get exciting for the crews, especially those in back of the line-up. The higher the temperature, the longer the take-off roll. And with black smoke from water injection pouring out of eight engines per aircraft, the visibility was much worse. Put several B-52s going flat out down the same hot runway, not too far apart, and with the guys in BUFFs at the back of the line guessing at decision speed and take-off speed, the pucker factor was a variable number, subject to temperature. The best the pilots could wish for would be a decent crosswind, to blow the heat, jet-wash, and smoke some place else. The worst was having the wind blowing the black smoke straight down the runway, right at you.

The 'BUST-OUT'.... B-52s departing using Minimum Interval Takeoff, (MITO.) Black exhaust is the result of water injection into the engines. Photo courtesy USAF.

The BUFF's crew navigator (NAV) is primarily responsible for the aircraft's position at all times. He must get the aircraft and the bomb close enough to the target to allow the RN to place the bomb on target at the right time. TOT (Time On Target) was a critical event. One reason: there was a policy of multiple strikes on the same target, and you didn't want to be over the target when some other SAC bomber or missile ahead of you happened to be early or late. That was the reason for the computer-generated master timeline for all bombers, to insure the other aircraft would be safe from other SAC bombers in going to, from, and at the target area. Several crew members wondered what they would do if they got to the target and it already had a mushroom shaped cloud over it. Would they drop another one into the fire or go to the alternate target? Would they "make the rubble bounce?"

Radar bombing was a skill in itself. Practice targets known as 'show' targets would be identified by radar returns from known large, stationary objects, like bridges or buildings. When missile silos went underground, with no discernible structures, a new skill set was devised: offset bombing. By using the known distances and known direction from 'show' targets, the hidden 'no show' targets would be offset, and identified on the radar navigator's screen. In practice bomb runs on America's prairies it would appear they were bombing an empty spot on the windswept plains, but they would know if they hit the practice 'no show' site. It was estimated that 90 percent of all Soviet targets were 'no show.'

SAC crews practiced bombing the same practice radar bombing sites in the US so often that they became too well known, so the 'RBS Express' was invented. The radar bombing targets were put in sealed boxcars on three trains traveling around three parts of the country. The sealed units would transmit electronic images identifying them as targets. The purpose was to eliminate crew familiarity with permanent practice sites, to create real-time mission planning.

Most SAC crews could agree on one thing: the navigator was the hardest-working man on the airplane, always figuring and rechecking. Captain Brown had to be very proficient and extremely accurate in several types of difficult long-range navigation: celestial, pressure pattern, grid navigation in the Arctic, dead reckoning, and radar navigation at very low altitude. Pressure pattern navigation was part art, part science. It proved that the shortest distance between two points is not necessarily a straight line, but knowing where the atmospheric highs and lows were, or going to be, and how to best utilize current and future winds associated with them. It was sort of like windsurfing, where the surfboard has an attached sail. In this case however, the surfboard weighs about a half million pounds and carried several buckets of Hell.

These six men made up a new configuration called the *battlestation* concept of the B-52 G placing the defensive crew (the EW and gunner) facing aft on the upper deck, and the offensive team (the two crew navigation system operators), in The Hole on the lower deck facing forward. The flight crew, the pilot and co-pilot, were side-by-side on the flight deck. Surprisingly, a very early prototype of the B-52 actually had the pilot and co-pilot sitting in tandem, one behind the other, like the B-47. That was when General Curtis LeMay reportedly told Boeing during the development phase, "Change it. Put the pilots side by side and I'll buy a bunch of the damn things."

Refueling

The G-model B-52 had eliminated the ailerons, the primary wing control surfaces traditionally used on most aircraft. Wing control was now handled by a series of spoilers on the top of each wing, seven per wing. Spoilers were very distinctive in appearance, with long flat "fingers" off the trailing edge. The fingers had gaps between them and did a great job of "spoiling" the linear air flow over the wing.

When not in use, the spoilers, including fingers, lay down flat against the wing surface.

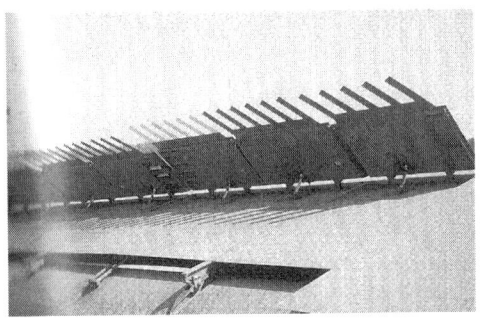

Wing spoilers.
Photo courtesy USAF.

Ailerons, the traditional controls for aircraft roll, are connected to each other in a cross-control way; that is to say, if the right aileron goes up a certain degree, the left one goes down by the same amount. Together, they work as a team, on opposite wings. To roll the airplane to the right, the pilot turns the yoke right. That raises the aileron on the right wing that impedes the air flow and reduces lift, lowering the right wing. At exactly the same time, the left aileron is lowered by the same amount, which makes the left wing more efficient, and raises that wing. Left wing up, right wing down, equals a roll to the right. Kick in a little right rudder, and you have a nice coordinated turn to the right.

Spoilers work by merely creating drag and spoiling lift on one wing at a time, causing that wing to drop and forcing the other wing to rise. B-52s had both ailerons and spoilers before the G-model, but the G-, and the later H-model, had only spoilers. Spoilers were excellent speed brakes when used in unison on both wings and were very effective in that role—the loss of lift slowed the airplane quickly and provided quicker and better control for safe descents. But some B-52 pilots were critical of spoilers for fine flight control, and most preferred the quicker feedback response of ailerons. Spoilers increased the tendency of the G-Model to go into a frightening gyration called a Dutch roll, a problem with all large, swept wing aircraft. When a pilot initiated a turn the spoilers usually caused a slight buffet and the nose would pitch up, which could be particularly troubling during aerial refueling.

Refueling was delicate enough even without the strain of fighting the controls. In a fighter plane, it was said, if you think about a turn, you turn. In a B-52, you think about the turn, you initiate the turn, and a while later, the airplane agrees. But then it keeps on turning until you change it. That was never more evident than during air refueling which was exhausting for the pilots wrestling with "the beast" below and behind the refueling tanker. Chrome Dome air refuelings were conducted day or night in radio silence, unless in case of emergency. At the rendezvous point, and about forty minutes before the specified time, the tanker would turn on a radar beacon for the B-52 to home in on. Usually, the two aircraft usually would begin the dance head-on, but at different altitudes, around 150 miles apart. Then, as the distance closed, they would turn in careful coordination so that both aircraft ended up on the correct refueling heading. The radar operator would report the closing rate down to one mile increments. After the bomber moved in behind the tanker, the boom operator used a series of signal lights on the tanker's belly to help the receiving pilot with his relative approach speed and to find the proper staging location. When the B-52 was in the right spot below the boom tip, the lights on the tanker's belly turned green, and the receiving pilot would hold that position while the boom operator flew the probe, using its small wings, above the four-inch-wide receptacle. The boom itself was 33 feet long and 2 feet in diameter. Inside was the 12-foot long telescoping tube that makes the hook up. The final connection was by the boom operator extending the probe down and in for a good lock-on, much like a harpoon being launched. Whoever was flying the bomber for the refueling (both pilot and co-pilot had to be qualified), used his own personal references, such as: if he could see the boomer's face in a certain corner of an overhead window, he was in the right spot. Once connected, it took about twenty minutes to complete the fuel transfer at the rate of 6,000 pounds per minute. That is, if there were no disconnects. The goal was to complete up to 120,000 pounds of fuel transfer at one time, and thus join the "One-Gulp Club." The last portion of the fuel transfer was always the most difficult because the center of gravity, or CG, was constantly shifting in both aircraft. The limits of the refueling area, or "box" were 20° up, 40° down, and 10 °on either side of the boom in its neutral position. Exceed the limits and you hear the urgent command from the boomer over the radio, "Breakaway-breakaway-breakaway!" as the probe was being quickly withdrawn then raised. Both the boom operator or the receiver pilot had the ability to disengage. There were always other dangers with two such large and heavy aircraft flying so near to each other. One danger was in juggling the changing fuel weight and pressure. Too much fuel pressure could actually force the B-52 backwards off the boom. Or if the alignment was shifted, the probe could actually penetrate the roof of the B-52 cockpit. There was no such thing as a small problem in aerial refueling.

The B-52 was bigger than the KC-135 tanker, but that usually was not a factor for the experienced tanker and receiver pilots, and as long as the weather was cooperating. Lieutenant Colonel Earl 'Mac' McGill, a highly qualified B-52 pilot and instructor pilot said that after you pushed through the tanker's downwash, you retarded the throttles very slightly to maintain a stable position and waited for the refueling nozzle to descend. Once it was hooked up, you controlled yaw by very slight wrist movements on the throttles to keep the nose from wandering from side to side. As long as big adjustments in flight controls could be minimized, and you could keep a good alignment with the tanker by differential throttle settings—staggering the power so the airplane maintained a straight-ahead orientation with the tanker, it could be like being towed around by the boom. But flying in turbulence while it took on a large, shifting weight of fuel could be a handful. Then it could be tough, even exhausting. If you had a "break-away," a disconnect, the receiving pilot fell back, got stabilized, and the line-up process started all over again. The key was making very small adjustments in relative speed and relative position. The tanker pilot was concentrating on flying exact heading and altitude, and exactly straight and level. The receiving pilot was frequently drenched in sweat by the end of the transfer of fuel.

Pilots also relied on the powered trim controls, which permitted continuous adjustments of nose up and down as well as aircraft heading by changing small tabs on the wings and tail. Trim was increased or decreased by small switches on the pilots' steering yoke or the larger knobbed wheel on the center console, and was constantly fine-tuned during flight. Making very small, continuous adjustments on the trim controls was a technique that makes any good pilot look better. It also helped relieve some of the stress in manhandling the airplane.

Colonel Walter J. Boyne, who was an Air Force captain when he first encountered the B-52, gave a comment about spoilers in his neat short description of what it was like to fly the BUFF: "The control surfaces were small so you used trim a lot… It responded to more than one gust variation at a time and hence was never in synch. The spoilers took some getting used to. It wasn't like having conventional aileron control… When you took off, the wings flew before the fuselage, so the flight surfaces had to be used while the wheels were still on the ground. Also, the crosswind landing gear [which could be turned up to 20° in either direction to counteract crosswinds up to 43 knots] took some getting used to. While landing, you could be looking out the side window to see the runway ahead."

Crew R-10 watched the inauguration of the new president, John F. Kennedy, on the black and white TV in the recreation room of the alert facility. Sergeant Barnish saw his former commanding general, Dwight Eisenhower, as he sat bundled in overcoat and scarf in the bitterly cold weather. After the ceremony, the old soldier and now ex-president would be driven with his wife the eighty miles north to their farm in Gettysburg, Pennsylvania. One Secret Service car led the two car procession. When they got to the gate of the farm, the Secret Service car turned around, honked the horn, and headed back to Washington. Eisenhower sat there waiting a minute, then got out and opened the gate for the driver to pull through. That night in the farmhouse he would try to place his first phone call in over twenty years. It did not go well and he would yell out, "Come show me how you work this Goddamn thing!"

That was on a Friday and the nation was at the height of the Cold War. President Kennedy had said in his inauguration address, "We will pay any price, bear any burden, meet any hardship, support any friend, oppose any foe, in order to assure the survival and the success of liberty."

On the coming Monday, January 23, 1961, Crew R 10 would fly.

B-52 H Model with landing gear coming down. Note the rotation of the 'bogies,' the main gear with two wheels each. Also, at the end of each wing, there are two outrigger wheels that have not yet started down.

Photo courtesy USFA.

Chapter 2. The Mission

Crew R-10 had completed their fourth day of alert duty in the facility that was (and still is) just 1,400 feet from the western end of Seymour Johnson runway 08-26. All runways use a system based on the closest ten degrees of magnetic heading of each of it's two directions. Runway 08-26 heads 080 degrees in one direction, and 260 degrees going the other way, almost due east and west. The crew was near their waiting aircraft, Number 58-187, ready to go. Their aircraft occupied one of the alternating nine slots, or branches of the "Christmas Tree," the alert parking ramp for Seymour Johnson. The closest slot was just 250 feet from the alert facility, the furthest was 1,700 feet away.

The *"Christmas Tree" alert ramp at Seymour Johnson Air Force Base. The alert billet facility is at the southwest corner of the "Tree."*

Illustration by author

They had a briefing on the afternoon of Sunday, January 22 for a 'Coverall' mission in accordance with Eighth Air Force Order 20-31. It would be a twenty-four-hour, non-stop flight that included two heavyweight air refuelings. The purpose was to replicate a full alert mission in all aspects: elapsed time from takeoff to landing, total distance flown, takeoff weight, crew manning, planning and even weapons carried—to 'cover all' aspects of an actual airborne alert mission. They would be flying around a big portion of southeastern United States and the Atlantic Ocean. It was technically called a training mission.

That day started out warm for January at Seymour Johnson Air Force Base in Goldsboro, North Carolina. But during the day it turned windy and chilly, and by late night a cold front would come through in force. Crew R-10 would eventually be flying the new Southern part of Chrome Dome looping over the Atlantic to the Mediterranean. The route was named Southern because it began in the southern United States. Others were Northern, from the area around Michigan, and Western, from the northwest US. There was also a fourth route, the Thule Monitor, which circled around and around Thule, Greenland. The Chrome Dome routes would funnel one B-52 after another, a constant stream of bombers and tankers, spaced out for refueling, into several giant holding patterns on all sides of the Soviet Union. That's where they would wait for World War III to start.

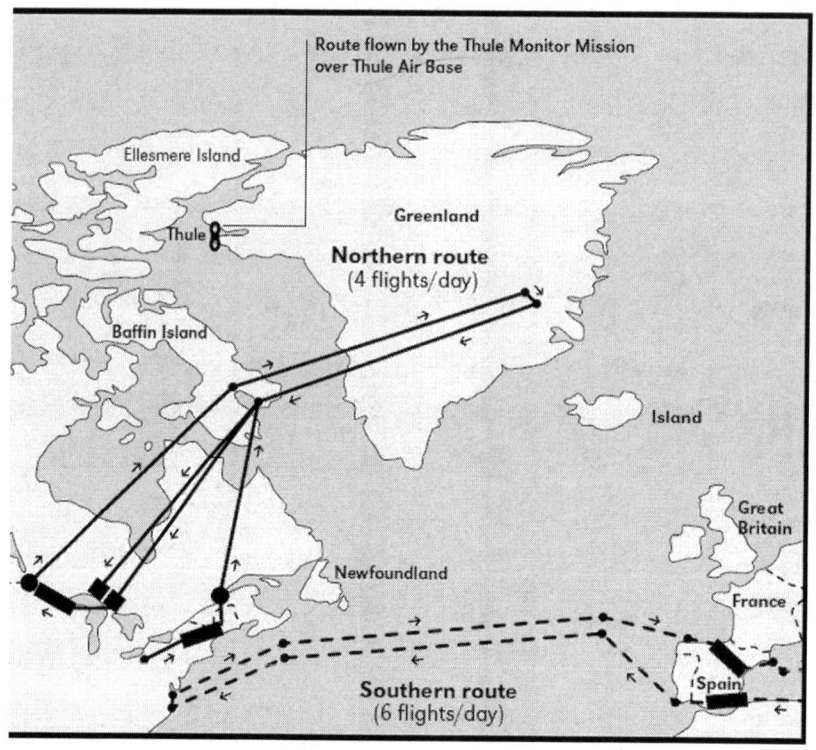

Chrome Dome Routes, showing Southern route from the East Coast. Courtesy of USAF.

SAC

General Curtis LeMay had built SAC into a powerful organization, and it was designed to be the elite fighting force for a new battle concept, total annihilation of the Soviet Union. The necessity for Strategic Air Command had its beginnings in the Northern Mariana Islands in 1944. That's when General LeMay, in charge of the 21st Bomber Command in Guam, unleashed the fury of massive bombing on the mainland of Japan. Hundreds of long-range B-29's hammered the enemy with a pace never before seen in history. The only pause was when LeMay ran out of bombs, and he had to wait while the Navy resupplied his airfields from their supply ships. On the night of March 9-10, 1945, LeMay launched what would be the deadliest bombing raid of World War II. It was a big gamble for LeMay, who had only been on this job for two months. He had discovered that B-29s fighting the headwinds of the jet stream at 35,000 feet would permit only three tons of bombs per plane to be delivered to the targets in Japan. This raid was planned for a lower 10,000 feet, which would require less fuel, and with guns, gunners, and ammo removed from the aircraft, the bomb loads could be doubled. LeMay had put Brigadier General Thomas S. Power in charge of this raid and a total of 325 B-29s took off from the runways of Guam, Saipan, and Tinian. Even with the airplanes crowding the minimum takeoff wartime interval of one minute apart, it took three hours just to get them all in the air.

General Power led the first bomb run, dropped his bombs, and circled Tokyo from 10,000 feet. At about 2 a.m., he sent a message to LeMay: "Bombing the primary target visually. Large fires observed, flak moderate. Fighter opposition nil." Fires from the napalm bomblets started a raging firestorm and destroyed sixteen square miles of Tokyo and killed almost one hundred thousand people. LeMay would later say that he might be hung as a war criminal if Japan had won the war. The Joint Chiefs of Staff in Washington found his military successes hard to comprehend. How could just one bomber command, on a few tiny islands in the Pacific, thousands of miles from America's shores, singlehandedly be so effective against the powerhouse of Japan?

It would be two single B-29s, with two single bombs, that brought

Japan to its knees without an invasion, but it was the overwhelming air power that laid the groundwork. When General LeMay stood on the crowded decks of the *U.S.S. Missouri* in Tokyo Bay on September 2nd, and after the formal surrender of Japan was signed, the silence was broken by a massive, deafening formation of 462 B-29's in a fly-by. General James H. "Jimmy" Doolittle said, "The Navy had the transport to make the invasion of Japan possible; the Ground Forces had the power to make it successful; and the B-29 made it unnecessary."

General Hap Arnold said, "The influence of atomic energy on air power can be stated very simply. It has made air power all-important."

There in the Pacific, with the B-29 and the atomic bomb, air power entered its primacy. It showed what massive air power and the atomic bomb could do. The seeds for the Strategic Air Command were sown. After the war, LeMay returned to the US by piloting a B-29, non-stop, from Hokkaido, Japan, to Chicago.

LeMay had the nickname Old Iron Ass. When he took over a B-24 bomber group earlier, in Europe, the mission abort rate was high. He told the crews that he would fly the lead on every mission, and any crew who aborted would be court-martialed. After the war, when the national need for the intercontinental delivery of atomic bombs became paramount, SAC as born. It was actually born as a separate command (1946) before the US Army Air Corps became the Air Force (1947). General LeMay was not the first commander of the Strategic Air Command, but he is considered its father. The first commander was General George C. Kenney, commander for two years. When LeMay took over as SAC commander on October 19, 1948, he had the headquarters moved from Washington, D.C. to Omaha, Nebraska. He said Washington was just too easily hit by the Soviets on the East Coast.

SAC had just a few untrained B-29 groups that were World War II leftovers, and only half of them were operational. The officer force was demoralized and training was far from adequate. As an early exercise in January 1949, he had his planners set up a simulated bombing attack. The target: the city of Dayton, Ohio. It was to be a practice radar bomb run, at night, from thirty thousand feet using the entire SAC fleet of five hundred bombers. The accuracy of the bombers would be measured by the radar operators on the ground at nearby Wright-Patterson Air Force Base. They would record the point where the bombers would have released the loads, and calculate the area where the bombs would have landed. As an operational test, it was a disaster. Not a single plane accomplished its mission. Only 303 planes reached the target, none hit it, and the average miss was 10,090 feet, almost two miles. The bombardiers had been used to aiming at the large radar reflectors on practice bombing sites, not the actual profile of an urban cityscape.

LeMay had his work cut out for him. By July 1950, the circular error, or CEP, was down to 2,600 feet, then down to 1,925 feet, acceptable for nuclear war. CEP is an acronym for "circular error probable." It is a term to describe accuracy: one-half of all shells, bombs, or missile warheads will fall within a specified radius of a circle centered on the target. Thus, a one thousand foot CEP would mean that one-half of all the weapons aimed at a specific target would fall within one thousand feet of that target. In the fall of 1944, only seven percent of all bombs dropped by the Eighth Air Force on Europe fell within one thousand feet of the target.

LeMay had promised that he would defeat Japan from the air in World War II, and he kept that promise. He promised he would keep Berlin open from the air at the start of the Cold War, and he did it. He promised that SAC could deliver annihilation from the air against our enemies under any condition, at any time, and he was keeping that promise too. He had stated, "The objective of our national defense police is deterrence. In the public mind—both ours and the Soviets—deterrence is rooted in fear of nuclear devastation of population centers."

There were two large paintings in his office at Offutt, both showing humiliating retreats from Moscow, one of Napoleon's army, one of Hitler's army. The message was to show that only airpower could take Moscow. LeMay would be a general for seventeen years, longer than any other man in the history of the United States military. He was the youngest four-star general since Ulysses S. Grant. He would be awarded every medal but one, the Medal of Honor. His ever-present cigar was partly to hide a sometimes drooping lip from Bell's Palsy, which was caused by flying high and cold in B-17s during World War II. The palsy would sometime cause the General's speech to be slurred, causing him to rely more on a cold glare, instead of a long sermon of displeasure.

Two months after LeMay took over SAC, Air Force Chief of Staff General Hoyt Vandenberg called a meeting to be held at Maxwell Air Force Base in Montgomery, Alabama. The three-day meeting started on December 6, 1948, seven years after the attack on Pearl

Harbor. All the Air Force commanders were there to discuss force readiness in a darkened conference room, complete with impressive slide discussions. General John Montgomery, the SAC planner, in somber and unflinching tones, spelled out the tactics and timelines for destroying the Soviet Union's cities. One attendee remembered, "It was the voice of doom."

LeMay was in the conference room, but his part of the meeting had not yet arrived at Maxwell. Without telling his boss, LeMay had scheduled a performance that would nail down the role of air power. He had two bombers launched from Carswell Air Force Base in Texas, not stripped down, but in war configuration, to haul a load of dummy bombs to a spot just off the shores of Hawaii to the approximate longitude of Pearl Harbor, and drop them in the sea at about the same time of day the Japanese attacked seven years before. It was a round trip of 7,700 miles, and several refuelings were necessary. The two planes were supposed to land back at Maxwell, right at the site of the conference, but they had to divert at the last minute due to a base-scheduling problem. LeMay wanted them to taxi right up at Maxwell and he would then brief the commanders on what just occurred. The point was well made however. SAC could deliver an atomic bomb anywhere in the world.

At another meeting, LeMay would make the point that Strategic Air Command would deliver the bomb more effectively than all the other US forces combined. On 21 May 1957, he addressed the USAF Advisory Board at Patrick Air Force Base in Florida. He announced to the board that a recent appraisal of what each Joint Chief of Staff command could actual do in the critical first hours of the *air power battle* as he called it.... the opening first shots of World War III. Of all JCS Commands only SAC could "underwrite the destruction of 100 percent of the DGZs (designated ground zeros)." There were 1,539 at that time.

SAC alone	100 percent
All other JCS commands including Navy	11 percent
Navy alone	5 percent

At its inception SAC had an original response time based solely on World War II experience: six hours. They would assemble the crew, fuel the bomber, sign the bomb out from storage, load it, and take off. The goal was to speed things up where ever possible. One of the first goals was to gain control of the nation's nuclear weapons for the bombers. The weapons had always been under the control of the Atomic Energy Commission, a civilian agency. LeMay wanted a faster way to get his hands on the weapons, to get *bombs-on-base*, so they would be available immediately on his Strategic Air Command bases, and not have to wait for them to be checked out of the civilian stockpile storage facilities. He not only wanted them available on base, he wanted them on the bombers. He achieved 'bombs-on-base' in 1956.

The six-hour ground alert was soon reduced to one hour for one-third of the armed and ready bomber fleet to be off the ground. When it was anticipated that the Soviets would have an operational ICBM with a detection-to-detonation time of fifteen minutes, this became SAC's goal: launch of bombers in fifteen minutes. That was the reason for the fifteen-minute ground alert. Response was measured by two exercises: *Bravo,* where the crews raced to the aircraft and started engines, and *Coco*, where they started engines and taxied to the takeoff position. There were times when SAC went to a higher intensity DEFCON, or defense condition, and the twenty-four-hour airborne alert would be put into effect, in which a classified percentage of bombers, tankers, and flying command posts were in the air at all times. The airborne alert program was officially announced on January 18, 1961 and would continue for seven years.

There was a national fear in the 1950s that the Soviet Union was prepared to wipe American cities off the map. In 1950, the Gaither Commission predicted that the Russians would pull ahead in the number of bombers and they would be ready to strike by 1954, and that was when the US would be the most vulnerable to attack. We demanded, and got, a massive expenditure for defense. Over five years, it amounted to more than forty-four billions dollars, half of it going into bombers and missiles. "It was like looking into the abyss and seeing hell at the bottom," said Robert Lovett, a member of the Gaither Commission.

When 1954, the projected date of Russian bomber attack came and went, the biggest threat came from missiles, ICBMs. Intercontinental Ballistic Missiles. (The 'C' was added when the IBM Company objected to the first abbreviation, IBM.)

Many people in the 1950s and 1960s believed with almost religious fervor that it was SAC alone that kept them safe from the Soviets. Most believed we were always on the brink of nuclear war. This was the time of underground fallout shelters, *duck and cover*, and schoolchildren wearing their dog tags, so their bodies could be identified after the coming nuclear holocaust. The Cincinnati Reds baseball team changed their name to the Redlegs for several years. Miss America contestants were asked their opinion of Karl Marx. When the television networks went off the air at 1:00 a.m., they played the National Anthem, and it was frequently a flight of B-52s that flew across an image of the flag.

LeMay's thinking, based on his World War II experience, was that massive, overwhelming force was the only way to fight a war. It certainly worked in Japan. Career military officers, especially those in the Navy, were amazed at how fast Strategic Air Command was growing, both in size and political importance. The new United States Air Force would soon get 46 percent of America's defense budget. The US Navy used to carry the big stick, but now, with the introduction of new weapons that could travel through space itself, the Navy was clearly worried. SAC doubled its personnel in five years, from 1950 to 1955. The new president, Dwight Eisenhower, joined LeMay's view of "deterrence," and saw that America could prevent nuclear war only by showing spectacular strength. Handling the workload of this responsibility was on the bombers alone, the B-36, the B-47, and the B-52. ICBMs were not fully in the picture yet. Even though the Atlas missile was declared operational in 1959 by General Thomas Power, a year later he would say, "Missile reliability… still causes me deep concern. As a result of our experience at Vandenberg with Atlas, our probability of a successful launch… is almost zero."

More years later, this concern over the missile force would continue. LeMay would comment in 1988, "We had dropped atomic bombs; we knew what we could do with them. We have never as yet fired a missile with an atomic warhead on it. In other words we have never gone through the whole cycle. So there is always some question: will they work?... In the back of one's mind: Is that first outfit going to go into combat for the very first time screwing up the mission?"

The Bombers

In the 1960s, the prime weapons carriers of SAC were the B-47, the B-58, and the B-52. The B-47 would fade away from SAC bomber inventory, the B-58 Hustler would be added, then dropped after a spectacular but brief ten year service, but the B-52 BUFF was destined to live on for decades.

The immediate predecessor of the B-52 was the B-47 Stratojet, the swept-wing bomber with six jet engines, which first flew in 1947. But it would have a relatively short life in the Air Force, and many said it had a deplorable safety record. Roughly twelve percent of all production B-47s crashed and never flew again—251 total losses at a cost of 470 lives. But it was indeed a beautiful airplane. The B-47s were phased out rapidly after 1961, and the SAC inventory fell from some 1,100 in that year to none in 1966.

Here is what Lieutenant Colonel Earl McGill said about the B-47:

> "When it was first wheeled onstage, the B-47 presented a whole new family of heavy aircraft... Boeing engineers had set out to make a bomber that looked, handled, and performed like a fighter. To achieve this goal, they hung on thin swept wings that could literally flap like a bird's, six sleek J-47 engines that even at full power could not lift a fully loaded B-47 safely into the air.... Her engines

were as fickle as she was. They were slow to wind up, and if impatience won over wisdom and the pilot moved the throttles too rapidly, the engines would overheat and fly apart. They'd been designed to do the job with nothing to spare. This zero margin for error resulted in situations where the pilot was strapped to a fast moving machine on the ground and could do nothing but crash. (Any problem on takeoff meant) he would not take off and could not be stopped on the remaining runway. Faced with the choice of a certain crash if he aborted and the chance that the airplane might fly, the aircraft commander usually selected the latter. An accident, he realized, meant the end of his career while saving the airplane was the kind of event heroes emerged from. His chance of becoming airborne was inevitably a bad one. There was no way the B-47 could fly under those conditions, even though the bitch would make you think she was flying....That she became a killer, we had no one to blame but ourselves. We made her trim, alluring and graceful as seductive, wild, and unforgiving. Seduced by her beauty and the character we gave her, we forgot that from the tip of her nose to her twin 20 mm cannons she was every inch a lady. She would not tolerate abuse and when we abused her she killed us. And when she had killed so many of us, we condemned her to an early grave."

B-47 alert crew responding.
Photo courtesy USAF.

As part of SAC's new push for power, a subtle change in the wording of the *Emergency War Plan* was made in the late 1950s. The title was changed to the *Emergency War Order,* implying they were through with planning—they were now ready for orders.

Another view of the SAC philosophy was revealed years later in an interview with former Soviet officials. It concerned land-based ICBM missile silos that were not hardened by constructing them as underground facilities; instead they were grouped tightly together, and considered *soft* targets, easily taken out by the Soviets. They knew the Americans "were not stupid" they knew the silos were easily visible to Soviet satellite photography. The Soviets then realized these ICBMs were not designed to ride out a strike. Instead, they were meant to be used as *first strike* weapons. Not only that, but SAC wanted the Soviets to know they were meant to be first strike weapons.

General LeMay demanded hard work, pride, but most of all, professionalism from every person in Strategic Air Command. He was somewhat 'less than tolerant' for failure to perform. He was famously quoted, "I can't afford to differentiate between the incompetent and the unfortunate." Even the slightest deviation from any established SAC policy was a cardinal sin. "Zero tolerance" was the by-word. Writing a bad check was like stealing, and thieves would not be trusted with a nuclear weapon. LeMay insisted on rigorous training and extremely high standards of performance for his aircrews. SAC's official historian once explained, "If you weren't in SAC you simply did not have the high sense of urgency. You could not keep up." The annual written proficiency tests required a score of 100 percent to pass. A 99 percent score failed. Alert crews were constantly being tested on their specialties and any score below 100 percent required more lectures, more study, and another test. The testing during alert duty became so frequent that crews asked to be tested before lectures. If they passed with 100 percent, they would sometimes be allowed to skip that day's lecture.

At the beginning of SAC in 1948, bombers could not be refueled in the air, and so had to be based at forward bases which were much more vulnerable to Soviet fighter attacks. The ability to refuel in flight erased that security issue, and allowed nuclear loaded bombers to be based on American soil where they could be better protected. LeMay was a ham radio hobbyist, and he incorporated his knowledge of single-sideband radio into practice. He knew that combined with midair refueling, constant radio communication with his bombers was absolutely essential for a worldwide airborne alert system. Single-sideband modulation (SSB) was the only convenient system at that time to have almost unlimited range. LeMay had an SSB transceiver put on a bomber and told his deputy, Lieutenant General Francis Griswald, also an amateur radio operator, to "go fly around some." Griswald flew to the Far East, while chatting with LeMay in Okinawa. A larger test involving a dozen ham radio stations on the ground and in airplanes, proved the viability of constant radio communications with SAC bombers. It met General LeMay's requirement to reach any wing commander in 30 seconds, and was the means for voice communications from SAC headquarters to be transmitted directly into the cockpit.

In the years to come, communications systems would become increasingly complex and more reliable. But in the year 1960, the vulnerability of SAC communications to nuclear attack was of great concern. SAC had developed what it called its "full pipeline philosophy," which meant that the command's communications lines should be kept busy, even loaded, at all times. It should be noted this is in direct contrast to Air Force policy. LeMay wanted his operators trained, equipment ready, and the system operating beforehand as it would be in an emergency. There was to be no increase in traffic to be detected by an enemy during an actual emergency, and the enemy's interpretation would be much more difficult by the sheer volume of traffic to be read. Wartime conditions were simulated by deliberately saturating the teletype system. Also, knowing that any intelligence monitoring by the Soviets would measure the amount of military radio chatter as a degree of force activity, SAC added white noise (meaningless messages and raw data) into the mix of true communications to fill the gaps. The right equipment on the other end filtered out this noise.

Other systems were added to cover the possibility of SAC headquarters being wiped out in a Soviet strike:

—The airborne command post was known as 'Looking Glass,' constantly manned with a General officer aboard. That came about after discussions with the other military branches. The Army wanted a railroad train as an alternate emergency command post, to roll around the country. In November 1960, Admiral Burke presented the Navy's proposal—the cruiser *USS Northampton*, arguing that the ship could cruise around on the Chesapeake Bay and on random routes in coastal waters. The President and his staff would move to the ship by car, helicopter, speedboat, or submarine. The Air Force was highly critical of the Navy's proposal, stating the *Northampton* was very visible, confined to the surface of known navigable waters, and thus vulnerable. The Air Force proposed what would become LOOKING GLASS, the flying command post. They submitted this idea to the Joint Chiefs on 26 January 1961, four days after the Goldsboro crash.

—A network of rockets to be launched that would carry powerful

UHF transmitters for pre-recorded Go Codes was approved. The first Emergency Rocket Communications System was comprised of four sites, with three rockets each, located around Omaha. The first rockets were Blue Scout Juniors.

—A low frequency radio system used the Earth itself as the transmitter; so-called *Earth waves*. This last system unofficially was known as Thumper, for the slow, measured *thump* of each letter received at wing command posts and missile silos.

Voice radio messages received by aircraft and at command posts would sound something like this: "Sky King, Sky King, do not answer, do not answer. This is Grand Slam, standby to copy. Message is in three parts. Authentication Code Zulu, Four, Hotel, Zulu. Part one: India, Bravo, Tango, November, Juliet. Part two… " In aircraft and wing command posts all over the SAC net, people would write down columns of five letters, which would be converted into columns of five numbers, which would be converted into English words. The five-digit code was old school, as old as the Civil War, but it was still used in the 1960s alongside the newer encrypted messages systems.

LeMay was a tough commander, but he wanted to create special benefits of being a member of SAC. When SAC first started it sometimes operated out of tar-paper shacks on overseas bases, now LeMay was having modern buildings constructed within the continental United States and decent housing built for crew members families. The alert facilities had fenced off swimming pools and picnic areas for family visits. It was said that some alert facility cooks even trained in fine hotels to learn how to create culinary masterpieces, although I haven't found any crewdogs who could attest to that. SAC was following the same policy the Navy used on submarines: If the troops were going to be cooped up, they had better have good chow. SAC had a million-dollar telephone and Teletype network to link all bases to Omaha headquarters. Crew members wore white ascots with their flight suits. LeMay had turned SAC into an elite outfit. And they were the big dogs with the nuclear hammer.

LeMay had his own method of testing his wing commanders' response to pressure. It would work like this, according to his aide, Colonel David C. Jones. General LeMay would tell him, "Miami. Ten a.m. tomorrow." When the general and his staff showed up at the aircraft at 10:00 ready to go to Miami, he would cancel the plan and instead fly to some SAC base. "Don't tell them I'm aboard," he would order.

When they arrived at the SAC base, he would want to see the wing commander at once. One showed up wearing a golf shirt one time, surprised at seeing the CINCSAC there. "Execute the war plan," LeMay would tell the wing commander. Complete chaos on the entire base. After about an hour and a half, including a MITO 'bust out,' LeMay would cancel the exercise.

The interesting point is, he would never bring the subject up again, to the wing commander, or anyone else.

Six weeks later, "Savannah. Tomorrow, 2 p.m." Same procedure: Cancel the Savannah trip at the flight line, instead go to another SAC base. Another wing commander would get a surprise visit. Sometimes a wing commander would be fired on the spot. He would be instructed to report to an office at the Pentagon where someone would find another job for him.

Each bomber crew on alert could get a dark blue Air Force station wagon or four-door pickup truck whenever they needed to be away from the alert facility, as long as they stayed on base and within the sound of the Klaxon. They had to be able to get back to their aircraft and meet the required take-off time, so everywhere they went on base, there were special parking spots marked with yellow paint, and signs that announced ALERT CREW PARKING ONLY. Such spots were at any place they may need to go and were closest to the building's main entrance: the base exchange, the commissary, the credit union, Officer's Club, library, movie theater, even the base chapel. If it was a place with seats like the chapel or theater the last two rows of seats closest to the exit always were reserved for alert crews, and marked in yellow. Their families could meet them there, but would know to quickly step out of the way when the horn went off, or if the movie stopped and the words ALERT CREWS RESPOND appeared on the movie screen.

I remember once being at the base chapel for Sunday Protestant services. There were some alert crews with their wives and kids sitting in the back two rows. The chaplain was in the middle of a prayer when a soft buzzer went off on his pulpit, right next to a signal light. He said Amen, then, in a different voice with more authority said, "Attention: Alert Crews respond." The organist played something while the crews left, jumped in the blue trucks, and headed toward the flight line. The chaplain had the congregation stand in silence for a moment, then gave probably the most moving and heartfelt prayer I have ever heard. It sounded like he may have practiced or given it a time or two. Then he gave the benediction and we were dismissed.

During alert period, if one of the crew needed to do something on base away from the alert facility, like cash a check at the credit union, the entire alert crew would drive over to the credit union in the alert vehicle, and proceed to the head of the line to take care of business. Whenever an alert crew member broke line, if anyone behind them had a problem with that they would certainly keep it to themselves. Anyone driving on base knew to pull to the right and stop if a blue alert truck with flashing yellow lights came up behind them.

The author witnessed during the days of the 1962 Cuban Missile Crisis the priorities of alert crews, such as the right to break line at the commissary, the base grocery store. I had gone to the BX commissary to pick up some popcorn for snacking in my BOQ (Bachelor Officers Quarters.) The commissary was packed, yet strangely quiet. There were a lot of wives and children of alert crewmen, quietly waiting, each with several shopping carts filled with canned goods and staples. It was a nervous, somber occasion. When the alert vehicles arrived, each crewman searched out and went to his family and had a very serious quiet talk with them. The large crowded grocery store had all checkout lanes going and was very busy. Then the alert crew families moved to the head of each line. Everyone in every line stepped to the side, and this new group of shoppers just moved in ahead of them and checked out. They got a lot of help from the other shoppers in unloading their shopping carts. These were our guys, and they might be going to war.

Outside, the alert crews loaded the boxes of food into family vehicles, mostly campers on pickup trucks. There was another serious, emotional talk with the kids and wives, and a few tearful goodbyes. Then, the families drove off to someplace thought to be safe, to preselected areas in the mountains. The crew members watched them go, then got in their blue trucks and drove back to work, down at the alert facility.

Every New Year's Day the annual Commanders' Reception was held at Officer's Club on SAC bases. Officers' wives would dress in formal wear, the male officers not on alert would wear the infamous *mess dress* uniform, which had a short tuxedo jacket that looked like it belonged to a waiter. That was for the male officers. Female officers' mess dress uniforms looked like they belonged to another waiter.

All would meet at the O Club at noon, New Year's Day, for cocktails, hors d'oeuvres, and strained social small talk. The officers would leave their card, an actual embossed calling card, in a silver dish at the entrance. This is the only time the card was used in the history of the US Air Force as far as anyone knows. Those on alert stood out just a wee bit. They wouldn't drink, and they always tended to stick together. They would meet their wives at the front door of the club, and escort them through the reception line of all the commanders and their wives. The wives would be in classic formal wear, the husbands on alert would be in stylish rumpled green flight suits, sometimes with pistols in shoulder holsters.

Combat and support crews went through enough stress just to be in SAC: long periods of time away from families, the stress of the constant maintenance of the nuclear weapons, working long hours on the flight line, often in terrible weather. Maybe it just seemed like SAC bases traditionally were located where there was extreme weather. In fact, many were, to be close to the Soviet Union via

Arctic routes. But the East Coast route went to the milder climes of Spain and the Mediterranean. A guessing game of crews concerned the source of the name Chrome Dome. The B-52s at that time were painted the *nuclear blast reflection* pattern: light grey on top, brilliant white on the bottom. And supposedly there would be so many of them flying overhead that from below it would look like an aluminum overcast, a "chrome dome."

General LeMay put great emphasis on teamwork and professionalism of his people. He knew the important mission of SAC would require the best individuals and he developed a temporary spot promotion system to inspire incentives. There were four types of SAC bomb crews: the non-combat ready was the lowest, then combat ready, lead, and select at the top of the ladder. The temporary spot promotion policy for SAC select crews was certainly an incentive, but it could also have a negative effect. If anyone on a crew screwed up badly, and it reflected on the crew's performance, that entire crew could lose their temporary spot promotions and get knocked back to their permanent grades with the lower pay. This certainly adversely affected the morale of that crew, but that was nothing compared to the morale of the wives. If somebody on the crew caused a drop in the grocery money, there would definitely be problems on the home front, directed at whatever crew member was *the goat*.

The air police on a SAC base had a very important job: to protect the nuclear weapons and the airplanes and missiles that carried them. They were called Combat Defense teams and took great pride in their presence, their uniforms, and their professionalism. The crisp salute rendered by an Air Policeman on a SAC main gate to any officer, in uniform or in civilian clothes, as he approached the gate was always a perfect salute. As long as that officer was in a vehicle with the blue SAC sticker with the "O" in the lower corner, he got the salute. Even wives of officers would get the salute as they drove through the gates in the family car, on the way to the base library, or base exchange.

Base security became a matter of vital importance and was tested by disguised inspectors who tried to enter bases without the necessary documents or approach the flight line without authorization. LeMay himself once tested the security of the alert aircraft by seeing how far he could get, dressed in civilian clothing, without showing his credentials or asking permission. He was immediately stopped by an armed guard, an Airman Second Class, on guard at an aircraft.

"Don't you know who I am?" LeMay roared.

The guard pointed his weapon at the intruder. "Sir, if you do not stand where you are, I will shoot you!" The guard was terrified. He thought a maniac had somehow gotten on base and was in front of him.

LeMay wisely stopped pretending, asked if he could show some identification, and promoted the astounded guard on the spot. The story spread through all of SAC immediately.

Helen LeMay, the general's wife, was not immune. Once a guard asked her for identification, which she immediately produced. She was in the backyard of the General's quarters at Offutt Air Force Base at the time.

Most SAC bases were located near towns whose citizens had good public relations with the Air Force personnel. Many bases did not have enough on-base housing where families could live, so there were quite a few military who lived off-base, usually renting apartments, houses, or mobile homes. Local merchants and businesspeople usually appreciated the dollars generated by the military in the local economy.

There was at least one town however, where the military was not appreciated as much. Landlords tended to 'gouge' the troops, who usually were young enlisted people—on their rent, insurance policies, appliances and car sales, even to the point of the local police setting up speed traps catching Air Force personnel and heavily ticketing any questionable violations. Morale among the troops who lived off base was not good.

But then, a new base commander was assigned. He made a point of asking questions and listening to his people. Then he called a meeting of the town mayor, along with all the community leaders: town board members, clergy, newspaper publisher, and police chief. They met in the big conference room on base, the one with nice leather seats, an impressive conference table, and a lot of maps and charts on the walls that were covered up with locked covers marked SECRET. The setup was designed to impress. The new base commander introduced himself, expressed his findings from his discussions with his people and the concerns about the way the town people was treating his troops. Then he reminded them how much the Air Force had spent the previous year in the local economy. He reminded every one in the room that his base was fully stocked, and it was within his authority to declare the entire town and county outside the base as OFF LIMITS. The Air Force people who lived off base would be permitted to drive to and from their homes every day, but that's all. Every can of beans, every loaf of bread, every drop of gasoline, and carton of milk would be purchased on base. The base had a bank, dry-cleaners, restaurants, library, bowling alley, several bars, a movie theatre, chapel, and auto repair shop. Everything they needed. And if they didn't have it, he would get it. Every nail, screw, car tune-up, hamburger, case of beer or baby diaper would be bought on base. Then he excused himself for a few minutes and asked them to discuss the situation among themselves.

When he came back to the conference room, the mayor announced there would soon be an Air Force Appreciation Day, with free entertainment, hot dogs, events for the kiddies and there should be no further such complaints. And things were pretty good from then on.

TRAINING MISSIONS

During the 1950's, military and political leaders were becoming more and more concerned about the threat from the Soviets. A later paper written by SAC historians said, "Given the inferiority of Soviet forces, SAC planners thought it reasonable that in time of war the Soviets would resort to the most basic military principle to quickly gain superiority—*surprise."*

LeMay and Power firmly believed that the most important way to counteract that element of surprise was for SAC to have a portion of the armed bomber fleet in the air at all times, ready for instant retaliation—an airborne alert. The bombers would be safely off the ground and in the air: a big part of nuclear deterrence. In 1959 in a closed meeting of the House Committee on Armed Services, Congressman Stratton asked General Twining, the Chairman of the Joint Chiefs of Staff, about the importance of nuclear deterrence and if the airborne alert aircraft were considered part of our capability to retaliate if needed. General Twining, concerned about security, answered that we have no airborne alert aircraft with armed weapons and have never had them. Later, Congressman Gruber asked the question another way, "Could SAC aircraft on normal training missions proceed immediately to strike Soviet targets if the balloon were to go up at any given moment?" General Twining thought a moment and answered, "Generally, yes."

Seemingly, General Twining was agreeing that we had nuclear weapons on board airborne alert training missions, missions that could be turned instantly into retaliation strikes if necessary, but those weapons were not considered armed until the crew armed them. The question of when exactly does a nuclear weapon become 'armed' would continue for years.

During the previous two years, a series of tests showed that the "sealed pit" system had been proven to be much more straightforward than the "pit insertion" method of nuclear weapons. In the older method, the weapon had to be armed in flight with the insertion of a nuclear canister, or pit. The older bombs were not fully armed until the pit insertion was complete, but the newer weapons were complete systems within themselves. The sealed pit weapon was loaded into the 'cocked' aircraft then left alone, functionally complete. All other arming was accomplished in flight without touching the weapon itself. Both General LeMay, as Vice Chairman of USAF, and General Power, as Commander In Chief, SAC, thought the sealed pit weapon would improve their chances of getting congressional approval for armed airborne alerts. Congress was very skittish about the thought of B-52s flying around America and other parts of the world with armed nuclear weapons aboard, twenty-four hours a day.

In January 1960, General Thomas Power took his case to the public. He gave a publicized, but cleared, talk in New York where he stated if the Soviets had 150 ICBMs and another 150 IRBMs (intermediate range ballistic missiles), they would have a 95% probability of wiping out our entire nuclear strike capability within 30 minutes. He added that an airborne alert offered at least a partial solution to the threat. In his book, *Design For Survival,* he said those statements caused considerable discussion and controversy, and the then Secretary of Defense, Thomas S. Gates, told him later that this matter had caused him more trouble than anything else he had encountered during his tenure of office.

A few weeks later, General Power stated his case before the Air Force and also Congress that the airborne alert program should be permanent, not a test program. If we were to survive a surprise attack from the Soviet Union, he said we must have a portion of our defense in the air at all times. He told Congress, "I feel strongly that we must get on with the airborne alert…We must impress Mr. Khrushchev that we have it, and that he cannot strike this country with impunity."

"After detailed testimony, I received wholehearted support for the airborne alert concept. This proved instrumental in bringing about action by other committees which gave the Department of Defense virtually a blank check for creating an extensive airborne alert capabilities—an unprecedented action indeed."

The 'blank check' General Power received came with a caveat: the airborne alert flights would have to be referred to as "indoctrination," or training missions.

On 18 January 1961 SAC finally obtained permission to publicly announce that B-52 bombers were conducting airborne operations, but the activity had to be characterized as airborne training missions.

Four days later, on Sunday evening January 22, 1961, the members of Seymour Johnson crew R-10 were released from the alert facility to go to their quarters for rest. They had completed the standard four days of alert duty and were now ready to fly. The following morning, at 8:00 a.m., they reported for duty and had the traditional hot breakfast in the alert facility mess hall. After breakfast, they gathered for the pre-takeoff briefing at 8:45. All six regular crew members of R-10 were present, plus the extras, the third pilot First Lieutenant Mattocks, and Major Richards. During the weather portion of the briefing, the gunner, Sergeant Barnish went to the base in-flight kitchen as usual to pick up the preordered flight meals and put them on their tabs. Officers paid $1.35, enlisted paid 95¢ per meal.

They boarded their waiting aircraft and became *Keep 19*, the radio call sign for the mission. The call sign "Keep" was the next random name in the operations missions book, and this was be the nineteenth of the series. It was applied to that mission on that specific date, when aircraft tail number 58-0187 would carry crew R-10. *Keep 19* had an on-time takeoff at 10:56 a.m. on Monday, 23 January 1961.

They would crash about thirteen hours later, shortly after midnight, 24 January 1961. Five of the crew would survive. Three would die.

The Last Three Hours And Six Minutes of *Keep 19*

Keep 19 completed the first scheduled midair refueling without incident, but now turbulence was picking up along the assigned refueling corridor. The cold front was behind them and moving them along to the east, both tanker and bomber, like surfers riding a ground swell. The winds aloft would later be estimated as out of the west at over 150 knots at 40,000 feet. *Keep 19* was assigned twenty-nine thousand feet.

Midair refueling was absolutely essential for SAC's mission of worldwide bomber coverage. It had its awkward beginning with a British concept called the *looped hose,* method in which a tanker, trailing a hose behind it, flew in front of the receiver aircraft. The receiver would fly a dangling grapple hook over a loop and haul the hose aboard. It was installed on the B-29, and proficiency training began. The Air Force finally had its global reach. A new day had dawned.

Two methods of midair refueling were soon developed: the *probe-and-drogue* and the f*lying boom,* a forty-foot telescoping boom from the bottom of a tanker that could be maneuvered into the refueling receptacle of the bomber. The Navy and Marines still use the probe-and-drogue, because their tankers are not large enough to accommodate the boom and it's operator, but SAC wanted the flying boom, and wanted the receptacle of the receiving airplane placed outside the pilot's field of vision whenever possible. Refueling formation flying was difficult enough and SAC did not want the pilot to be watching the nozzle as it approached. Best to leave that to the refueling boom operator. On the B-52, the opening is in the top of the fuselage, behind the pilots and forward of the EW and gunner.

In 1960, an average of 122 bomber and tanker aircraft were airborne every day, with one SAC refueling done every 6.8 minutes somewhere in the world. Twelve B-52s were authorized for the first three Chrome Dome routes to be in the air for every minute of every day in early 1961. To refuel these twelve bombers, tankers were expected to pump a minimum of 634,000 gallons a day, or over 50,000 gallons per day per bomber. Tanker aircraft and crews stood alert just like the bomber crews: airplanes ready and cocked, pointed at forty-five degrees to the runway on their herringbone, or *Christmas Tree* parking ramps. Just like the bombers, the tankers would be ready—fueled up, departure frequencies pre-set on the radios, navigation charts, checklists, and sunglasses on the seats. Headsets were plugged in and on the seats. The hatch was open and the boarding ladder pulled down. The aircraft were ready for the crews to dash to the plane, pausing long enough to give the correct number code to the armed security guard. SAC Combat Defense guards didn't assume that just because you had a flight suit on and the correct flight-line badge that you were legit: you still didn't get past them without knowing the daily code. One pilot remembered: "If we were running out to the aircraft we wouldn't cross the red line until we knew the number. If the number was five the guard would hold up two fingers and we'd hold up three and he would let us through on the run. If you crossed the red line without the guard approving, you might just get shot." At the very least, you would definitely be standing in front of a desk later, getting yelled at by someone with a lot of insignia on his collar and the silver clouds and lightning bolts, known as "farts and darts," on his billed hat.

The KC-135 jet tanker was a big improvement over the older prop-driven KC-97 which struggled to match the much faster B-47 Stratojet. The pilots of the two-plane formation worked out a ticklish maneuver to compensate this difference in speed. The KC-97, going 'balls to the wall'—the throttles shoved full forward toward the instrument panel wall, at the maximum speed; while the streamlined B-47 slowed to near stall speed. Then the hook-up at high altitude was followed by a shallow dive, in tandem. Both could speed up, making for better control of both aircraft while the refueling took place.

During that Monday at various times Lieutenant Mattocks had replaced Major Tulloch and Captain Rardin for rest and relief. They were now setting up for the second refueling scheduled for 29,000 feet near Columbia, South Carolina, at around 2100 hours, or 9:00 p.m. Their KC-135 tanker was designated *Addle 57*. The boomer (often called Casey, because he lowers the refueling boom) was in his pod, looking down on them from above, waiting. Boomers were enlisted men, and would brag they had a great job: ride in the back lying down while two officers drove them around.

According to the government document, "The History Of Flight," this is what happened next:

> Rendezvous was six minutes early. The initial (*refueling*) contact was held only for a few seconds with an outer limit disconnect being experienced. The second contact was made and held until 93,000 pounds of fuel had been

onloaded. At this time the receiver pilot (*Major Tulloch*) disconnected and returned to the observation position to rest a few minutes. It should be noted that the tanker was being hand flown by the tanker co-pilot for a short time during the refueling. After the receiver pilot rested a few minutes, the tanker was requested to increase airspeed to 260 KIAS *(knots indicated air speed)* and another contact was established. After three disconnects had occurred, the Boom Operator reported a fuel leak coming from the right wing behind the number three nacelle. (Italics added.)

Here is what was behind that government document. Major Tulloch was working hard on this second refueling. He was forty-six years old, and this flight had not gone easy. They never do, especially when you need easy. Electrical problems had been popping up all day and the boys were constantly shifting fuel around. They were a good crew, always on top of things. And they tried to protect 'the old man' from additional things to worry about. They would talk over a problem between themselves and offer the most logical choice to Major Tulloch. Usually they had the correct solution but the Major was commander of the ship. And he took care of 'his boys' on the ground too. They had an excellent relationship. It was said that in the Air Force there were two individuals you did not screw around with. One was any aircraft commander and the other was any chief master sergeant. People in these two positions did not get there easily, and they were the ones who ran the Air Force, they were really the people who got things done, and could be either the best friend or the worse enemy you could ever have. They could make things happen behind the scenes that you, and others, would never even be aware of. Those things could either be in your favor, or not.

This particular mission of *Keep 19* was different and extremely important. Headquarters Wing and 8th Air Force was counting on getting all crews and aircraft of the 4241st Strategic Wing ready for this new airborne alert policy and Chrome Dome. And the fact that *Keep 19* was hauling live weapons around today was always in the back of everyone's minds. The Major and the rest of the crew knew the pressure of completing this heavyweight refueling mission and get Crew R-10 qualified for Chrome Dome.

The first refueling went easy, about five hours ago. That had been in daylight and good weather. *Keep 19* had located the refueling tanker from over one hundred miles away by using the electronic beacon, and had swung in behind in a giant graceful turn while it was still out of sight. The alignment maneuver covered hundreds of square miles as the KC-135 tanker and the B-52 aligned themselves, with the bomber about twenty miles behind the tanker, in trail and closing. Major Sheldon, the radar navigator was giving constant radar readings to the flight deck on range and direction to the target, which, in this case, was the tanker. The two aircraft never made radio contact with each other, but that was by design. This profile flight of *Keep 19* was to replicate all aspects of an actual Chrome Dome mission, down to hauling the actual thermonuclear weapons, both of them in SAFE mode in the bomb bay, but very much active weapon systems. These sealed pit bombs did not require the awkward in-flight pit insertion, where the bombardier on some missions crawled back into the bomb bay with the 'bird cage,' a heavy wire enclosure that contained the nuclear capsule. The MK-39 bombs were self contained and ready to go from the moment they were loaded into the BUFF. They needed hooking up and careful checking as they were married up with the airplane, but they were ready to be used in nuclear war.

There were a total of three boom disconnects on this second refueling, in the dark and being bounced around by winds aloft. Each disconnect was due to exceeding the outer control limits of the refueling boom. This exercise was turning into a frustrating contest between an insistent man and his flying machine, fighting the delicate flight control response in air turbulence from the weather front. Each disconnect meant a fall-back by the bomber, the stabilizing of both aircraft, and another retry. Line up, get the speed and attitude just right, then slowly move into position and hold. Major Scott Tulloch was determined to successfully finish this second heavyweight refueling. To the major, there was no other option. This mission *was* going to be completed as planned. He was determined that when they returned to Seymour Johnson they would be signed off for Chrome Dome.

The official report stated that Major Tulloch "returned to the observation position to rest for a few minutes." This means Major Tulloch backed the B-52 away from the tanker and moved it to the observation position, which was several hundred feet behind and over to the side of the tanker, safely away from the possibility of collision, where he "rested for a few minutes." Then he requested the tanker pilot to increase speed and he moved back into the refueling position where another connection was made.

Lieutenant Mattocks was looking over the shoulders of the two pilots and scanning the instruments. Major Tulloch watched the refueling 'environment,' the entire area of the bomber's nose combined with the tanker's boom, concentrating on keeping the right 'feel,' everything in the correct relationship. He knew Rardin and Mattocks were doing continuous cross checking, looking for any problem on the instrument panel. Mattocks saw a slight drop on Number 4 fuel tank gage and announced it. Major Tulloch reset the gauge to test it. He tapped the glass with his gloved finger... an old habit from the B-17. The boomer in the tanker also reported the leak. While Major Tulloch and Lieutenant Mattocks were concentrating on flying the airplane, Dick Rardin, the co-pilot was doing what a good co-pilot was supposed to do at a time like this: not watch them. His eyes were scanning all the other gauges. Never get too concentrated on one problem, that's why they called him the co-pilot. There have been too many cases where everybody in the cockpit is working on one problem while the airplane runs into something. Like another airplane. Or the ground.

The needle on the gauge dropped to zero like it was supposed to, then slowly began to climb, but it never showed full. Something was going on and it was not good.

The B-52 crew could not see the fuel leak from the cockpit since the wing was behind them. Major Tulloch had Captain Rardin ask the tanker to drop back and under them to take a look, but the crew of *Addle 57* couldn't see very well in the dark. Major Tulloch requested that Seymour Johnson get a chase plane ready to come up at dawn and get a good look. The three pilots worked the lengthy checklist for *Fuel Leak, Refueling.*

Major Tulloch at first did not think they were in immediate

danger, but agreed with the Command Post to head closer to Seymour Johnson. *Addle 57* moved out one mile ahead and one thousand feet above them, well out of range of an explosion. The boom operator was watching them closely through binoculars. Tulloch made sure that Seymour Approach Control was keeping the Command Post informed of the fuel problems.

It was later determined that the initial fuel loss amounted to thirty-seven thousand pounds, or about nineteen tons, in a little over two minutes. That would be at the rate of *thirty-six gallons per second.* This is comparable to the water drop ability of the huge Martin Mars airborne forest firefighter, now used in Canada. Over the entire three-hour period of the emergency, total fuel loss would be fifty-four tons. Whatever hole, or break, or rupture in the fuel system had to have been a big one in size. The rupture could not have been just a few square inches, it had to have been the equivalent of about a foot square to allow that much fuel pour through and out of the right wing. It may have been a long slit between metal panels, or a ragged broken gap in a fuel tank, or several fuel connectors failing at once.

They were now ten hours and thirty-three minutes into the planned twenty-four hour mission.

Once again, the tanker was asked to take another look from behind and above the bomber. This time, *Addle 57* got a better angle and reported the leak to be between engine pod Number 3 and the fuselage. That is at the root of the right wing. The decision was made to leave the refueling area and get out to sea beyond Wilmington, North Carolina, not far away. By deciding to go out over the water, the level of the emergency just went up one notch with the crew. An attempted emergency fuel purge of tank Number 3 was unsuccessful due to pump failure. There now seemed to be a cascade of problems centered around the fuel system. They would have to get rid of the fuel in that tank by using it up in the engines by watching the tank as it was running dry, then quickly switching over to another tank.

The wing commander had been called at his quarters at Seymour Johnson, and he was now in his staff car on the way to the Command Post. He used his car radio to talk directly with Major Tulloch. Headquarters SAC and 8th Air Force were notified of the in-flight emergency. The full expertise of the Air Force was up and running. Boeing was notified, and also nearby military bases and even the Wilmington and Oak Island Coast Guard Stations. Major Tulloch wanted to hear from the chief of the standardization crew, similar to an airline's chief pilot. He was a trusted and knowledgeable friend.

Major Tulloch said, "It would probably be a good idea to shut down the two engines." Normally fuel venting at that altitude was not combustible, but that amount of fuel pouring out into the atmosphere near the exhaust of jet engines is another matter. The two closest engines on the right wing, Number's 5 and 6, were shut down to reduce the fire risk. However, shutting down those engines stopped the hydraulics and generator systems for the right side, disabling controls for the right wing. Lieutenant Mattocks quickly opened circuits from the left side generator to run the right side controls.

By this time, they were out over the Atlantic Ocean and *Keep 19* was instructed to orbit at thirty thousand feet with the in-bound turning point no closer than ten miles east of Wilmington. The intent was to keep the aircraft well away from populated areas, but close enough for Coast Guard rescue if necessary. They now had to use excessive trim to maintain control. They were fighting the airplane.

Major Tulloch needed someone to check out the bomb bay. The only access to the bomb bay in flight was through the forward wheel well via the small door which was Major Richards' backrest. That would mean breaching the pressure bulkhead and depressurizing the aircraft. Any trip to the bomb bay in flight would require going down into the Hole, passing through the forward wheel well and squeezing around the stowed landing gear, a tight fit. Sergeant Frank Barnish, the smallest man on the airplane, was just the guy.

This meant leaving his parachute on his ejection seat because there wasn't going to be enough room to wear it where he was going. He first switched his oxygen mask connection over to the walk-around oxygen bottle, for that was required when they were depressurized above twelve thousand feet, and they were at thirty thousand. Frank climbed down the ladder into the navigators' Black Hole. Major Richards probably wanted to know what was going on up on the flight deck. The major had moved out of his spot at the back of The Hole while Frank waited for the airplane to be depressurized. Frank looked through the round porthole widow in the door, just to be sure nothing bad was waiting for him, like fire or an open wheel well, then he unlatched the bulkhead pressure door. This depressurizing process is similar to what happens at the end of each flight when the engines spool down and the ground crew puts the wheel chocks in place. Before cracking open the crew door hatch in the bottom of the airplane, the navigator calls the pilot on the interphone: "Navigator to pilot: Is your window open?" Unlatching the crew hatch without first completely depressurizing the airplane could cause the crew hatch door to blast downward with disastrous results—either an injured ground crew, or a damaged hatch with sprung hinges, or both. Opening the pilot's side window after parking insures equal air pressure throughout the airplane, and that's why it's on the engine shutdown checklist. If the hatch blew open and sprung, the bomber could be taken out of the alert rotation while the door was repaired or replaced, just because the pilot's window was not opened the specified two inches. Of course opening a window in flight was not an option, so depressurizing was done by the cabin pressure valves, controlled by the co-pilot.

Keeping a B-52 pressurized during flight is an essential function, and it is powered by a very complicated system. A former BUFF crewman, Lothar "Nick" Maier, facetiously explained it like this: The B-52 is a masterpiece of engineering, but a big part of its nervous system is determined by the quality of duct tape mending of the single greatest concept of aircraft design: the *air bleed system.* This is a complex monstrosity of four-inch wide piping and manifolds carrying air at about 750 degrees Fahrenheit and 250 pounds per square inch of pressure. The air pressure starts at the final compressor stage of each of the eight jet engines. This superheated pressurized air is then circulated throughout the entire airframe in a twisting, pulsating, screaming manifold of threatening, potentially dangerous hot air leaks. An *internal inferno* designed to deliver essential operating pressure to where ever required, such as the horizontal stabilizer movement and the crew compartment pressurization and air conditioning and heating. It is also the power source for secondary engine start. All from the windmills in the engines.

This hostile environment is what awaited Frank Barnish

as he entered the forward wheel well. The noise must have been unbelievable—the whistling of the outside airstream, the screaming of the air bleed system manifolds, the stink of the JP-4 jet fuel that had poured down from the massive leak above. He struggled aft through his inspection tour, crawling around and over the big rubber wheels on the landing gear, slippery wet with jet fuel, along the shuttering crawlspace, constantly on the lookout for dangerous air bleed leaks, on into the bomb bay. He made sure he had good hand grips at every step since he was not wearing a parachute and one big lurch and he could be flung down against the bomb bay doors. Sure, the doors were latched, but right on the other side of them was thirty thousand feet of nothing but air. And if he was flung down and the doors held closed, he would be wallowing in a pool of JP-4 and looking straight up at three tons of H-bomb above him, wobbling in it's chain. He returned to the flight deck stinking of the fuel on his flight suit. He would have killed for a cigarette right then but knew that was not in the cards for quite a while.

When Frank climbed back up the ladder to the flight deck, he reported to Major Tulloch that the bomb bay was covered in jet fuel. The entire wheel well was soaked, and it was covering not only the bottom of the hull but much of the electronic equipment. Frank went back to his ejection seat and refastened his parachute and changed his oxygen supply back over to the connection on the seat. He and Lieutenant exchanged nervous glances. Wilson had listened on Frank's report to the boss and knew what was going on. One spark could turn the aircraft into a massive fireball, and both he and Frank wanted very badly to be ready to punch out, quickly eject—through the fireball if necessary—but just get out of the airplane. Frank must have had very bad flashbacks to that bailout over Germany seventeen years before. That didn't go so well back then, in World War II. He went from a flying sergeant to a prisoner of war in a German POW camp.

The crew began pulling circuit breakers, including most interior lights, trying to minimize the chance of fire and to stabilize the giant aircraft. They flew on in a wide loop shaped like a racetrack out at sea. The refueling tanker, *Addle 57*, stayed on the scene. Now another problem cropped up: the EW had been having trouble with the High Frequency radio, and now the ARAC 58 radio was on the blink.

As they made gentle turns out over the dark Atlantic, the pilots had to increase the trim controls to help maintain attitude and altitude of the bomber to compensate for the changing weight. During this time the Command Post was relaying instructions to *Keep 19* in regards to fuel management. The fuel transfer pumps were acting erratically or not at all at times which created a series of continuous adjustments for Rardin and Mattocks. They would pump fuel and switch tanks, trying to balance the airplane by using the consumption of fuel by the engines alone where possible.

Everyone on board was very aware of the slow growth of things going wrong: the huge fuel leak, the pump failures, and now radio failures. Could they all somehow be connected? Is this how accident reports are written up? Pilots and flight crew are a suspicious bunch. They were always on the lookout for unusual events, noises, smells, and vibrations—anything unusual gives them pause. They are also extremely aware of time and its passage and are very superstitious. It is said the three most useless things to a pilot are altitude above you, runway behind you, and two seconds ago.

The crew tried everything they knew to resolve the crisis. After more than two hours, Washington Center cleared them to depart the Wilmington area, and head north to their home base, Seymour Johnson. Major Tulloch thought they were still too heavy for landing and told Captain Rardin, "Tell them I said I intend to stay in the Wilmington area to use up more fuel." This led to a long discussion with the wing commander, who wanted him back at the base due to all the electrical problems mounting up, so Major Tulloch lost in that discussion. After one more orbit at sea, "radar revealed the coast line."

Major Tulloch would later say in his narrative that he agreed with the decision to land. He had always said it was his responsibility and all decisions were up to him as aircraft commander.

He had recently read a report of another bomber that had made it down safely under similar circumstances but the plane had burst into flames on the runway after it landed. It exceeded the safe landing weight and the brakes caught fire before it could be stopped. He was very concerned about that and warned his crew to be ready to "make tracks" as soon as they could land and get stopped. *Keep 19* now crossed the North Carolina coast near Wrightsville Beach. All of them had been to that beach at some time. It was called the Crystal Coast—bright white sand on a wide beach. They wondered if any fishermen were down there now, looking up at this big airplane in the night. The crew had some time to think and knew they were in trouble, but the aircraft at least at this point appeared to be balanced and was handling well.

Paul Brown's clock on the navigator's panel reached midnight. Twenty-four hundred hours. Monday was over and Tuesday was starting. The crew thought the airplane was under control, fuel management appeared to be working, and airspeed was not an issue even with the two right side engines out. They loosened the tight, uncomfortable chin straps of their helmets and tried to relax. In the clear moonlit night above the Carolina countryside and towns, *Keep 19* was heading north toward home, early.

But on the right wing, above and behind the crew, a metal fatigue crack was growing inside the second panel of wing section number 556. The crack could not have been found by the ground maintenance people on pre-flight inspection. The inspection for *Keep 19* had been done exactly as specified. Sure, there was a general statement about looking for wrinkles and cracks in all exterior wing, control, and fuselage skin, just as it has always been for every airplane, from the Piper Cub to the Boeing 707, and all crew chiefs knew all about metal fatigue cracks and how to fix them: drill 'em and stick 'em. Carefully drill out an exact size hole and insert an exact size rivet. They always found stress wrinkles, but it was always the seriousness of any problem that was the tough call. If every aircraft was grounded for every skin defect found, few would fly, especially in the B-52 fleet. In fact, the hidden weakness in this wing design was already known at higher levels of Air Force command during cyclic testing. A test wing had broken during a static load, where weights are applied and the bending measured. But the results of that test were not announced. Raising the issue of a wing problem would mean taking many B-52s out of service, and Chrome Dome and the Airborne Alert were just starting. Anyway, this airplane was scheduled to go out of service and to the repair depot in four months: on May 5, 1961. That would fix the known wing weakness of the G model.

Right then, in the first minutes of that Tuesday, *Keep 19* crew's immediate concern was to finish this ride and prove that this crew was proficient enough to haul two MK-39 thermonuclear devices around, ready to drop, for a period of more than twenty-four hours, the length of time it takes to fly to the Mediterranean and stand by on station. That would put them as Qualified, Chrome Dome.

The crack in the wing panel was growing.

Also growing, like an aortic aneurysm, was a weakness in at least one of the fuel lines couplets. This was part of the system that connected together the big fuel compartments that made up the interior of the wing, known as a wet wing. When the wings moved in flight, and they did a lot of moving, the flexible lines and couplets had to take up any slack and move in any direction. The first type couplets used were known as Marman clamps, and they broke down from the start of G-and F-Model operations. They caused "fuel gushers" whose name alone would indicate a very serious flying hazard. Several repair projects were tried such as the CF-14 Blue Band, and the CF-17 Hard Shell, but were obviously not foolproof solutions. We are not sure which clamp was used on this aircraft. Marman clamps were invented by Herbert Marx, better known as Zeppo, one of the Marx Brothers movie stars.

Each crew member mentally went through the bail out drill, just in case. The four crewmen on the top level would eject upward, and the two on the lower level would eject downward. It was specified that as soon as the navigator on the lower level had ejected, the *extras*, the men not in ejection seats, would make their way to the lower deck hatch opening and drop through it, then manually deploy their parachutes. That was the general concept, and there was a recommended bail out sequence to follow if the bail out was elective and they had enough time. Since the crew is confined to a relatively small portion of the aircraft, in a controlled bail out it would be better if they did not go out all at once, but one at a time to prevent the possibility of high speed midair contact with each other. The navigator, Paul Brown, would go first. Reason: they needed an opening in the bottom of the airplane for the two *extras* to jump through—Richards and Mattocks. There was no other way out for those two guys without ejection seats. That is why the navigator went first: he happened to be sitting directly over the ejection hatch which was the closest to the ladder between decks, and that was the best egress point for the extras. So the best way to open a hatch for the 'extras' was for the navigator to eject downward. Gene Shelton was to stay put for a short time, right beside that opening, to render assistance to anyone who needed it. He was the guy who made sure that anybody who was supposed to go through that opening in the floor did so.

Next in the controlled bail out sequence would be the two non-pilots on the upper deck: Sergeant Barnish, the gunner, and Captain Wilson, the EW. They would pull their ejection handles and be fired upward. Then Major Shelton would eject downward. Next, the co-pilot Captain Rardin would go. Last would be the commander of the ship, Major Tulloch, after assuring that all others had left the aircraft. All this was making the assumption that the crew had sufficient time, and the bomber would be under reasonable control and flying horizontal. Bomber ejection seats were catapults, powered by explosive-powered compressed air cylinders rather than the rockets found in the single-seat fighters. Bomber crews sat side-by-side, and the flaming exhaust of a rocket taking off right next to someone is not a good idea for the second guy—much better to have a compressed air catapult.

PLANNED BAILOUT ROUTES

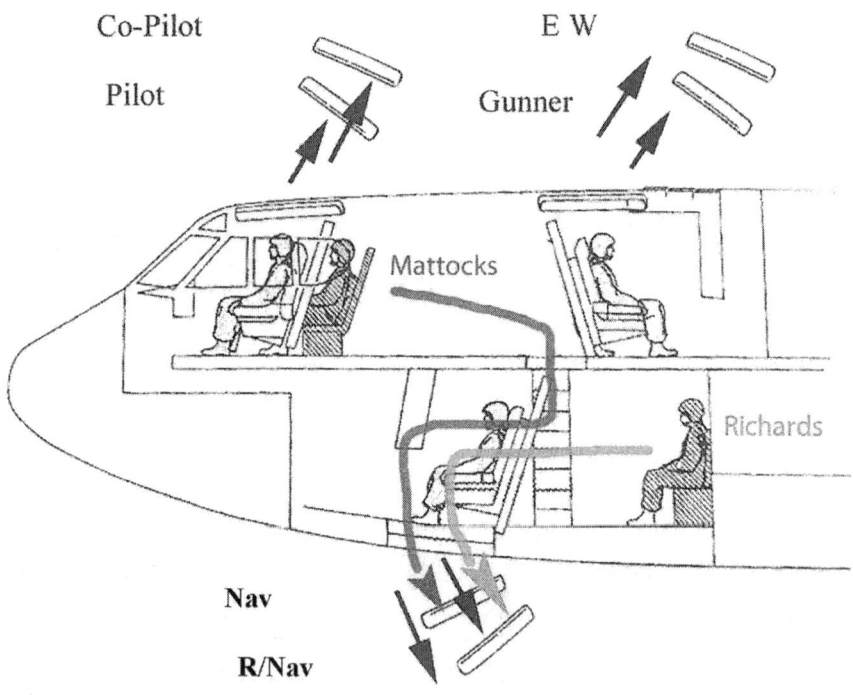

Illustration by author.

There was also another very good reason for the order of a controlled bail out, it had to do with the consequences of fire. If there was an in-flight fire, especially in the wheel well, and an upwards firing escape hatch was jettisoned, the resulting vacuum would cause smoke and fire to be drawn violently up into the crew compartment through the ladder opening, like a giant chimney. The basic flight crew manual "Dash One" stated emphatically: "WARNING. The jettisoning of an upward escape hatch prior to the egress of all lower deck members and extra crew members could seriously hamper their escape." But if there were a fire on board, it would probably be considered an emergency, and not a controlled bail out. If it was an emergency bail out of course, there was no preferred sequence, just get out. It was every man for himself, as quickly as possible. The command to bail out would be given by the pilot two ways: by interphone and a two inch bright red ABANDON light at eye level on the panel in front of each crew member. There was also the highly popular but unwritten rule that if you ever saw the pilot eject you had permission to leave.

At the beginning of flight safety training, the typical pre-flight instructions given to the new crew members by the aircraft commander would be something like this:

"If it becomes necessary to abandon the aircraft in flight, I will give the command, firmly and in clear King's English. There will be no anticipation of this action, which is to say any statements or questions over the interphone are never to include the word BAILOUT in any form. For example, if you accidentally dump the contents of the coffee jug into the forward hatch hole, you will not 'bail out' the forward hatch hole. You will 'clean out' the forward hatch hole.

Misuse of the word BAILOUT in the heat of an emergency can easily result in a misunderstanding leading to tragic consequences. I repeat, the word BAILOUT is to be used only by your AIRCRAFT COMMANDER in the context of an actual order to begin the activity. Is that CLEAR?"

If he did not hear a lot of "YESSIRS", the lesson would be repeated.

When each member of the crew went through that bail out class back in flight safety training, they were taught another important lesson: don't touch the yellow handle until you are ready to leave the airplane. In fact, anything painted yellow and black had something to do with your own personal safety. The instructions were split into two classes—upper deck and lower deck. First the upper deck: If you were in an upward firing ejection seat, the magic handle is a six inch by seven inch yellow and black metal frame on the end of each arm rest. Its release is imbedded in the top of the metal frame. Squeeze it and the frame will rotate upward into your hand and several things will happen all at once: the ejection seat is armed, the firing trigger flips into position, the overhead hatch is released into the slipstream, ankle restraints secure your feet, your work station stows itself, (control columns for pilots and gunner, table for EW), and your shoulder strap inertial reel locks. The firing trigger itself does only one thing, it fires an explosive charge into a gas cylinder that will catapult your ejection seat up and outside, sort of like a very large potato gun.

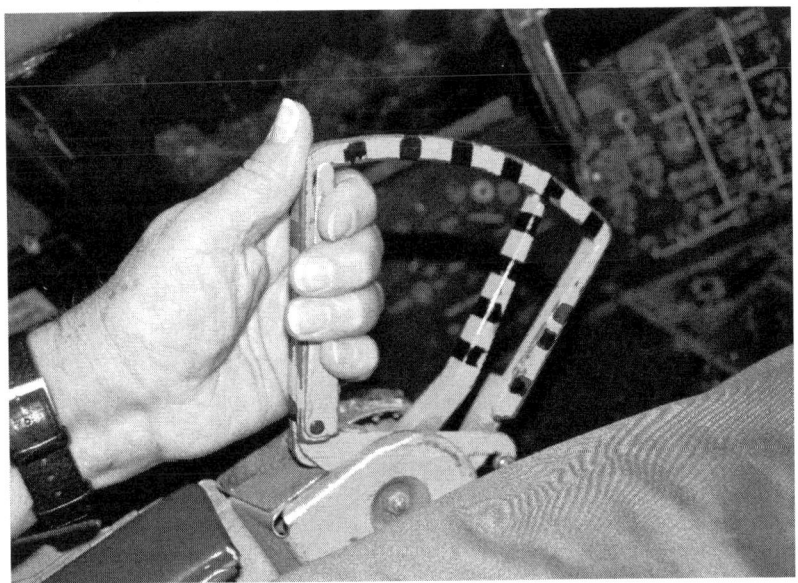

The ejection seat Magic Handle. Step One: Depress top lever with thumb, which rotates the handle upward and begins the seat arming process and secures the crew member firmly to the seat. It also releases the overhead hatch into the slipstream.

Step Two: Pull trigger. There is no Step Three.
Photo by author

Downward ejection seats for the two navigators on the lower deck worked basically the same way, but the yellow D trigger was between the legs at the front edge of the seat. Downward seats don't have armrests. Holding tightly onto the trigger ring with both hands keeps the navigator's arms from flailing around on the way out. Plus, there were ankle restraints that rotated around your ankles and tucked them in. Moving your feet back against the spring-loaded triggers activated the ankle restrains. Every new BUFF navigator triggered these restraints many times during normal flight before he learned not to bring his feet so far back under his seat—unless he's serious about ejecting, of course. When ready to eject, pull the yellow D trigger up in one continuous motion. That would rotate two paddle-shaped leg guards up and around your hips and into position beside the thighs to keep the legs tucked in. That would force your legs inward to be narrower than the width of the hatch opening, which was a very good idea. The continued pull of the trigger would release the hatch below your feet, arm your seat, lock your shoulder straps, and fire the ejection seat. It was said that if you are not completely within the confines of your seat, you are going to lose "whatever is hanging out there."

When you are reminded about the hatch being released and carried away by the slipstream, you realize there is nothing beneath your feet but air, and that all this time you have been sitting on a seat on rails, not unlike that of the dunking booth at the county fair. And you are the guy in the dunking booth chair.

For any of the ejection seats, either upward or downward firing, one second after you eject, your seat belts will release; a small explosive-powered reel in the seat back will quickly tighten up the two nylon straps that you are sitting on, and you will be flipped away from the ejection seat like a pancake and your parachute will automatically open. Your seat cushion is still attached to you. It is your *global survival kit*, containing, among many other things, a rubber life raft. As you are floating down beneath the parachute canopy, the survival kit will fall away automatically and it will stream out fifteen feet and inflate the rubber life raft, just in case you come down in water and need something floating nearby. After all, the earth's surface is 75 percent water, so the odds are three out of four you will get wet.

The life raft will hang about fifteen feet below and the surviving kit about twenty-five feet. The survival kit will hit Mother Earth first and hopefully reduce your landing weight. If you were sure you would not need the raft or anything else in the survival kit and it was in your way on the way down, there was a way of releasing the string of two drop-lines. But you needed to be sure, for the kit did contain a lot of needful things including medical supplies and a firearm, a fold-up .22 caliber rifle suitable for small game hunting, just in case you are out in the bush somewhere long enough to get real hungry.

At some point in the evolution of flight in B-52s, it became apparent there was a need for a second set of basic survival supplies, not as bulky, but attached to the crew member himself instead of packed away inside his seat cushion. That way, even if he dropped the global survival kit too early, he would still have some essential supplies close by, tucked away in a nylon garment for the torso and legs. In each 'chap kit' there were pockets containing a direction-finding beacon, dehydrated food, a flashlight, a two-way radio, shark repellant, minimum first-aid kit, twenty rounds of .38-caliber cartridge, and a pistol.

There was also the possibility that you might need to get out of the airplane in an emergency without using the ejection seats, such as in a crash landing where the upward firing ejection seats could not carry you high enough for the parachute to function. If you were part of the bottom deck crew, downward ejection would definitely not be an option. In that situation, where the airplane was already on the ground (or water), the four crewmen on the top deck would pop their hatches off, throw ropes out, and climb down. Those on the lower deck would go up the crew ladder to the top deck and climb down one of the four outside escape ropes. Sometime after 1961, a warning was placed on the cloth bag that held the escape rope beside each hatch: WARNING. DO NOT HOLD THE ROPE END AND JUMP. THROW THE ROPE OUT THEN CLIMB DOWN THE ROPE. The story behind the need for that warning would probably be interesting. It might have been that the rope was just a little bit longer than the distance from the top hatch to the ground, possibly resulting in someone falling at a high rate of speed onto a concrete runway while tightly grasping the rope end.

Emergency water landings would also have another hazard that had to be addressed for the B-52. The fact that two decks were on this airplane, and at least two people, sometimes three, were on the bottom deck, a sure-fire method had to be devised to get those people safely seated on the upper deck to survive a crash landing on water. The upper deck did not have any more room for seats to provide enough protection against forward "G's" during a water 'landing.' The lower deck would probably not be waterproof for very long after the landing, and may not even be intact. Any extra upper deck seating would only be used in an emergency water landing. The solution was the "Ditching Hammock," a brilliant invention of nylon webbing construction that could be quickly fastened with a single attachment point at the top, and two at the bottom. The fittings on the bottom of the hammock are studs that snap into receptacles on the walkway floor.

Stowage for the hammocks, which fold well and do not take up much space, is on the side of the chemical toilet, located at the top of the crew ladder. It is a canvas bag, marked clearly enough: DITCHING STATION HAMMOCK STOWAGE. When advised there was going to be a 'landing, water,' everybody on the bottom deck would go up to the top deck and grab a hammock off the chemical toilet. They would quickly attach it top and bottom in the walkway behind the pilots, climb in facing aft, and buckle up. The hammocks were designed to withstand a floor load of 8 "G's" forward and down and 4 "G's" up and aft.

Another emergency, even though the probability was very low, was how to deal with an severely injured or unconscious crew member without an ejection seat, but who needed to bail out of the airplane. There had been occasions in WWII where fellow bomber crewmen, knowing they were going to crash, desperately tried to get an unconscious member out of the plane, usually by pulling his ripcord and tucking the spilled parachute under his arm before throwing him out. It seldom worked as planned. But the knowledge that the need had occurred during the war drove the Boeing engineers to offer a solution.

It was the parachute static line and it was stowed in a pouch behind the radar navigator's ejection seat. It would be the navigator, just to the R/N's right, who would have to create an opening by ejecting downward, just like he would in order to get the 'extras' out. The static line is used to facilitate an injured crewmember though the navigator's hatch. Above 14,000 feet, the line would be connected to the automatic parachute arming lanyard. Below that level, directly to the ripcord T-handle. They would hook him up, throw him out, and hope for the best.

There would be one other way, if there was enough time. The navigator could give up his ejection seat, fellow crew members work the injured man into the navigator's seat and strap him in, then fire the seat.

The emergency hatches on the B-52 did not actually "blow." When activated by the ejection seat trigger for an in-flight emergency, six latch clamps would rotate out of the way and two small gas cylinders would push the leading edge of a lifter about two inches into the slipstream, where it would be carried away, taking the hatch with it. The two pilots' hatches had windows in them to provide vision for banking turns and during refueling.

Winston Churchill once said there was nothing like the fear of being shot at that clarifies the mind. The instant before you release the hatch and hurl yourself into space there is nothing like visualizing the open space directly beneath your feet or above your head to clarify the mind. But then, in an emergency, the training takes over and you probably won't even have time to think.

As they proceeded northward over the North Carolina countryside, *Keep 19* descended to ten thousand feet and did an emergency lowering of the landing gear with all the normal gear circuit breakers pulled. They had asked the Command Post for the best altitude to lower the gear with the least chance for a spark igniting the fuel. After the landing gear reached the down and locked position, all normal gear electrical circuit breakers were reset. They had just passed a major test: getting the landing gear down without blowing up.

Keep 19 was still under Raleigh Radar control, and they were being directed in from a point forty miles south of the base. The Command Post wanted the crew to activate the airplane's flaps to check out the aircraft's control in the landing configuration, with both the landing gear and flaps down. Major Tulloch certainly knew that in combat the rule had been to never lower the flaps if you had a damaged wing. But here, the experts on the ground "must have decided the wing was OK, and our only problem was the fuel leak." Flaps are essential for landing at that heavy weight, but timing was going to be a factor, and they could not wait until they got to the lower altitude during final approach to see if the flaps worked. The situation did not seem so critical, as they thought the main tanks had drained themselves.

Major Tulloch began to slow the airplane. The tension of the crew members would be at a peak, for they knew they were now going to attempt a night landing with a wounded airplane that had been leaking a whole lot of fuel. Mattocks was helping the pilots with circuits located on the overhead panel behind them that they couldn't reach. They wanted to shut off anything electrical that was not essential to landing. He would also be leaning forward between the pilot and co-pilot, searching for the runway lights. Wilson and Barnish would be twisting around in their backward-facing seats, trying to see down the narrow passageway and out the cockpit windows up front. The two navigators down in the Hole also didn't have any way to see outside. They would have put away any loose objects and cleared their writing tables to remove any obstacle between themselves and their downward ejection paths. If they had to eject, the spring-loaded table would snap forward into a slot in the panel in front of them and anything left on the work-table at that time could make for a nasty airborne projectile during ejection. Major Eugene Richards, behind them in his small jump seat, could only listen in on his headset to the events unfolding beyond his control. There he was, tucked away back in this very snug hide-away, trying to visualize what was going on outside the airplane, or even on the upper deck. His only way of trying to figure out where they were, what the altitude was, how far away from landing, anything, was what he was hearing over the interphone headset. In the event of a bail out, he would at least be the second man out, diving through the hatch opening made by the navigator, Captain Paul Brown, a few feet to his front. He visualized watching Brown and his entire ejection seat disappearing downward, then him unbuckling, taking two steps, and going out the bottom hatch, to safety. That's all he wanted to do—get out of this airplane safely—and maybe think about his retirement papers.

After Raleigh Radar turned *Keep 19* over to Seymour Johnson Approach Control, Major Tulloch ordered the flaps down as requested by the Command Post. They were at nine thousand feet. It takes the massive thirty-foot wide flaps a full minute to reach the extended position. Just as the flaps started down he was instructed by Seymour Johnson to turn left from the current heading of 320° to a heading of 260° to line up with Runway 26. This is a heading change of sixty degrees, somewhat sharper than similar intercepting turns for civilian aircraft. It is possible that Major Tulloch may have preferred a more gentle turn, starting much further away from the runway. Now there he was, doing a banking turn to the left, with his right wing higher than the left. But the turn was completed without any control problems, and the final heading of 260° would be later confirmed by Raleigh Radar and witnesses.

They were on a very high, very long final approach. A radio message from the base would have sounded like this: "Keep One Niner Heavy, Seymour Johnson Approach. Cleared for the ILS,

Runway two-six. Altimeter two niner niner six. Advise the runway in sight. Good luck, sir."

"ILS for two-six. Keep One Niner," Tulloch acknowledged.

The "good luck" comment would have been a courtesy offered by the Seymour Johnson approach controller to an aircraft in trouble. It was to let the pilot of the landing B-52 know that this was indeed being considered as an emergency, that firefighters would have been notified and their equipment was rolling into position, and the airport would be closed to all other traffic. There would be no other takeoffs or landings during this emergency. *Keep 19* "owned the field."

During flap extension, the speed reduced from two hundred and twenty to one hundred and eighty knots. The landing gear was already down and locked. Adam Mattocks said that the turn was completed and the aircraft was flying straight and level. Tulloch did a quick check of the indicators. Stabilizer trim zero; rudder trim, approximately zero; airbrake: position two. Flaps indicator showing 100 percent. Then… there was a loud noise from under the airplane like it had struck something and there was a violent jerk to the left. The pilots got the plane leveled but then a worse noise came from below. The right wing dropped slightly and the aircraft began a turn to the right. Adam Mattocks thought then and now that somehow the lowering of the flaps during the turn had jammed the control surfaces of the right wing, damaged from the huge fuel leak. Major Tulloch tried to correct this unexpected right turn… The turn increased… He and Dick Rardin had both yokes hard left, both were stomping hard on the left rudder pedals, trying to stop that turn…. Major Tulloch yanked off all power to the four engines on the left wing, and increased power to full on the remaining two outboard engines on the right wing. The big aircraft did not respond. Six of the eight jet engines were either spooling down to idle or already idle on a heavy aircraft with landing gear and flaps down. Major Tulloch was running out of airspeed. He was doing everything that nineteen years of flying had taught him—all his skills, his hundreds of hours of combat, everything he knew—he was putting up the fight of his life and that of his crew. It was coming down to this one instant in time; his eyes and hands were flying over the myriad of throttles, instruments and controls. Get the nose down to pick up airspeed… airspeed coming back up. Worry about heading later… looking good. Just maybe… Then, there was a loud cracking and thumping noise and the aircraft began an uncontrolled barrel roll to the right. A loud explosion was heard. The right wing was folding up. "The beast was rolling over on her back."

Adam Mattocks had recently gone through a session as pilot in the ground training simulator where the instructor had set up the exact same configuration: an approach to landing, gear and flaps down, six of the eight engines out, and loss of airspeed. Adam crashed the simulator every time.

He had also, just the day before, gone through in the same simulator the exact steps he would make in order to leave the instructor pilot's jump seat on the top deck and bail out of the opening in the lower deck. He knew it would take him more than the few seconds like the others in the ejection seats. While the airplane was starting this last, fatal maneuver, he put into action what he had practiced. First he unplugged his headset, for he did not want to be connected in any way to the airplane. He kept his hand on the belt release. Then he turned in his seat to his right as far as he could, to be in a better angle to his route of escape: the ladder behind him to the lower deck. While mentally preparing for what was to come next, he quickly realized he would not be able to hear the bail out command over his headset, so he quickly plugged back in. That command came immediately from Major Tulloch, "Bail out!" Amazingly, someone answered back on the interphone, "Did you say bail out?" "Yes!" shouted Major Tulloch, "Bail Out!" It would be determined later that the person who asked for confirmation was Major Gene Shelton, the Radar/Navigator.

Mattocks simultaneously disconnected both his headset and his seat belt and immediately was flung to the floor, on his knees, facing aft. He grayed out from incredible G-forces. He said he thought he was out for two or three minutes, but it must have been only seconds. When his vision fully returned, he was somehow facing forward, and he saw Major Tulloch, while fighting the violently shaking controls, turn his head and look back at him. He said that look between them agreed on one thing: Adam Mattocks was a dead man. Scott Tulloch's eyes sent the worried message, "I'm sorry... ." Adam nodded his head as if to say, "It's OK." Then the co-pilot, followed quickly by the pilot, ejected—each departing like a small, savage, single-passenger rocket ship, a loud bang, but without flames. Mattocks knew he could not make it to the lower level, so he tried something truly desperate. He tried to jump straight out the open overhead right-hand hatch... but due to the aircraft's spin actually went out the opening on the left. He was hung up, with only his head and shoulders out. Then it was inertia, or something, that popped him outside the aircraft, stationary, with no wind sounds. He and the aircraft were momentarily suspended together in a bizarre ballet in space, forward motion ceased by the huge wing surface, which was now vertical, instead of horizontal, and was acting as a big air brake.

We know that when Major Tulloch gave the bail out command the aircraft was in a nose down position and had rolled to the right past 90° of vertical, with the tail now forward of the nose. The aircraft could not survive this incredible attitude. "Complete aircraft breakup occurred at this time," three hours and six minutes after the crisis began. The right wing broke off, the fuselage cracked in the middle, and the two thermonuclear bombs spun out of the disintegrating, crumbling aircraft.

Total flight time was thirteen hours and thirty-nine minutes. It was 0035 hours, 24 January 1961.

"Night scene over Faro, North Carolina. The crash of Keep 19."
Illustration by author

Chapter 3. The Bail Out

Lieutenant Bill Wilson, electronic warfare officer, said that in the minutes before the crash, "There was a lot of chatter going on. The next thing I knew, they said, bail-out. I took their word and bailed out." He said he told himself, "This can't be happening to me. It's all a dream. When I looked up and saw the chute open, I knew I had it made." When he ejected, his ejection seat separated from him and his parachute opened as advertised. But on the way down, the life raft somehow inflated early—inadvertently, tangling him in the rigging. He found himself in the unusual position of fighting with a boat that was somehow tied to him in midair after bailing out of an aircraft. He was able to reach the knife strapped to his leg, cut the lanyards and free himself before reaching the ground. He tried to be very careful and cut only the boat cords, not the parachute cords. The inflated life raft quickly blew away in the wind and was never found. Somewhere in North Carolina, a hunter or farmer has probably been surprised by finding a rubber life raft, miles from the ocean.

Lieutenant Wilson landed in a plowed field of soft mud. He said later, "I don't know how it happened. I know that when I landed in the field I felt awfully good. I felt like running." Then he thought he saw a bull. He thought it started chasing him in the dark, so he ran to a fence and jumped it, breaking his ankle in the process. He limped to a nearby house, where a pot of coffee was started on the stove and a Mason jar of clear 'medicinal spirits' was made available. "They thought at first I was a prowler when I told them I had jumped out of an airplane. I must have been bad-looking." His broken ankle would prove to be the most serious of the injured survivors. Adam Mattocks, told me in his interview, "Bill Wilson was from New Jersey. He didn't know a bull from a cow. It was an old cow."

When Major Tulloch ejected, the plane was rolling over and he was hanging suspended by his seat belt. There was a gap between him and his ejection seat, and when the catapult fired, it slammed hard against his body. He found himself tumbling out of control, losing his oxygen mask and helmet. It was like being overpowered inside a big wave at the beach. His parachute opened and he was surrounded by flaming pieces of wreckage as he was coming down. He would say later it was a fine physical sensation, this floating, and he could see why people would do it for sport. He was probably already in shock from the blast of the exploding aircraft. He found himself floating down alongside someone, and found out later it was Gene Shelton, the radar navigator. Tulloch called out, talked to him, but got no response from the limp form. Tulloch came down in a swamp and was hung up in a tree. He could not see clearly in the dark, but he thought he was only a few feet off the ground, so he released his parachute harness. The drop was over twenty feet into the cold waters of the Nahunta Swamp. Shelton was nowhere to be seen. The wind was very strong and they had separated during the parachute fall of over a vertical mile. He was thinking surely that all the boys had gotten out, he could hear the seats firing off before he ejected. When he first heard the muffled explosions he thought it was more trouble, but then he heard the shell that fired the co-pilot's seat and realized that was a good sound—"The lads were firing their seats off and were safely away."

He was alone in the dark swamp and could see no fires or house lights, so he checked himself for broken bones, found the North Star, and started wading out of the swamp. But each direction he tried he encountered deeper icy water. He blacked out several times and once found himself face down in the water.

He had flown every available heavy bomber in the Air Force inventory during his career, from B-17s to the B-36 to the B-52. He had flown thirty-one combat missions over Japan in B-29s. It would be ironic, he thought, to survive an exploding B-52 only to fall out of a tree and drown in a swamp. That might be the way his fellow pilots would remember his demise: "Tulloch got out of the plane OK, but he came down in a tree, fell out of it, and drowned in a swamp."

He decided this would be a good time to climb out of the water and just wait a bit.

Part of the parachute was hanging within reach, so he pulled on it, and retrieved the orange and white cloth from the tree. He spent the rest of a cold, wet night wrapped in it, teeth chattering, waiting hours for daylight to arrive. For years he had carried with him on every flight a pack of government-issued waterproof matches. Now that he needed them they were lost. He had also lost that often joked-about black eye patch. It was issued to SAC pilots to use when they were going into combat so they would have at least one eye, in theory, functioning after the nuclear blast. He heard rescue helicopters coming over but had no way of signaling in the dark, with no flashlight, no matches. He had lost everything from his pockets, things he always checked for, before every flight. He started blacking out again. A slow, cold dawn crept into the swamp. When it had accumulated enough daylight to make out items, he tried moving east, around and away from the deep swamp, where he found a road. He did not know which way to turn. A milkman for the Wayne County Dairy, Mr. Robert Ham, was making his morning deliveries and came upon a person walking down the road. Mr. Ham said he stopped, with this "pretty rough looking" fellow in his truck headlights. He "did not appear to be armed," and was muddy, dazed and disheveled. Mr. Ham thought he might have been in a car wreck, so he offered him a ride. When he found out Major Tulloch had just survived an airplane crash, he drove him to the first farmhouse that had a telephone. The Major called the Wing Command Post to report in, and to find out if the rest of the crew made it. His first concern was Lieutenant Mattocks, for the young man had been up on the flight deck helping with circuit breakers that the pilots could not reach. Major Tulloch was transported by the farmer about a mile to the crash site at Faro where he "made a dramatic appearance," according to the newspapers. His commander was certainly happy to see him. He was then transported by ambulance to the hospital at Seymour Johnson Air Force Base twelve miles away.

At base housing, Betty Tulloch had been awakened around 6:00 a.m. by the visitation team of two senior Air Force officers and a chaplain. That was the rule: the Casualty Affairs team must be made up of at least two people of equal or greater rank than the service member, along with a chaplain. They were the official notification team, the bearers of bad news. For years, Betty expected them each time Scott flew—visualizing in her mind's eye their slow walk up to the door, how they would watch her closely, ask permission to come in, ask if anyone else was in the house, and then gently sit her down. That was important, to get the wife sitting down. They did all that, but now, somehow, it was all in slow-motion. She was wondering why was it all so slow? She was focusing hard on what they were saying.

They told her the Major's plane had exploded and crashed, and he was missing.

Air Force wives, especially SAC wives, had an unusually tight support group. Back when their husbands raised their right hands and swore to support and defend, the wives didn't raise their right hands, but they were just as much a part of the SAC family. They all were. They knew this notification drill, and over the years have had to get very good at handling it. Two of her best friends quickly came in to be with her, somehow they got the word and just knew to be there. Betty decided not to wake up the boys, Scottie and Andy.

About an hour after she was officially notified that her husband was missing, she got a telephone call from someone at the Wing command post: "Betty?! Just a minute—I've got someone who wants to speak with you.... Hold on... I'm transferring the call...."

It was Scott, her husband, now at the farmhouse. Betty was incredulous, speechless. "Why are you crying," he asked, laughing. "Did you spend all the insurance money already?"

Years later the boys would admit they knew what was happening that morning. They were awake, watching from a hiding place, and saw all the people and the cars arrive, they saw the silver cross on the chaplain's uniform, and saw their mother quietly shaking.

Betty met Scott when she was sixteen-years-old and a junior in high school in Phoenix, Arizona. He was a dashing twenty-six-year-old Air Force pilot in flight school at nearby Luke Air Force Base, and they met at a Brethren Church social function. They dated some, on and off, nothing serious. A year later he wanted to take her to San Diego to meet his parents. Nothing doing, said her parents. Two more years went by and Scott was stationed at various bases around the country, but somehow he would find reasons to fly to Phoenix to see her every now and then. He made another request for her to meet his parents, since he was going into combat. He really wanted to see them, and for her to meet them. Finally, her parents agreed she could go to San Diego, but only after extensive late night talks and with the plan of her staying at her aunt's house. Her first inclination that he was serious was when he asked her, "Do you want to make it a honeymoon?" She said it took three years to get her. When they were married on February 3, 1945, she was nineteen, he was twenty-nine.

*Scott and Betty Tulloch on their wedding day, February 3, 1945.
Photo courtesy of Betty Tulloch*

Adam Mattock was not hit by the tail assembly when he jumped only because the tail was not there—it had just broken off.

"I didn't want to open my parachute and have the plane run through it, so I did the count to one-thousand-three and then pulled the D ring," he said. When his parachute deployed, big pieces of falling burning debris narrowly missed him. He looked up and saw he had a big, beautiful chute. "Thank you, Lord."

That's when the plane blew up.

The concussion collapsed his chute and he had a streamer. After he straightened out his parachute and got air back into it, he tried to get oriented. He saw two parachutes above him. He was blown over two fields and tracks of woods by the stiff, westerly cold wind. He could see the moon over his shoulder. Then he realized he was coming down in one of the fires of the burning wreckage. He had already prayed twice before, on his knees in the aircraft and then and under the parachute. He knew the Lord was still with him, but if He needed him to go Home, he was ready. Mattocks yanked his parachute riser controls, slid around the fire, and soon came down right next to a dark house that he had not noticed earlier. His first hint that he was near civilization was when he saw electrical wires go between him and the lighted horizon. When he landed, he didn't even do a roll, he just stuck in the mud standing up. He had somehow gotten out of an airplane without an ejection seat, narrowly avoided being blown up and hit by flaming debris, and now he was just standing in some mud. He just stood there for just a minute staring at the ground in amazement, trying to realize the fact that he was really alive. He gathered up his parachute and walked over to the house where three people were out on the far end of the front porch, looking away in another direction at the fire. They had not seen or heard him land upright in the soft mud.

"When I stepped on the porch I made a little noise and they turned around and looked at me. I said, 'It's just me. I just bailed out of that plane… I'm not from Mars.'" This shocked family, jarred by the burning wreckage falling from the sky all around them, appeared to be afraid of him, so he took his helmet off. He wanted to show that he was just a man, not a space alien. He told them that he was from Maysville, North Carolina, and he needed their help badly. The mother said they would drive him to the air force base, but would have to wait for Brother who had the only car, to return from the store. He did not arrive for another fifteen or twenty minutes. Mattocks sat stunned on the edge of the front porch, holding his parachute and helmet under his arm. Finally Brother returned. The quiet family then drove him to the main gate of the air force base at Goldsboro. It took about fifteen minutes. They arrived at the gate, let him out, and drove away. Adam never did find out the name of the family.

The guard at the gate of Seymour Johnson Air Force Base looked over the disheveled black man who was approaching. He did not see any evidence of him being a military person, and he appeared to be holding a bundle under his arm. "Where're you going, buddy?"

Mattocks said, "My name's Adam Mattocks. There's been a plane crash."

The two guards exchanged glances. "We don't know anything about a plane crash. Where's your military ID?"

Mattocks, still in a daze and in shock, began to search through his torn pockets without success. The guard said, "Well, if you don't have military identification, we will have to arrest you for stealing government property. Step into the guard house."

Mattocks moved forward, then realized what was going on. "What? What did you just say, SERGEANT?" The instincts of an Air Force officer were kicking in.

"That parachute," mumbled the guard, now putting things together fast. "Uh…. Where'd you get it?" Mattocks shook his head in disbelief. The confused and bewildered Air Police didn't know what else to do, they didn't know anything about a B-52 crash, so they were arresting him for stealing government property—the parachute. It was still strapped to his back.

Co-pilot Captain Dick Rardin also safely ejected. His later report would be in true test pilot format, short and to the point: "I could see three or four chutes against the glow of the wreckage. The plane hit ten or twelve seconds after the bail out. I hit some trees. I had a fix on some lights and started walking. My biggest difficulty was the various and sundry dogs I encountered on the road."

He also was driven to the base, where the gate police, who still thought this was some sort of bizarre hoax, apprehended him too. As Captain Rardin expressed his loud and very flavorful opinion to those at the main gate, Mattocks was quietly reciting the names of the crew, the time they had taken off, and other details to one of the guards to convince him that they really were Air Force crew members. Then he asked the security police officer in charge to call the tower and tell them to "Go code Twenty-Seven." That confirmed what people in the tower were suspecting from the sudden loss of communication, and the fact that *Keep 19* never landed long after being cleared for the final approach. They thought *Keep 19* had lost radio communications, and was still flying around somewhere—there had been no Mayday call. Now they scanned the entire horizon with binoculars and found an unusual glow to the north, far away from the flight path, and they knew they had a serious aircraft accident. An accident involving a B-52 bomber carrying nuclear weapons… A Broken Arrow.

Broken Arrow: The accidental or unauthorized detonation, or possible detonation of a nuclear weapon, including the non-nuclear detonation or burning of a nuclear weapon; radioactive contamination; or seizure, theft, or loss of a nuclear weapon or component (including jettisoning).

There are other definitions of situations involving nuclear incidents and weapons: *Dull Sword*, a minor incident that could impair a nuclear weapon's deployment; *Bent Spear*, a more significant incident such as a breach of security or requiring major rework; *Empty Quiver*, a missing functioning weapon which was usually an inventory-keeping problem, and *Faded Giant*, a nuclear incident involving a nuclear reactor or other radiological accident not involving nuclear weapons.

Broken Arrow was the most severe incident, other than NUCFLASH, which was a detonation that had the potential to create nuclear war. The Command Post initiated their part of the Broken Arrow notifications: to SAC, Operations, Wing HQ, Fire, Security, and the Medics. At base headquarters the Officer Of The Day continued it by calling the first on his list of people in quarters who had the need to know. Each person in the Broken Arrow 'telephone tree' would in turn call more people, and so on. Quickly the entire organization would be brought up to speed by the recall alert. Every function on the base that had any responsibility in a nuclear accident or serious incident would cover their duty station and be prepared to meet that responsibility; everyone from base commander, communications, public relations, personnel, chaplains, civil engineers, etc. Even the base veterinarian, who had responsibility of caring for the guard dogs, was part of a Broken Arrow alert, and would be notified through the telephone tree.

Adam Mattocks and Dick Rardin were finally driven from the main gate to the base hospital while the fire and rescue equipment from the base were rolling. The fire trucks had been called off the runway and were thundering out the main gate, black exhaust pouring out, toward Faro at their maximum speed, forty-five miles per hour. One of the firemen on board was Airman Second Class Fred Johnson.

Fifty miles away in Maysville, out in the rural area called Belgrade, Anne Mattocks was pregnant with their third child. She and her extended family had been up all night long having a good time, playing cards, and laughing together, girls versus the boys, sisters and brothers. It was a big, happy family. Anne had eight brothers and sisters, and when both parents died when she was two, aunts and uncles raised all the children. She grew up with an aunt near Hatteras, North Carolina, on the Outer Banks. When Anne was fifteen, her aunt began developing heart problems, and started taking Anne to spend time with other relatives near Jacksonville, North Carolina. "My aunt wanted to make sure that I knew the rest of the family." The aunt died two days after Anne's sixteenth birthday.

She went to high school with Adam, but they really didn't care too much for each other. Anne said, "He thought he was going to be the high school valedictorian, but my grade point average *took him out!* When we both started to college at A&T University, several of us would ride back home to Jacksonville with him. He was the only one with a car."

Early that morning, around 5:30, her mother-in-law who lived next door, was up preparing breakfast and the biscuits were ready. She came over with the news from the TV that a plane had crashed. An Air Force jet bomber had crashed in "the Snow Hill" area, east of the air base.

They were staring at each other when bright red lights appeared outside in front of their house. Soon, a very nervous North Carolina state trooper appeared at the door and told them there had been a plane crash. Adam's sister and brother asked him if Adam Mattocks was in it. "I really can't say, I know that not everyone was alive. I'm just supposed to take you to the air base." Seymour Johnson Casualty Affairs had decided that because of the distance away from the base, it was better to quickly use the state police instead of the personal visit from the Casualty Affairs Team.

"I've got to take a shower," said Anne in a daze. Neighbors from all over were coming into the house. One of them made a very inappropriate remark about how Anne was now going to "get a lot of money." That's when she came apart.

The trooper said, "Now wait a minute. I didn't say anything about your husband being dead, did I?" He was very calm now, and got everyone else calmed down. "Let's just get ready and go."

When Anne got in the police car and they pulled out, it seemed like everybody in the community was following in a long string of cars. When they reached La Grange, someone remembered the mother-to-be had not eaten, so they stopped at a fast-food restaurant. The entire convoy pulled in after them. Sitting in the parking lot, the car radio came on and gave the names of the survivors. Adam

Mattocks' name was read. There was much rejoicing in that fast-food parking lot in La Grange.

At the base hospital, the doctors and nurses were amazed at Adam Mattocks' miraculous escape, but were watching him very closely for signs of stress and shock. Newspapers would call Adam Mattocks "the luckiest man in North Carolina." He says he should have died several times that night, both in the plane and out. He prayed each time, and he was in a state of peace. But he wanted to see his children grow, to train them. He saw his entire life pass by his eyes. He said he survived due to one thing: the continuous prayers of his entire family to a merciful God.

Many other pilots and SAC airmen would later say there was no way he should have gotten out of the airplane in that manner.

Paul Brown, the Navigator, safely ejected downward and landed in some trees east of the crash in an old graveyard. A Mr. and Mrs. Singleton picked him up and took him to the base. He had some minor injuries and was glad to see Adam and Dick Rardin at the base hospital. They were comparing stories, trying to piece together what had happened. The idea of a wing breaking off a B-52 was so foreign to them, but they gradually began to consider it in their discussions.

It was not known why Frank Barnish did not use his ejection seat. He may have been thinking back to that very bad experience over Germany seventeen years earlier. He at least could look out of his B-24 gun turret on that sunny day. But that night, perhaps he was stunned, covered in jet fuel, strapped into his ejection seat in the dark, thinking about bailing out of yet another bomber. Or maybe he just ran out of time. He had started the ejection process, "press the top lever and rotate the ejection handle upward"… the overhead hatch was gone, but the second lever, the seat trigger, was never pulled.

The bodies of Technical Sergeant Francis Barnish of Greenfield, Massachusetts, and Major Eugene Richards, of Toccoa, Georgia, were found in the main wreckage at the edge of Big Daddy's Road. It was later told that after the fire was extinguished, a Faro volunteer fireman named Add Edmundson saw Frank's remains in his ejection seat and covered his son with his coat; he didn't want him to see. Father and son stood quietly near the steaming wreckage for a few moments in the smoke and haze of that cold, wet dawn, heads bowed. Frank Barnish left behind three children and a sick wife. Eugene Richards left behind a wife and son.

Adam Mattocks said later he thought that Major Richards had actually gotten out of the aircraft, but was pulled back inside by the same inertia that somehow had helped him escape through the top of the aircraft. The inertia would have forced Richards in the same relative direction as Mattocks within the aircraft, which would have shoved him up against the ceiling of the lower deck. He would have been very near Major Shelton, the man who was responsible for the safety of the extra crew members on board.

The body of Major Gene Shelton was found the next morning three miles away near Bullhead Bridge, caught in a tree, his neck was broken. It was later be reported in the official findings that he was jerked against his ejection seat when the parachute inflated and after his helmet was lost. Gene Shelton, a native of San Antonio, Texas, left a wife, three sons, and a daughter.

When Major Tulloch gave an interview at the base hospital to *The Goldsboro News-Argus* managing editor Eugene Price, he said, "If there was a hero, it was Gene Shelton." He said Major Shelton was apparently trying to assist Major Richards down in the Hole, and delayed his ejection until it was too late.

Major Tulloch had a rough time at the hospital. He had collapsed several times, blacked out from the pain and shock. At first they told him that the others were being collected and were in a room down the hall. "I even thought I heard some of them outside my door. Relief and exhaustion helped me to drift off to sleep. The next morning, when I kept insisting that I wanted to see them the doctors told me the grim truth… three of them had perished. That next night I was alone with my grief. This loss sorely affected me, and I was stricken with remorse. Why had I tried to save that cursed plane? I had lost three men I loved like brothers. Black despair dragged me down… ."

The above quotes are from a narrative written by Major Tulloch a few months after the crash. In it he recalls how he struggled within the grip of despair and how his faith helped him recover. His narrative is included in this report, graciously provided by his widow, Betty Tulloch.

Chapter 4. The Crash Site

Billy Reeves was an eighteen-year-old senior at Eureka High School. He spent a part of his school day at the Industrial Education Center, a technical school, where he was rebuilding the engine of the family car, a 1957 Ford. This wasn't a hobby; it was a necessity, for it was the family's only vehicle. He lived with his family on Big Daddy's Road in Faro, a tiny community in Wayne County, North Carolina. He helped his daddy on the sixty-acre farm, which is not a big farm, and it was a tough go. His dad was ill and had asked his son to try to get a part-time job. Billy found one in nearby Freemont, at the Esso station. The Esso was also the bus stop and it had a grill where Billy got the job of cook. He was a hardworking young man. He closed up the station about 11:20 that night in January and Mr. Saul, the owner, gave him a lift home.

His room was on the south side of their single story white frame house and it looked out over the flat farm fields and woods. This part of North Carolina was mostly farmland, but also had a lot of woods and a wetlands area called the Nahunta Swamp. Billy got home that night before midnight and went straight to bed. He had already eaten a hamburger that he cooked for himself on the grill, and the next day was a school day.

He had just started to doze off when he heard a noise like he had never heard before in his life. He jerked wide-awake and looked to the south through his bedroom window as his room lit up in bright red from ceiling to floor. "I was scared to death. I was looking at the plane when it fell. I saw it hit the ground, and it exploded twice." He bounced off the door frame as he ran out of his room and found his mother, a deeply religious woman, praying. She thought it was "the end of time."

His daddy hurried next door to the house of his uncle, William Edmundson. Both his dad and his uncle were members of the Faro Volunteer Fire Station, which was a mile away in the opposite direction from the fire. Everybody was excited and tried to talk all at once. Then they calmed down a little bit and knew that others would be rushing to the station and getting out the fire trucks, so the two men headed straight for the biggest fire, which was just to the south of their houses. It looked like several fires spread out for miles.

Earl and Mary Lancaster still live at the intersection of Big Daddy's Road and Shackelford Road, and Earl was the assistant chief of the Faro volunteer fire department. Mary saw the plane just as it crashed to the south of their house and she woke up her husband. Earl jumped up, got dressed, and headed out to the fire station, and, with some other volunteers, cranked up both the ancient two-seater fire engine and the tanker truck. That's all they had, but it was time to go with it. When they opened the wide doors and pulled out of the fire station they were staring straight down Big Daddy's Road into a giant wall of fire a mile away. It looked like they were going to be driving straight into Hell itself.

"We could see it clearly, it just lit up the sky. We knew it was a military plane that'd fell," he said. It was the biggest fire they had ever seen. "It was really something."

Volunteer fire chiefs and assistant chiefs had attended safety meetings given by Seymour Johnson Air Force Base representatives. They emphasized that the volunteers should try to avoid any close contact with military aircraft fires; they could be in extreme danger. The volunteers should not try to approach the aircraft itself unless further loss of life on the aircraft was imminent, but they were to protect the lives of the citizens and their property. The tanker trucks for the rural volunteer stations did not have foam, but contained only water, which could result in disastrous consequences if it made contact with certain chemicals and materials on board military aircraft. They were instructed over the radio that night to fight only structure and grass fires and to hold short of the crashed aircraft until specialized Air Force fire equipment could arrive from the base.

Rudolph Tyndall got a call from a friend that night. "He said, 'Rudolph, I have some bad news. I think a plane has fell on your daddy's and momma's house.' It scared me to death." he said. As he rushed out to Faro, he could see the bright glow from miles away. It was with great relief that he found his parents safe, the house unharmed. But amazingly, seemingly right outside the house, right next to it, flames rose hundreds of feet straight up in the air, a frightening catastrophe. "My daddy said when he looked out the window that all he could see was fire… fire everywhere," Tyndall said. "He said he thought the whole world was on fire, and my mama, she said she thought it was the end of the world." The Tyndall's were quickly gathered up and brought to safety, just as helicopters began to land in the field across the road. Tyndall said, "It was amazing. It really was a miracle that this thing happened and no one got killed in the neighborhood."

That white farmhouse still stands on Big Daddy's Road. Its only damage was one cracked window glass. It was less than three hundred feet south of a crashed B-52.

The safety instructions about not putting water on military aircraft wreckage may not have gotten through to at least one volunteer fire station, which had approached the fire from the south. Ellen Tyndall said, "Firemen reported that water behaved like gasoline on the flaming aircraft. They were unable to put out the fire until the Air Force arrived with foam to extinguish it."

The neighbors were very concerned about the Howards, whose house was just one hundred fifty yards away north of the main crash site, especially since George Howard was blind. Mr. and Mrs. Howard were evacuated from the scene by the military. The flames were scorching their house.

There was heavy smoke, the thick smell of kerosene in the air, and burning debris was hanging and dripping from the trees. Forty-five minutes after the crash, another helicopter appeared with a searchlight "as big as a car" and began announcing over a loud speaker for everyone in the crash zone to evacuate immediately. One gentleman dashed outside into the horror of the night and was frightened to the point of losing control of his bowels. He was extremely embarrassed to be caught in the spotlight out behind one of the tobacco pack houses with his overalls down. The glaring spotlight was bad enough, but then his hat blew off in this strong wind and a loud voice from above asked if he was all right. Across the road another neighbor opened his front door and his small dog ran out of the house and was never seen again. The people of Faro were out in their yards, twisting around, dazed and dizzy, trying to figure out what was happening to their world.

Billy ran as fast as he could down the road to where his daddy and two uncles, Add and William Edmundson, were at the biggest wreckage. They could tell it was an enormous fuselage lying across the road. They had never seen anything like it. His daddy told him to go get the uncle's truck and take everybody in the family to safety at a relative's home, that this was really bad. Billy took off running hard back to the house, avoiding the smoking, jagged wreckage and craters and loaded up the 1946 Ford flatbed truck. The roadway itself was burning. He somehow jammed all five relatives, all four of the adults being "good sized," into the cab and began working their way around the back roads to safety since Big Daddy's Road was completely blocked. They would stay at a relative's house for three days without a telephone, hoping the family firefighters were safe. They watched the terrible news about their small community on TV. All the major networks carried the story and they gathered around the television. They couldn't believe this was happening to them. Everything looked so different when they saw their houses and family members on TV.

Federal Agent Tom Dority, had been in his car near the Greene and Wayne County lines on a stakeout, waiting in the dark to catch a moonshiner and shut down his illegal liquor still. Suddenly the sky lit up for miles. He saw a big fireball fall from the sky and knew immediately what had happened. He called Mike Rouse, a journalist for *The Goldsboro News-Argus.* Mike and Eugene Price, his editor, got out to the crash scene at Faro before the military arrived.

Eugene Price said, "It was eerie as hell. Part of the fuselage lay across the road. I was told that one of the crewmen had been impaled on a tree and that a big box was found attached to a parachute hanging from another tree."

Willie Shelton, who lived just west of the Big Daddy's Road bridge over the Nahunta swamp, saw and felt the crash and for some reason immediately thought his old car had somehow blown up. He had been having some trouble with it, but then he realized, it hadn't really been *that* much trouble. He opened his front door and looked out, put on his coat and started walking toward the fire. Then he stopped, turned around and went back to the house. He had no idea what to do, so he just stood on his porch and watched. The boys in the fire trucks would be there soon, he could hear the tinny sirens, getting closer. They would be from the volunteer stations coming from all over the county. It seemed like every dog in the county was howling. He was thinking: *What in the world....* A while later huge red fire engines from the Air Force Base came lumbering by his house. He had never seen fire engines that big.

Evan Keel was a young college student who lived with his parents in Goldsboro, not too far from the east end of the runway, Runway Two Six. *Keep 19* would have passed very near their house on the final approach to landing… If the right wing not folded up and caused the plane to veer off to the north. Evan and his father, Paul, were volunteers at the Elroy Fire Department, where Paul was assistant chief. Late that January night the Wayne County dispatcher had called Chief Farrell Williams and asked for his fire department to help look for survivors of a plane crash. They did not know if it was a civilian or military aircraft. Evan, his father, and two others joined the fire chief in his personal car, a red and black 1956 Ford Fairlane, and the five men rushed out Highway 13 over to Saulston then out the Snow Hill Highway.

When they got to the intersection of Bull Head Road they saw helicopters with searchlights off to the west, so now they knew a military aircraft was involved. They moved slowly over the small bridge at Bull Head Creek, windows down, flashlights out in the cold air, shining up in the trees, down into the black water of the Nahunta Swamp. As they moved slowly up a short incline out of the swamp they saw something orange and white in the trees on the left.

"See if anyone's there!" cried the Chief. They piled out of the car just as a helicopter clattered to a hard, fast landing in a nearby clearing, showering them with dried tree leaves and pine needles, and someone jumped out running. The parachute harness was empty, with straps hanging down. The Air Force man looked it over carefully and said, "Nothing is torn… It looks like it was released by the guy who used it. Let's look around for him." They searched the area but found no other evidence.

Based on later information this was most probably the landing spot of Captain Dick Rardin, the co-pilot, who had somehow gotten a ride to the base and passed the volunteers on the road going the other way.

The group of Elroy firemen climbed back in the Ford and drove toward other searchlights that were now a lot brighter and closer together. They turned left down a dirt road that is now called Shackelford Road. They were out of the swamp and into cultivated farm fields of brown winter stubble. They stopped and looked at a really big object hanging from a huge white parachute in a group of trees. Someone whispered, "What the hell… ?" They did not get out of the car this time. Where there was a lot of chatter going on before but now they got really quiet. They thought it just might be a bomb, but this thing was huge, bigger than any bomb they had ever thought possible. Maybe it wasn't a bomb; maybe it was some kind of dropped fuel tank? They drove on to the intersection of Big Daddy's Road where they could see fires a half mile to the south. They checked around, flashing their lights around in the trees, but did not see any more parachutes at the small settlement. With the finding of those two parachutes and this big fire they knew they were witnessing something very unusual and very disturbing. People were out in their yards asking each other what on earth had happened? How was it possible for this much fire and destruction to come from the air? Had two airplanes collided in midair?

After about twenty minutes a big Air Force truck arrived, loaded with armed troops. Two men jumped off and set up kerosene smudge pots as temporary warning lights. They lit the wicks and created a roadblock with feeble, smoky flames. Evan and the others got together, talked it over, then decided to double back down Shackelford Road to search for survivors in the area to the south-east where there were more helicopter searchlights. Guards had been dropped off at regular intervals along the road, and one was now at that thing in the tree. In a field nearby they found a long length of metal pipe that smelled of jet fuel, then a hatch cover with a first aid kit still attached, and then a helmet. The helmet had a piece of tape on it that read: RARDIN. They waved their flashlights at the helicopters to let them know of the find. All those in ejection seats lost their helmets due to the extreme violence of their bailouts. Only Adam Mattocks, who did not have an ejection seat, was still wearing his helmet after bailout.

Charles Davis owned property in the area and had been asked by an Air Force major to ride with him around in his station wagon. They arrived at the object on the north side of Shackelford Road, on land owned by William H. Lane. It was a twelve-foot long cylinder hanging vertically by its parachute in a group of trees and they got a good look at it with flashlights. It was indeed a large bomb, and it appeared to be intact, but had spiral marks and scars and had a big dent in its nose where it had driven two feet into the ground. They went back to the spot on Big Daddy's Road where most of the wreckage from the aircraft fuselage lay burning. Charles Davis owned the cotton and tobacco farmland there. The major reported to the on-scene commander what they had seen hanging in the trees over on Shackelford Road.

Soon, there were ten volunteer fire departments from the surrounding area, ready to go into action if civilian lives or property were in danger. As far as they could tell no one on the ground had been killed or injured, and aside from some minor damage and the scorched Howard house no other houses or barns were involved. Considering the size of the wreckage area of several square miles that in itself was a miracle. The people of the Faro community were slowly coming to grips with what had fallen out of the sky and into their lives. State and military police were setting up roadblocks trying to control and quarantine the area.

Fred Johnson was a twenty-one year old Airman Second Class from middle Tennessee. He had always wanted to be a fireman and now he was one, assigned to the flight line fire department at Seymour Johnson Air Force. He was bouncing along in a large swaying fire truck heading north on the country roads of Wayne County toward Faro. They had gotten word there was a big crash, a B-52, possibly loaded with nuclear weapons. Fred was in his aluminum fire suit, holding on to his headgear and face shield. They could smell the burning jet fuel long before they saw the flames. Soon they stopped right in front of a white farmhouse, the home of Buck Tyndall. Then they turned left off Big Daddy's Road down into the muddy field to get to the main part of the crash, a few feet north of the road. They wanted to fight the flames from upwind.

After they got the foam going from the tanker trucks, they had beat the fire down and Fred went back to his truck to get a long handled hook to use in turning over burning wreckage. He left his headgear on the seat, he wouldn't need it for the time being. He and some others turned over a big piece of curved aluminum, and saw beneath it an upside-down partially melted ejection seat. He notified his sergeant who checked it out to see if it was still armed. An armed ejection seat, without the safety pin inserted, could be very dangerous for everyone in the area. When the cables and tubes were cut, it was determined to be safe. He and another firefighter lifted the blackened seat frame and tossed it aside, and saw under it an unused black parachute pack with a triangle of bright white nylon sticking out with some blood on it. Fred was wondering why the parachute was not burned, everything else was. He tugged at it, then realized the parachute was still attached to something. He called for the medics, who came with the black body bags to do what medics do.

Frank Barnish had returned to earth.

Fred stepped aside and looked toward the east. The sun should be coming up soon and maybe it would burn some of this cold mist away. He was thinking this wind would bring in some bad weather. That's the way it usually happened back home in Tennessee. Fred thought about Tennessee and God for a while. He tried not to think of too much else right then.

Nearby, other firemen were helping other medics recover more human remains. A chaplain was kneeling down beside the body of Major Eugene Richards. Some firemen joined him, kneeling in the wet ash for a few minutes.

Two photos at crash site. Both are the main site of the fuselage crash on Big Daddy's Road. *Photos courtesy USAF.*

Three miles east, near Bull Head Bridge, a group of firefighters were wondering how they were going to get the body out of the tree. The tree was one of many, in a thick patch of green pines. It was about fifty or sixty feet up, right near the top, and draped with the shroud of the parachute. The nearest ladder tall enough was back at the base, so one of the firefighters called up the Air Force rescue and fire-fighting helicopter, the Huskie H-43B. It was made for fire fighting. Its twin intermeshing rotors would allow it to hover and blow flames back from a crashed aircraft. It could get in and out of some tough places. This morning the twin clamshell doors at the rear had been removed, and a mesh screen snapped into place. The helicopter had two pilots, plus a medic and a fireman aboard.

A question over the helicopter intercom, "Fireman to pilot. Sir, do you think you can get close enough where we could grab the parachute?"

"Yeah, I think we can do that. Looks like there's enough clearance for the rotors. Watch me back there." The downwash blew the tops of the nearby pine trees around like a small hurricane. Soon, they were hovering over the tree. The fireman and medic had snapped themselves in safely, and removed the mesh screen at the rear of the helicopter. The helicopter slowly maneuvered until the top of the pine tree covered with nylon parachute material was brushing against the opening between the tail section and the fuselage. The medic and fireman reached out, grabbed a handful of parachute cloth each, and pulled. When both had a good grip of parachute cloth and were well braced against the frame, the fireman reported to the pilot over the interphone and the Huskie gently climbed straight up, lifting the body out of the tree, but with a tree limb still attached. Then it moved slowly over the open road nearby, and lowered it's special cargo. The body was slowly turning. The firemen in the road gently took hold, stopped the turn, and the recovery crew took over.

Major Gene Shelton had returned to earth.

After the biggest blazes were put out on Big Daddy's Road, the Air Force people had gone to the volunteer firemen and asked them to pull even further back, in order to conserve the water in the tankers, they were told. But it might have been for far more serious reasons. Specialists with handheld instruments were very concerned, saying they were looking for missing crew members, but they were actually looking for the bombs. The Air Force quickly announced that there were two bombs aboard but both were unarmed and had been recovered, that there was no danger.

Actually, only the part about there being two bombs was true.

The Air Force firemen were following the procedure known as *Moist Mop* for crashes of this nature. The first Air Force people at the crash site were the firefighters, wearing the aluminum hot suits, working side-by-side with the radiation teams with Geiger counters. Then EOD teams would find and secure any high explosives. These people wore full face masks and yellow coveralls for alpha particle radiation protection. Security forces kept anyone else, including civilian authorities, at least fifteen hundred feet away from the primary accident site. Red flags marked the boundaries of the site. In later accidents, the color of the flags changed from red to green "due to psychological factors." Even if there were evidence of radiation, the teams were forbidden to post the warning signs with the yellow and black international symbol of radiation. "Don't scare the locals" was an edict of *Moist Mop*.

The bomb in the trees on Shackelford Road was secured by Air Force personnel and vital components removed. A quantity of jet fuel had been found inside the supposedly sealed bomb case, indicating the volume of fuel that showered down in the bomb bay. Fred Johnson along with two other firemen had been dispatched over to the Shackelford Road site in one of the trucks to stand by as the thermonuclear weapon was 'safed.' He saw an Airman First Class holding a loose-leaf binder reading instructions to a man with a screwdriver working on an open panel of the bomb. Fred thought, "What am I doing standing here holding a two inch hose at the biggest bomb I've ever seen? What exactly am I supposed to do with this hose?" Then he found out his presence wasn't needed just because this thing was a nuclear weapon, it was because this nuclear weapon had some jet fuel inside it, and it might catch fire.

Bomb Number One, just north of Shackelford Road, Faro, North Carolina, with its retardation parachute. The nose is buried about two feet into the ground. It is tied off to keep from toppling over. Trees to the right of the bomb are covered in parachute material.

Photo courtesy of USAF.

Later that day the bomb was considered as "rendered safe" and loaded on a truck and hauled away to Medina Air Force Base located outside San Antonio, Texas. That was one of six nuclear weapon National Stockpile Sites, each located deep inside a military installation for an extra layer of security.

A farmer reported that he and his wife had driven down Shackelford Road several times that morning, just looking around, and had seen something white over on the right-hand side of the road. His wife's right side "just burned and burned," after finding out it was a nuclear weapon hanging in the trees.

At daylight, air traffic quickly became a problem. A yellow Marine helicopter with a movie cameraman hanging out the open door had a close call with a civilian single-engine airplane, which also had a photographer in the open door. The on-scene military commander banned all aircraft except for those involved in the emergency. It was now a Temporary Restricted Flight Area.

Throughout the day the conditions changed. Where the weather had been clear, windy, and moonlit at the time of the crash, it soon grew cold, and blowing snow and freezing rain turned the soft field into mud and delayed recovery efforts. This was the beginning of a winter storm that paralyzed some parts of the state for days. On Wednesday, January 25, the high temperature was 28°, the low was 10°.

The weather had changed for the worse just as Fred Johnson thought it would.

Wreckage was scattered for miles. The tail section and a wing were in an open field about a half-mile south of the bomb on Shackelford Road. Another part fell ten to fifteen feet from a family's house. Two of the eight engines were in the woods a half mile east of the main wreckage on Big Daddy's Road. And out in the middle of a plowed field a few hundred feet from an old cemetery was a fifteen-foot-wide crater six feet deep in the soft earth.

Explosive Ordnance Disposal (EOD)

"Jack, I've got a real one for you." The early morning phone call came to the young lieutenant at his apartment in Fairborn, Ohio. His squadron commander was assigning him to the Broken

Arrow at Goldsboro, North Carolina. And he was doing it without any of the planned elaborately coded wording that was the official terminology. The phrase, "Jack, I've got a real one for you," cut right to the chase.

Air Force First Lieutenant Jack B. ReVelle was commander of Detachment Four of the 2702nd Explosive Ordnance Disposal Squadron at Wright-Patterson Air Force Base at Dayton, Ohio. His team's job was to be ready at a moment's notice to go anywhere to deactivate anything, including the largest thermonuclear device in the world. ReVelle was a young bachelor, a man-about-town. He drove a 1959 black MG convertible with red leather seats, and had one of the first car phones on base. He had been in ROTC at Purdue University, and played trombone in a Dixieland band called the Salty Dogs. At college he lived in the Tau Epsilon Phi fraternity house with enough beer flowing to rival anything in "Animal House." Before he went into munitions ordnance, he was a USO escort officer at an Air Force base in Japan. The ladies called him "Kuma" which means bear.

At Dayton, Jack and his team usually spent a lot of time at Wright-Patterson doing intensive classified training, along with maintenance of their specialized equipment. Occasionally, they gave assistance to the Dayton, Ohio, fire and police departments acting as the local bomb squad. It takes a special person to be in the EOD: calculating, smart, and able to focus intensely on the task at hand.

*First Lieutenant Jack ReVelle, EOD Team Commander. 1960.
Photo courtesy USAF*

Just the previous July he had worked a Broken Arrow adjacent to McGuire Air Force Base, New Jersey, when a BOMARC missile caught fire and exploded in a ready-storage unit, which was also the launch site. The nuclear core of the anti-aircraft missile didn't detonate but the fuel tank fire it sure melted it. All of the missile's safety devices functioned as designed, but there was a lot of radioactive contamination from the firefighter's runoff.

ReVelle and his team tried to keep an even balance in their tense jobs. These fellows depended on each other in moments of extraordinary crisis, like any other battlefield brotherhood. A highly unofficial but favorite clothing item was a black tee shirt that had this message printed on the back:

I AM A BOMB TECHNICIAN.
IF YOU SEE ME RUNNING,
TRY TO KEEP UP

When he got the word about Goldsboro that morning, Jack grabbed his Remain Over Night kit that contained a few personal items. He kept the satchel close by him at all times. At the base a two-seat Lockheed T-33 jet aircraft was already warming up and the pilot waiting for his single passenger. On the flight line, Jack hurriedly put on the helmet and parachute that was handed to him and climbed up the ladder and into the rear ejection seat. Two ground crew people were helping him strap in as another person secured his bag in a small compartment of the jet.

"I don't know who you are, or why you need to get to Goldsboro in such a hurry, but I've never been cleared for a 'takeoff when ready' while sitting on the ramp," said the pilot, as soon as the intercom was plugged in. "The field's shut down to everybody else until we get wheels up."

"Sorry, Captain, but I can't tell you," the lieutenant replied. "'Need to know,' and all that."

"Roger that," said the pilot. There was no safety briefing. Jack had already been checked out in the required aircraft's emergency procedures as part of the job, including bail-out procedures and the high altitude chamber training. About an hour after takeoff he had *boots on the ground* at Seymour Johnson Air Force Base North Carolina at 8:30 a.m. Quite a morning's commute of four hundred and fifty miles.

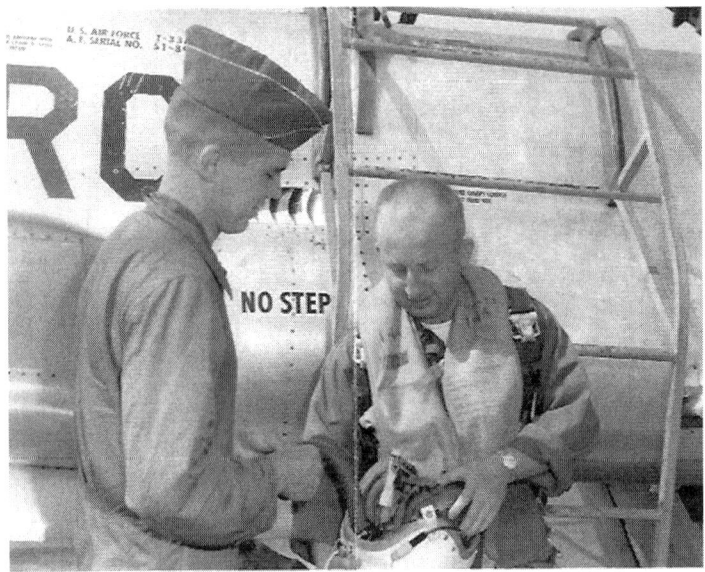

Lt. Jack ReVelle, at a familiarization flight in a jet trainer, similar to the one that delivered him to Seymour Johnson Air Force Base, Goldsboro, in 1961.

Photo courtesy USAF.

Within three hours of notification, and about ten hours after the crash, the rest of his team of fourteen EOD technical specialists arrived on a C-54, a four-engine cargo plane. They would be working very long hours in the cold and wet snow. The first task was to safely disarm Bomb Number One, the bomb that came to rest in the center of a clump of three gum trees that grew wild in the ditch between two cultivated fields on Shackelford Road. The bomb clearly had spiraling marks and scars where it rotated out of the aircraft holding chain when the fuselage broke apart. The chain resembled a very large bicycle chain that permitted movement only in a one directional plane: down—and it held the bomb tightly up against the bomb rack.

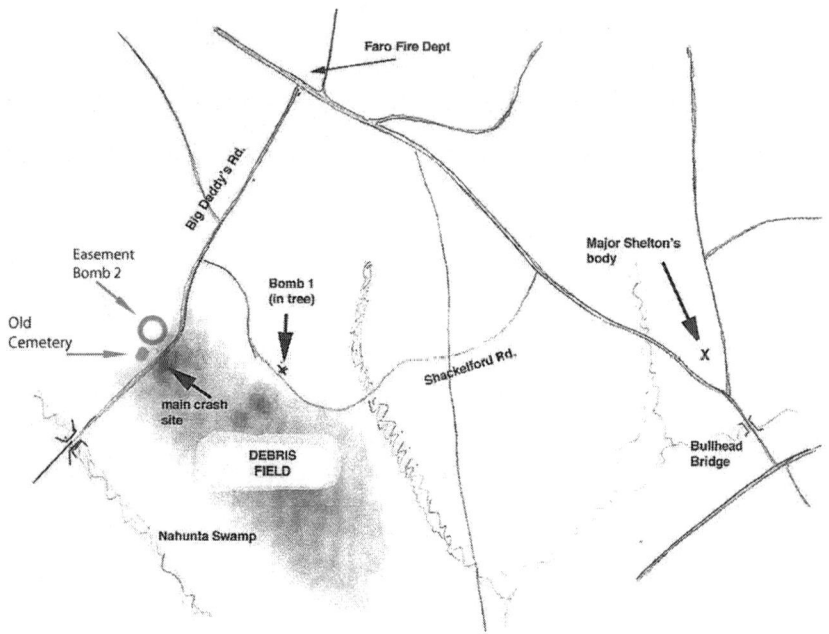

Debris Field at Faro

When the *render safe* task had been completed, ReVelle and his team focused their attention on Bomb Number Two, the bomb buried in the plowed field. They began by locating the hole of entry where the bomb had penetrated the ground's surface. The crater was fifteen feet wide and had a center six feet deep. It was 420 feet northwest of Big Daddy's Road, and about 600 feet north of the fuselage wreckage. The team started this initial recovery effort with hand shovels, gingerly removing and analyzing each clump of muddy earth. It wasn't long before they would ask for large equipment to be brought in. Eventually very large equipment, such as bulldozers and huge mining draglines, whatever could be rounded up, was used. They did a lot of digging and would spend a lot of time down in the dirt over the next eight days.

A local ham radio operator, who was also the engineer for a local radio station near Goldsboro, heard and recorded a Radio Moscow news report that claimed there had been a detonation at Goldsboro, North Carolina, and that "the whole area was incensed with radiation." The recorded Moscow report was replayed on local radio. Once.

After three days Billy Reeves decided that it was time to get the family back home. They had not heard anything from his daddy or uncles. They knew the men had plenty of experience fighting fires; they had to have that skill to protect their homes this far out in the country. Volunteer fire fighting was just something that neighbors did. There were several families around Faro with three generations of firefighters, as there still are today. But this was something entirely different, a fire like none had ever seen before. This one was really bad.

Billy loaded up everybody into the truck again; they began to work their way through the woods and swamp, successfully evading the roadblocks, for the Air Force didn't exactly approve of what they were doing. In some places the path through the woods seemed barely wide enough for a person, let alone a flatbed truck, but Billy was in his element, he knew the trails. The family was very thankful to make it back safely to their own warm homes and to just be together again. The thanks they said at mealtime took on a new meaning. This had been the most frightening thing ever to happen to them. The night it happened, they had been told by the Air Force, "Leave. Leave. Leave. You don't know how dangerous it is." They left.

For the people around Faro, things now began to fall into a routine. They could still smell the strong kerosene fuel, and the aluminum foil counter-measure strips called chaff were still hanging from trees like tinsel. On cold nights with sleet and snow falling, Mary Lancaster would prepare hot coffee for the troops manning the checkpoint in front of their house at the intersection of Big Daddy's and Shackelford Roads. The troops left the empty coffee cups in her mailbox. On several occasions, she saw the change-of-shift fellows checking the cups in the mailbox for any residue. She quickly offered refills to the new fellows.

At the Buck Tyndall home, a knock at the door came that cold night when it was sleeting. It was one of the Air Force policeman assigned to the road in front of his house. He said, "Mr. Tyndall, we will be spending the night on your front porch out of the sleet, so don't be alarmed if you hear us moving around."

"Son, would you like to stay inside the house?" asked Mr. Tyndall.

"Thank you sir, but we can't do that."

Rudolph Tyndall visited his parents every day to see how they were doing and to help feed the farm animals. He also wanted to check out what was going on in the big field, all lit up by portable lights from Carolina Power and Light. It was amazing. Their house was right besides a crashed B-52 jet bomber and yet the only damage was one cracked windowpane. The digging in the field continued twenty-four-hours a day, seven days a week on the far side of the old cemetery.

Morris Cruise was nine-years-old, one of nine kids, and they lived close to the middle of what was called the debris field, just to the west of Short Road and south of Shackelford Road. When the plane fell, they ran to a tobacco pack house thinking its tin roof would offer more protection from the falling pieces. The rain of metal on the roof was deafening. Amazingly, the debris from the sky hit no one. He saw a wing hit the ground and roll over and over several times. In the morning, they saw an ejection seat in the yard, and it remained there for two days. They were afraid to go near it. They remember finding containers of orange juice and cereal scattered around in the woods, and tasted it. They found big belts of ammunition and ran around with the ammo around their necks playing soldiers. They had to spend the first night with relatives but were back in their house after that. A big brown tent was put up just to the north of their house, probably the temporary command post. They could see the aircraft's big vertical fin, still attached to the horizontal stabilizer, just sitting out in there in the middle of the plowed field. It looked so strange, this piece of a great big airplane, something so foreign, that had somehow entered their world.

The military asked Billy Reeves to help identify neighbors who wanted to come through the intersection checkpoint near his house. The neighbors all wanted to get back to their homes. His mom's specialty for the troops was mugs of homemade hot cocoa: fresh milk, chocolate, and plenty hot. Schools started back up, and Billy prowled around the area in the afternoons getting to know several of the military people who were guarding the area and searching for wreckage. He and some pals found a metal box of "really big bullets"... .50 caliber from the four tail guns. He and the others took one bullet each, but the military confiscated them.

A Goldsboro civilian excavating company, T. A. Loving, was quickly contracted to bring in heavy digging equipment, and security clearances were required and passes were written. They ended up using two dragline cranes, one cable rig backhoe, sixteen wellpoint pumps, bulldozers, and a lot of trucks. Due to the mud, the EOD team needed a wide hole around them and room to work as they went deeper. At 3:45 p.m. on Day Two, January 25, at twelve feet down in the boggy, sandy soil, they found the remnants of the unopened parachute pack, parts of the nose, and pieces of the conventional explosive which originally surrounded the nuclear core. The HE, or high explosive, was collected in oil-soaked burlap bags and stacked about two hundred yards away.

Retrieval of Bomb Number. Two. The Arm/Safe switch was found between the two sections of this bomb.

Photo courtesy USAF.

One of the people assigned from Seymour Johnson digging through the dirt was Airman Second Class Guy Altizer, an Air Force nuclear weapons technician assigned to the 53rd MMS. He had recently finished specialized training at Lowry Air Force Base in Denver. He cared for and loaded bombs on B-52s at the base, he now was out at the crash site searching for one of them: Bomb Number Two. When he was worked on his "toys" back at the base, he was not beyond leaving a handwritten message, a little personal note inside a bomb.

Thermonuclear bombs at that time had a choice of three types of detonation: air, ground contact, or laydown, which has a delay of up to three minutes. One story told of a message stenciled on the outside of a laydown bomb in Cyrillic: "Hey, Dmitry, how far can you run in three minutes?"

If there was a message left, there had to be at least one other person who knew about it. The two-man program applied to the work area; it was a *no-lone* area. No one got near a weapon all alone. And no one did anything to a weapon without at least one other person there who knew exactly what the first person was doing. While Guy was taking care of the weapons, he also sanded and painted the bomb casings to keep them looking professional. Now he was out at Faro at the edge of the muddy crater with classified documents and the Top Secret bomb manual. Someone in the hole would wipe the mud off a part and Guy would check off the bomb component by part number and serial number as they were brought up the ladder and identified. That way, they knew which parts they had and which were missing.

Jack ReVelle remembers that the Air Force did not have any food service at the site for the first few days. But the Salvation Army was there. From the very start they had hot black coffee and donuts. He still appreciates their service, and makes a contribution every year because of what they did fifty years ago at Faro. He said he first learned to drink black coffee from Salvation Army mugs. Guy Altizer said the highlight of his night shift was the hot food served up at the Air Force field mess tent at midnight, available for everyone at the site including the civilian workers. The truck drivers and equipment operators really liked that. Somehow the cold, muddy environment made the hot food taste pretty good and there were no complaints. There was also a large heated tent with bunks for sleep between the work shifts and for breaks from the extremely cold winter weather.

Over the next several days the EOD team found more pieces of the MK-39 weapon as it peeled apart on the way down through the soil. On Day Three, they discovered dark water in the hole, not just run-off. Lieutenant ReVelle performed a critical but disgusting test. He tasted the nasty water and found it salty. ("Needs a lot of lemon…." he thought.) The salt meant they had hit the water table of the nearby Nahunta Swamp. They had penetrated a peculiar seam of clay that lay over the water level. He said, "We were pumping water out and digging the hole deeper. If we were not able to pump, we never would have found what we did."

The key *tritium bottle* was found intact on Day Four at a depth of seventeen feet. This contained a very toxic compressed gas that provides boost to the *primary*, the atomic bomb part of the weapon. More essential components were found the following day. When the primary, the volleyball-size pit of plutonium and uranium, was found, Jack brought it out of the hole in his gloved hands. His gloves were taped at the wrists. An Air Force photographer snapped a picture and Jack would later see that picture at the National Museum of Nuclear Science and History in Albuquerque, New Mexico. He was holding an atomic bomb in his hands.

On Day Five, Saturday, January 28, Lieutenant ReVelle heard a nervous voice from the hole, "Lieutenant!" ReVelle went down the ladder to Sergeant Lack, who was ashen-faced. "Lieutenant, we've found the ARM/SAFE switch. And it's on ARM!" They were finally able to carefully remove the parachute pack and there it was, right in the center of the firewall. The red triangle with the letter A was very visible.

The attitude of those down in the hole changed some that day. It got a lot quieter. People took time to come up the ladder and stare at the horizon for a while.

EOD Team from Wright-Patterson Air Force Base, at site of Bomb Number Two, on Big Daddy's Road. Photo courtesy USAF.

By Day Seven, January 30, the man-made crater was twenty-two feet deep, fifty feet wide, and seventy feet long. An attempt to wall up the hole failed. The wooden forms could not hold against the shifting of the heavy, wet mud. The only way to dig down more was to dig out more. The hole got a lot bigger.

Security and quarantine became a problem, but not from the local civilians. On one occasion Lieutenant ReVelle looked up out of the hole and saw an Air Force general poking about at the top of the ladder. It was obvious he did not belong there since he was in his blue uniform, not muddy fatigues like everyone else. The lieutenant came up the ladder, introduced himself, and said, "General, I will be glad to brief you away from the site, but I think you are putting yourself in harm's way. I strongly urge you to get the hell out of here. You are in imminent danger." He braced for the impact, which did not occur. The general thanked him, told the lieutenant he was doing a fine job, and left.

On the day of the crash, Brigadier General Herbert Loper from the Military Liaison Committee of the Atomic Energy Commission sent a letter to the Joint Chiefs of Staff in Washington, D.C. He said that one of the Goldsboro bombs was caught by its retardation parachute in a tree and was recovered, and the other bomb was destroyed by a one-point detonation. The sealed pit MK-39 bomb had ninety-two detonators carefully spaced around the high explosive lenses of its spherical surface. If any one of them detonated prematurely it would only set off a lopsided conventional explosion, enough to destroy the bomb and scatter its radioactive contents but would not cause a nuclear detonation. This was referred to as being *one-point safe.*

General Loper's letter on the day of the accident was incorrect, possibly in the haste to get notification to Washington. There was never a one-point detonation at the Goldsboro site. If there had been, it would indicate that a firing signal had reached a detonator and that in itself would be a sign that the safety interlock system had failed in some way. It would also indicate that radioactive material would probably be spread around the area. General Loper wrote the committee a second letter changing his comments from the first.

"There is no positive evidence to support the earlier allegation of a one-point detonation."

But then he added, "No high explosives have been found in the crater." Well, maybe at that time there had not been. But Jack ReVelle's EOD crew would remove numerous pieces of high explosives, and put it all in "oil-soaked burlap bags" and stack them two hundred yards away from the hole.

Two groups of people from Los Alamos left New Mexico on special C-47 flights and arrived at Goldsboro on Tuesday night after an exhausting eleven hours of flying. They did not wear name tags and were not introduced. One group, called W-7, carried special equipment to test the gas boosting system. The other group, called X Personnel, were made up of men from the Air Force, the Sandia Corporation, and the Atomic Energy Commission. Their report, "W-7-2717" dated February 20, 1961 which is now declassified, identified the two bombs by serial number. This is the first known declassified record of nuclear weapon serial numbers. Bomb Number One, the parachuted bomb was S/N 434909. Bomb Number Two, the buried bomb, was S/N 359943. The Los Alamos people finished their part of the investigation and departed Faro on Sunday, January 29, five days after their arrival.

The Air Force had announced they were digging for an ejection seat and asked for the public's cooperation if found. "It is black with yellow arms and has the word 'Co-pilot' printed on the back." It was not long before local people began to doubt the story about the missing ejection seat. That was a real big hole just to look for an ejection seat. People started to collect and hoard souvenirs so the

Air Force made an announcement that they could be prosecuted if wreckage material was not turned in. A great amount of wreckage materials was soon turned in. But not all of it.

Someone said a crane had the bomb in its jaws at one time but dropped it back into the hole. If this happened it was probably the parachute pack or another large component. The complete bomb was huge: 6,750 pounds and eleven feet long. When this one hit the ground without the parachute open it was traveling about 700 miles per hour, and components were peeled away as it traveled downward through the soft dirt. It was determined that the weapon fishtailed in the earth. The path was not straight down, but J-curved, and ended with the nose of the weapon pointing slightly upward.

It would be determined that when the aircraft fuselage broke apart between the two bomb racks, the bomb in the aft rack, Bomb Number One (so-called because it was first to leave the airplane), spiraled forward, out of the big bicycle chain that was holding it and out of the broken airplane. That's the bomb that was caught up in the trees by its parachute. It fell the furthest vertical distance, almost two miles. The second bomb that fell, Bomb Number Two, came from the front bomb rack and fell about a mile in free fall. Since its parachute lanyard was severed, the big chute never opened, and the bomb's 3.5-ton weight quickly brought it up to a speed approaching that of the speed of sound, according to a study group at the University of North Carolina at Chapel Hill.

At Day 8, January 31, at a depth of twenty-two feet, the hole of travel of the heavy Secondary was determined by probe at 1:30 p.m. Two hours later, in a conference, it was determined that "based on an estimate of the current situation, the principal hazards were under control and the AMC [Air Material Command] explosive ordnance dispersal support was no longer requested. Remaining operations concerned only the location and recovery of the secondary." The Secondary, described by those who know as about fourteen inches in diameter, about thirty-four inches long, and weighing between two hundred and three hundred pounds, had burst through the frangible nose of the weapon and the inertia of its mass carried it further downward into the water-soaked soil. It was not detected by probe down to a depth of fifty feet through the hole of travel. The EOD team from Wright-Patterson packed up their equipment and went back home, and the recovery was taken over by Seymour Johnson Air Force Base EOD.

Nine days after his arrival at Seymour Johnson, Jack ReVelle was back in his Dayton, Ohio, apartment, sitting at his kitchen table writing a letter to his parents. Then it hit him that he had just deactivated two thermonuclear bombs, each capable of leaving a 100 percent kill zone diameter of seventeen miles. At that point his hand started to shake.

Digging and pumping would continue for months, but the Nahunta Swamp water just kept coming in through the sandy soil. The sixteen pumps removing seven thousand gallons per hour could not keep up.

The issue of *need to know* had always been a point of contention between the military and the public, particularly the press. At the time of the Goldsboro Broken Arrow, the Air Force first admitted there were nuclear weapons, but there was no danger. Later, it would follow Department of Defense policy that neither confirmed or denied the presence of nuclear weapons in any accident. This was spelled out and later revised, in DOD Directive 5230.16, which basically gave local commanders the right to tell the public anything they felt necessary. President Kennedy addressed this at his first presidential news conference on January 25, the day after the Goldsboro accident, and five days after taking office:

> "I am anxious that we have a maximum flow of information but there quite obviously are some matters that involve the security of the United States, and it's a matter on which the press and the Executive should attempt to reach a responsible decision.
>
> "I could not make a prediction about what those matters will be, but I think that all of us here are aware that there are some matters which it would not be well to discuss at particular times so that we just have to wait and try to work together and see if we can provide as much information as we can within the limits of national security. I do not believe that the stamp 'National Security' should be put on mistakes of the administration which do not involve the national security, and this administration would welcome any time that any member of the press feels that we are artificially invoking that cover."
>
> President John F. Kennedy
>
> First Presidential News Conference
>
> *The Goldsboro News-Argus*
>
> January 25, 1961

"Both nuclear devices have been recovered."

>Captain Jerry Holland
>
>Information Officer
>
>Seymour Johnson Air Force Base
>
>*The Goldsboro News-Argus*
>
>January 24, 1961

"We are looking for an ejection seat."

>Captain Jerry Holland
>
>Information Officer
>
>Seymour Johnson Air Force Base
>
>*The Goldsboro News-Argus*
>
>January 28, 1961

Major Dick Manley, weapons squadron commander at Seymour Johnson, said that the Goldsboro civilian contractor T. A. Loving, provided the dewatering and excavation. That was confirmed by Jerry Smith of the company and also by former equipment operator at the site, Donald Robinson. Martin Richer was superintendent for the job. They had sunk fourteen wells about 50 feet apart along the edge of the excavation and were pumping 7,000 gallons per hour out of the underground seams located at 12 feet, 24 feet and 43 feet depths. The first contract was for a hole 100' x 100' x 20.' When that did not uncover all the bomb components a second contract was made for 250' x 250' x 40.' Soil had to be removed in two steps. A lower 'bench' level was dug out down in the hole twenty feet below surface level to support the primary dragline. A second dragline at ground level brought up the soil from the bench, to be spread by bulldozers. For every foot dug straight down about four feet of mud had to be removed at the sides of the hole.

By February 7 the crater was enormous: over two hundred feet in diameter and forty-two feet deep. It was at the northeast of the old cemetery, which was left untouched. The cemetery was so old no one knew who was buried there, it didn't have a name and there were no gravestones or markings of any kind. Rudolph Tyndall said he hunted rabbits there when he was a boy and at that time it had old wooden grave markers, but names and dates were not readable. By 1961 there was no indication of a cemetery, nothing there but briars and brush. It is not cultivated for farming simply because it is known by Rudolph Tyndall, and now his son, Brent, to be a cemetery, and it is respected as such.

The man-made crater had a circular road descending around the edge for vehicles and people. One person said, "The Caterpillars down in the hole looked like toys." Another said, "It looked like they were digging a lake. I have always heard they lost a bulldozer and it's still buried there." At one point there were six bulldozers working the site. Al Yelverton stated, "It was all anyone talked about. The hole was huge, taking up most of the field." Billy Reeves thought the whole area looked like a small city. A total of 93,000 cubic yards of dirt was removed, according to the Loving company records.

Major Manley remembers that the water in the hole was colored an unusual aqua blue, and a seam of clay around the hole was a smoky blue. He took samples of the clay to North Carolina State University in Raleigh for chemical analysis. He said he could not tell them what to look for; they just had to report on what they found. He wanted to avoid any mention of the words uranium, plutonium, or radioactive. The written report from the University said only that the sample contained bauxite, and was high in aluminum with traces of iron. The men operating the digging equipment knew what it was all along. They said this layer was common for the area and was called gumbo. It is the consistency of modeling clay and forms an impervious barrier to the water below. When it is penetrated the water level would tend to rise. The author found some handwritten notes attached to a declassified report that said, "The upward pressure from the Artesian well (REDACTED) at the 72' level is about 6 psi."

The day of the crash Major Manley and another officer were inspecting the wreckage of the fuselage that lay upside down across Big Daddy's Road. In the area where the cockpit would have been they found the melted remains of the pilot's readiness switch, set to SAFE. Major Manley took it along with a new spare to use for comparison to the wing commander, Colonel Osce Jones. Colonel Jones asked him if he had a safe in his office. "Yes, Sir," he answered.

"Then put this in it, and don't give it to anyone until I say so." The melted pilot's readiness switch stayed there until Colonel Jones said to turn it over to the Sandia Corporation in New Mexico.

By March 27, two months after the crash, the news had leaked out that the Air Force was digging for a missing nuclear device. At this point the Air Force revised their position and announced formally that they were looking for a harmless part. "All but one inert portion of the weapon has been recovered. The remaining portion is not explosive and there is absolutely no danger from it," stated Colonel Jones, commander of the 4241st Strategic Wing stationed at Seymour Johnson. The news was accepted at the time, but in later years the wording was reexamined. The three pages of handwritten notes referring to the artesian well is attached as Appendix H in a typed version. The last six items of "Random Notes at Goldsboro" are interesting:

"Item 16. Unit has been identified to the public as "a small portion of a weapon."

"Item 17. Little or no public interest now."

"Item 18. NC Public Health authorities consider it no problem."

"Item 19. Breaking through of the clay layer might disrupt the local water supply."

"Item 20. If we restrict well drilling we would by inference admit that there was a hazard."

"Item 21. DELETED"

It would be very interesting to know what Item 21 was.

The flooding at the crater was now uncontrollable and the high water table made further digging impractical and unsafe. The Raleigh Airport reported that an unusual amount of eighteen inches of rain fell in the area between January and May of 1961. The USDA Soil and Water Conservation Service say that the water table in the Faro area typically averages only one and a half feet below ground surface at that time of year.

Digging was halted on May 25, four months after the crash. The hole was filled in, finishing up in July. Heavily loaded flatbed trucks traveled the road from Faro heading back to Goldsboro. A study group at the University of North Carolina at Chapel Hill calculated that based on the weight and shape of the bomb, with the impact angle, velocity, and soil composition, the missing component was lodged at a depth of 180 feet plus or minus 10 feet. The minimum estimated cost of recovery was in the neighborhood of five hundred thousand in 1961 dollars. Dr. ReVelle says that frequent testing for radiation was done at both bomb locations and no radiation was ever detected.

Much later, when the farmers were allowed to start plowing again, they continued to turn up wreckage of metal and tubing buried in the ground. Years after the crash, people continued to find aluminum foil strips of chaff. Mary Lancaster found a pair of eyeglasses buried in her garden. The plastic earpiece was broken, and they were definitely military issue. They are believed to belong to Frank Barnish, since the size was for a small man, and most Barnish men also had poor eyesight, according to Jerry Barnish, of New Jersey.

The tip of the right wing being removed from crash site. This photo was taken by Mary Lancaster, who saw the plane crash from her window. Photo courtesy Mary Lancaster

When the excavation was filled in, the layer of rich topsoil was put in first instead of last, according to the farmers. The red clay on top made for poor crops for years. The summer after the accident, Charles Davis answered a knock on his door. An Air Force general had been flying over when he noticed thousands of sparkles on the ground, and became worried about what might be rising to the surface. He sent out a team to take soil samples. They found recently applied fertilizer pellets, shining in the sun.

The Army Corps of Engineers dug another hole north of the old cemetery and many fifty-five-gallon metal drums were buried there, probably containing tons of contaminated fuel-soaked mud and dirt. Compared to other aircraft accident sites where small pieces of wreckage have been found years after the crashes, this site of the Goldsboro Broken Arrow was picked clean. It took hundreds of military personnel, Air Force and Army, walking shoulder to shoulder and putting down little flags where anything was found. Specialists would go to each flag, decide if the piece of debris needed further study, and determine which category of wreckage it was. Most of the small stuff went into fifty-five gallon drums. The large pieces were marked with the location. It took several weeks, but they covered the entire area of several square miles. The bits and pieces of the aircraft were transported to Medina Air Force Base, Texas for accident analysis.

There has never been any sign of radioactive contamination at Faro.

The government, through the Corps of Engineers, bought an easement of the area for one thousand dollars to prevent digging more than five feet down. Crops could be planted but no digging or drilling was allowed beyond five feet, and "no structures of any kind whatsoever." There is nothing to mark the easement site. Based on the legal description of property records at the Wayne County Courthouse, the center of the 400-foot circle easement would be about 380 feet northeast of the center of the old cemetery on Big Daddy's Road.

The missing component, known as the *secondary* has never been found.

Crash Site, Then and Now.

By using the location of the Tyndall house and barn in the top photo (made at the time of the crash by the Raleigh Observer), the location of the photo on bottom (made in 2010 by the author), shows the site of the main wreckage. Both photos are looking south.

Top photo courtesy Raleigh News and Observer.
Bottom photo by author.

Chapter 5. The Chance of Nuclear Detonation

As human beings it is both our right and our responsibility to insist that the degree of safety in any weapon system be in direct proportion to the danger: the bigger the bomb yield the more safety we want built in. On the theory of probability of an accidental nuclear detonation, the Princeton nuclear physicist Frank Von Hipple said, "What isn't forbidden by physics is compulsory. It will eventually happen. If the probability is not zero, it WILL happen."

Since the inception of nuclear weapons there have been redundant and elaborate safety systems to try to prevent accidental detonation. One such system in place on *Keep 19* was as simple as pulling on a rope: a cable ran from the crew compartment to bomb bay to allow extraction of safing pins during flight and before the bomb release. Another system involved rigid arming rods that were extracted by the falling bomb when it dropped from the airplane. These rods acted like Wile E. Coyote's TNT plunger. When the bomb dropped off the rods, the rods generated an electrical pulse that started the fuzing and firing sequence. If the rods were not removed cleanly at bomb drop, the arming process never started. If the plane crashed with the rods in place then they would bend and the arming process would never start. But it is believed this Broken Arrow accident was unusual in a way never before experienced: the B-52 was vertical and breaking apart in midair. This bizarre position and the centrifugal forces from a spinning airplane allowed the departure of Bomb Number One to actually simulate in some ways a true weapons release. The Sandia report stated in their after-crash investigation of Bomb One: "There was no scoring or other physical damage to the assembly which would indicate that any unusual forces had been applied. Also, since the holes for the safing pins were not in any way damaged, it must be assumed that the safing pins were extracted prior to separation of the weapon from the rack."

Bomb Number Two, from the forward bomb rack, also had clean rod removal. But the parachute static line, which was attached to the aircraft, was torn and did not release the parachute, which in itself stopped the arming process of that bomb. But what was found later in the hole in the ground at Faro in the wreckage of Bomb Two, caused serious questions to be raised about the reliability of safety devices on all nuclear weapons.

According to the Sandia report of component behavior (Appendix D) in both bombs, the arming wires were pulled, which activated the pulse generators; the explosive actuators fired, and inside the falling bombs, timers started and ran, the barometric switches engaged, the low voltage batteries were actuated, and contacts closed. But one very important device, the ARM/SAFE switch at least on Bomb One, was still in the 'Safe' position. That one device was considered the gold standard of safety; there was no way the MK-39 bomb could detonate with that switch on Safe.

The very industry that created the switch would later examine that view more closely.

The government classified both of the 1961 Goldsboro bombs as *unarmed*. This should not be confused with the bombs being incapable of nuclear detonation. The arming of the bomb is a series of several steps. Chuck Hansen, who was a highly respected civilian nuclear historian said, "It was like a fully loaded pistol with the safety off, and the hammer cocked—it is not armed until the final safety mechanism, the trigger, is pulled."

Hansen considered both bombs to be unarmed but nuclear capable.

In a 1963 meeting with President Kennedy, McGeorge Bundy, and other senior officials of the Departments of State and Defense, Secretary of Defense Robert McNamara described a crash of a US aircraft in North Carolina where, "by the slightest margin of chance, literally the failure of two wires to cross, a nuclear explosion was averted."

Later, according to McNamara, the first bomb to leave the aircraft, the bomb caught in the trees on Shackelford Road, had "all but one of the arming devices engaged" and in his opinion was apparently extremely dangerous. In a 1983 press conference he said: "It ran through six or seven steps in order to detonate and it went through all but one, we discovered later."

Were these statements by Hansen and McNamara alarmist? At least now we have the luxury of viewing events from a historical standpoint. It has been better said of the fully loaded pistol statement that the ARM/SAFE switch was in fact, the pistol's safety, and it was

ON, and that any attempt to fire the pistol never got beyond that point. If the trigger was pulled it was to no avail.

However, as gun owners know, even a loaded pistol with the safety on can sometimes fire if dropped.

It is bizarre to visualize Bomb One, this huge 6,750 pound bomb, suspended by a parachute caught up in a group of trees with its nose stuck two feet in the ground. We now know that the trigger of this bomb is ground contact, provided that all safeties were satisfied. The Mark 39 Mod 2 had a specially designed *crush nose* switch, two metal plates separated by an air space, and with barium titanate crystals which, under pressure, produce a pulse of energy. Other types of nuclear bombs could be set to detonate at a certain altitude after the drop. This one would only detonate when it made contact with the ground and one metal plate touched the other, or the crushed crystals generated a pulse of energy. There was the option of timers, which would allow the *laydown* configuration, but it was the nose contact switch that initiated detonation. That's one of the reasons why it had such a big retardation parachute, to insure a controlled speed and to aid the fins in proper orientation for ground contact.

The other reason is to allow time for the bomber crew to escape the zone of destruction.

If the ARM/SAFE switch prevented detonation of the first bomb, detonation of the second bomb "may have failed because it apparently was a dud," at least those are the words that were used by Ross Speer of the Atomic Energy Commission. The second bomb to fall from the aircraft, the one buried in the field, essentially destroyed itself as it traveled down through the wet soil at high speed. At first they thought that process stopped all chances of nuclear detonation. But Mr. Speer, the official accident observer, gave conflicting information in his report. At one point he said, "We wondered why bomb No. 2 had been a dud.... Electrically, the MC-772 (ARM/SAFE) switch proved to be neither in the armed or safe position." Some people have interpreted this somewhat ambiguous report as Mr. Speer being shocked that there had <u>not</u> been a nuclear detonation upon ground contact.

A letter from Airmunitions, Ogden Air Material Area, Hill AFB Utah, said, "On the 28th of January, the Arm/Safe Switch of Bomb 2 was revealed and found that it was in the 'Armed' position, and the Low Pack had been energized." Other reports referred to it as "armed but damaged."

Chuck Hansen said that the first bomb, the bomb in the tree, was the closest to firing, because "The official reports claims that three of four arming steps were completed. Since the aircraft commander had not thrown the arming switch in the B-52 cockpit, and since that switch was not activated accidentally when the aircraft broke up, it was impossible for the weapon to fire, regardless of how uncomfortably close they came to doing so. This was a very dangerous incident and I suspect that steps were taken afterwards to prevent any repetition of it. I do not now know of any other weapon accident that came this close to a full-scale nuclear detonation (which is not to say that any such incident did not occur later)."

What we need is a definitive summary about the possibility of detonation of the bombs at Faro. Lieutenant Colonel Wilton Strickland, USAF (Retired), a former radar navigator on B-52s, wrote this one:

The internal fuses, switches, and timers in the arming systems for both bombs did not fail mechanically or electrically. They worked exactly as designed. Pullout switches and rods for both bombs were extracted during departure from the aircraft, initiating the fusing and firing sequence. The parachute static lanyard for Bomb One was still connected to the aircraft, causing the parachute to deploy automatically and allowing the fusing and firing sequence to proceed in the normal, planned manner, including production of a firing signal when the nose was crushed upon impact with the ground. Action of all of these switches was irrelevant, though, and there was no nuclear detonation, because the bomb's internal ARM/SAFE switch was in the SAFE position in accordance with Air Force policy.

The parachute lanyard for Bomb Two had been torn from the aircraft prior to the bomb departing the aircraft, therefore, the parachute did not deploy. Without the retardation chute, the bomb fell very fast, struck the ground 2.5 seconds before the fusing/firing sequence could complete, and destroyed itself and the fusing/firing system upon impact. Though the internal ARM/SAFE switch appeared at the crash site to be in the ARMED position, later analysis proved that the indicator had been rotated by impact damage, and the internal contacts were, in fact, still in SAFE position. Bomb Two failed to yield a nuclear detonation, then, for two reasons: the parachute failed to deploy causing fusing/firing sequence to be halted by impact damage and the <u>internal</u> component of the ARM/SAFE switch actually stayed in SAFE position.

The Investigation

This was really a whole new Broken Arrow scenario because of the way the airplane came apart in midair: spinning vertically as opposed to a nose-first crash. There were enough troubling elements in the weapons behavior that Sandia Corporation and the entire weapons industry would began an intense decades-long analysis. Sandia is still the Queen Mother of nuclear weaponry and this incident was at the rise of their reign. They were the premier US nuclear facility for twenty-five years, and 1961 was right in the middle of those years. Their analysis Number NND 922015-99 declassified June 18, 2004, showed that, indeed, the "safing pins were extracted from the Bisch generating action rods, and the rods themselves were extracted from the pullout assembly. On both weapons the fuzing sequence was initiated." The key that prevented detonation of Bomb One, the report maintained, was the internal component of the ARM/SAFE switch remaining in the safe condition.

Such troubling elements created another gnawing worry about one more critical aspect of the switch: the fact that electrical solder melts. A 1998 study by Sandia Labs (Plummer and Greenwood, "SAND-98-1184C" .2) said that:

> Elaborate computer models and fault trees were generated to calculate the probability of an inadvertent detonation [at Goldsboro]. Although the analyses became increasingly sophisticated, did they assure safety? The models focused

on the weapon response to a single environment. How could the effects of credible combinations of abnormal environments be addressed?

The methodology above suffered from a fatal flaw. There was no technical basis for some of the underlying assumptions. In fact, some were grossly misleading. For example, a fault to ground may not dud the system at all. It may simply create additional propagating damage leading to further unpredictability. The fundamental problem was expecting the accident to manufacture a 'safety device or feature' from charred insulation or melted solder instead of deliberately engineering these responses.

The experiences of the 1950s and the 1960s taught [weapons] designers some important lessons. First, accidents frequently mimic the delivery mode of the weapon. How is a bomb to know if it was deliberately or inadvertently released from an airplane? Second, wire insulation and printed circuit boards become unpredictable during a fire and it becomes relatively 'easy' to get a 28 VDC across the terminals of a safety device.

In trying to visualize how all this works, it helps to know about the first thermonuclear test, and how lightning was created in a bottle: an eighty-two ton, twenty-one foot tall bottle. As part of Operation Ivy, the MIKE test occurred on November 1, 1952 at Eniwetok Atoll in the South Pacific. This birth of thermonuclear detonation was analyzed by the use of five *hotspot light pipes*, tubes several miles long and absolutely level. These five pipelines carried neutrons and gamma rays from locations inside the device itself to measuring instruments in distant blockhouses as they were being vaporized. Cameras could actually see inside the bottle as it went thermonuclear. Also, a new phenomenon called *bomb light* was captured by a semicircle of seven mirrors sending images two miles to turbine-driven streak cameras. The cameras operated at the incredible speed of 3.5 million frames per second.

An observer described it this way, in the book, *Dark Sun: The Making Of The Hydrogen Bomb* by Richard Rhodes. The observer was George Cowan, a radiochemist from Los Alamos.

> "I was stunned. I mean, it was big. I had worked out a way to calibrate the shot. I would hold up a quarter to use as a measurement to cover the fireball. As soon as I could, I whipped off my glasses and the thing was enormous, bigger than anything I'd ever imagined it would be. It looked like it blocked out the whole horizon, and I was standing on the deck of the Estes, thirty miles away."

MIKE was 10.4 megatons.

Sandia came to the position that (a) some previous assumptions were grossly misleading, and (b) it was at least theoretically possible for electrical current to actually jump from one contact switch point to another in the molten solder of an aircraft flash fire or explosion, *even if the switch itself was on SAFE*. This may have been the perceived weakness of the ARM/SAFE switch that so concerned Secretary McNamara in his 1983 news conference. This possibility of safety device failure, although remote, was important enough that the weapons controls industry would study that possibility, and would make enormous capital investments in new and different *strong-link/weak-link* safety systems, systems which would further reduce the chance of accidental detonation while at the same time promoting reliability as a viable weapons system.

The physicists and engineers at two locations, Sandia and Los Alamos, were some of the brightest people in America. Los Alamos designed the warheads, Sandia engineered everything else: the firing and fusing sets, the arming devices, the safety devices, even the parachutes. The atmosphere at Sandia National Laboratories in Albuquerque, New Mexico, is best described in Barbara Moran's book, *The Day We Lost the H-Bomb*:

> Sandia in the 1960s was a secret paradise for the slide rule set. Every engineer who worked there had graduated in the top of his or her college class. They had cutting-edge equipment, seemingly endless funding, and a fairly loose rein. They also worked with a deep sense of mission. Nuclear weapons, most of them believed, kept their country safe from the Soviets. Sandia engineers considered themselves to be not only the elite of Albuquerque but indispensable to the defense of the United States.

There was an answer to the question, "Were we safe?" Yes, as long as the ARM/SAFE switch held, and a chance miniature lightning bolt didn't find its way through a splash of molten solder in a millionth of a second; or some other obscure thing happened that we had not even thought about. So the switch was the best thing we had at the time, and it did its job, it held. But scientists and engineers are well aware that any machine made by man is subject to failure, and they were working hard and fast to replace that switch with something better. The big question is, "What were the chances of nuclear explosion?" Some experts say we were very close to accidental detonation at Faro. Some say there was no way: we had the ARM/SAFE switch. We may never know the exact truth, it is somewhere in between, but it concerned Sandia enough to spend a lot of time and money making the bombs safer.

"How close was it to exploding? You're asking my opinion?" Dr. Jack ReVelle was responding to a reporter at a very unusual appreciation dinner hosted by Randy Gray, the Faro fire chief. It was on the anniversary of the Goldsboro Broken Arrow, held in the Faro Volunteer Fire Station, the very fire station that was first to respond fifty years and two weeks before, and one mile away. The fire station was having their monthly meeting, but this time, people from the neighborhood, firemen from nearby Eureka Volunteer Fire Department, people from Seymour Johnson, as well as a large number of other people were invited. We were having a nice dinner of barbecued pig, cooked up by the boys in the fire station. They had cooked it all night. Most of the visiting guests had never met before this dinner. There were so many people who wanted to attend that space became an issue, so a second presentation by the author was planned for a week later at a much larger Goldsboro church.

The guest of honor at the appreciation dinner, was Adam Mattocks, the last remaining survivor of *Keep 19*, who escaped from the exploding B-52 without an ejection seat. He was the third pilot, and he jumped through the open hatch where the pilot had just ejected. Also attending was Earl Lancaster, the assistant fire chief at the time of the crash, the first emergency official on the crash scene, about an hour before the Air Force fire equipment from Seymour Johnson arrived. Also Rudolph Tyndall, whose parents lived in the farmhouse right beside the crashed fuselage was there. Billy Reeves, Mary Lancaster, and Morris Cruise, were all eyewitnesses to the crash, which was close to all of their homes. C. T. Davis, who owns the land at the main crash site, and Brent Tyndall, who farms it, attended. Mike Rouse came, he was the first reporter on the scene. Many people attended who lived on farms in the area and saw the disaster as it unfolded; they wanted to know more about what really happened. Guy Altizer attended. He had loaded MK-39s onto BUFFs at Seymour Johnson—he didn't know if he loaded this particular mission, but he definitely helped dig the bomb parts up at Faro. Andy Tulloch from New York, son of Major Scott Tulloch the aircraft commander, came to the dinner. And Dr. Jack ReVelle—now a quality control author and aerospace statistical consultant in Orange, California—made the trip. He was the explosive ordnance disposal lieutenant that rendered safe two MK-39 thermonuclear weapons fifty years and one mile away from where he was now being interviewed by newspaper reporters, live TV, and Public Radio.

"How close was it to exploding? My opinion is damn close. You might now have a very large Bay of North Carolina if that thing had gone off," he said.

How Big Were The Goldsboro Bombs?

> *"The exploding weapon had created a crater abut 350 feet deep and some 3,700 feet in diameter. Beyond this enormous crater, a "lip" of radioactive debris extends*

outward for approximately 1,800 feet and to a height of 85 feet—enough to cover a six-story house.

"The resulting fireball would be about four miles in diameter, and the temperatures within that fireball would probably be around 8,000 degrees Fahrenheit. All matter within that area—animate and inanimate—has been pulverized. And lingering radioactivity would make it impossible to rebuild this area, at last within our lifetime.

"Large buildings as much as six miles from the impact point would now be nothing more than ripped-out shells of rubble and collapsing roofs and walls. In addition to the blast effects which have caused this damage, the intensive heat has sparked numerous big fires, and many more fires have resulted from broken gas lines, electrical short circuits and secondary explosions. Widespread devastation, raging fires, and casualties in the millions extend to about 18 miles from the impact point.

"Heavy radioactive fallout would start raining down on this area within twenty minutes after detonation and would last for approximately half an hour before subsiding. Radiation would prevent anyone from entering this area for the next 10 hours at least. And for 48 hours after time of burst, a lethal fallout pattern about 18 miles wide would extend downwind to a distance of some 130 miles, resulting in additional heavy casualties."

The above quote was written by an expert, someone certainly

experienced with nuclear weapons: General Thomas S. Power, who was the Commander In Chief of SAC at the time of the Goldsboro Broken Arrow. It is from his book, *Design for Survival.* He called the book the second edition—the first was never published—it was "banned by the Secretary of Defense, Neil H. McElroy." *Design for Survival* was written with Albert A. Arnhym, and was published soon after the General's retirement in 1964. In the above quote, he was describing the effects what he called a 'medium-sized hydrogen bomb' of around 3.3 megatons, if it impacted near the center of a metropolis.

Dr. ReVelle says that based on the information he was given at the crash site, the yield of each Goldsboro bomb was set at 3.8 megatons. In physical size, each Goldsboro bomb was eleven and a half feet long and weighed 6,750 pounds. But the basic measurement of thermonuclear weapons is the megaton, which is the equivalent destructive power of one million tons of TNT. Based on the published photos at the time, Chuck Hansen was first to identify the bomb in the trees as the MK-39. Seven hundred of these bombs were produced over a two-year period, from 1957 to 1959, and were retired from service in 1966.

Over the years, there has been reported a wild range as to the yield of the MK-39…from 2.4 to 24 megatons. The 24 MT number was picked up by Dr. Ralph Lapp, a well-known atomic scientist and the former executive director of the Department of Defense's Atomic Research and Development Board. He was the man who coined the phrase *The China Syndrome.* He published a book, *Kill and Overkill: The Strategy of Annihilation* the same year of the Goldsboro Broken Arrow—1961. In the book he states that each Goldsboro bomb was twenty-four megatons. Later, while at the University of North Carolina at Chapel Hill for a presentation about the Goldsboro incident, Mr. Hansen stated that he did not believe that Dr. Lapp was being disingenuous with his report of twenty-four megatons, rather it was a simple but very significant misplacement of a decimal point.

In any case, it is no less comforting to know that even a 2.4 megaton bomb would *exceed the yield of all munitions (outside of testing) ever detonated in the history of the world*—by TNT, gunpowder, conventional bombs, and the Hiroshima and Nagasaki blasts, combined.

To further complicate the question of yield of the Goldsboro bomb, others have called it a twenty-*five* megaton bomb. There was indeed a twenty-five megaton bomb in the US strategic inventory in 1961. It was the MK-41, and looked somewhat similar to the MK-39, except the MK-41 was a foot longer and almost twice as heavy (10,670 pounds). The biggest difference however, was internal. The MK-41 was a three stage weapon, in fact, the only three stage weapon fielded by the United States. The Goldsboro bombs were definitely two-stage, as described by Jack ReVelle. What's the difference between a two stage and a three stage? An extra Secondary. There was one three stage Russian weapon, called the *"Tzar Bomba,"* a one hundred megaton monster, that was 'dialed back' to half strength for testing by the Russians because they were afraid it would set fire to the entire atmosphere around the world.

If that is not scary and off-putting enough, the reader is encouraged to find and read the essay *"Late Night Thoughts on Listening to Mahler's Ninth Symphony,"* by Lewis Thomas.

Dr. ReVelle says the 100 percent kill zone would have a radius of 8.5 miles, or a diameter of 17 miles, meaning anyone caught in the open within the circle of 17 miles would die. That does not factor in the extreme damages done from the blast outward by base surge and overpressure. Dr. Dietrich Schroeer, nuclear physicist and professor of physics at the University of North Carolina at Chapel Hill, said that this blast from a ground-level detonation would have left a crater in the ground one-third of a mile wide at Faro.

Using these two data points (the one-third mile crater size from Dr. Schroeer and the kill zone diameter of 17 miles from Dr. ReVelle) along with the interactive simulator found at www.MeyerWeb.com/eric/tools/gmap/hydesim.html you can see the effects of a 3.8 megaton bomb if it exploded, say, at the Empire State Building in in New York, City. That location was picked simply because the actual Faro location is more difficult to get a sense of scale.

The simulator is based on information in The Effects of Nuclear Weapons, 3rd Edition, by Samuel Glasstone and Philip J. Dolan.

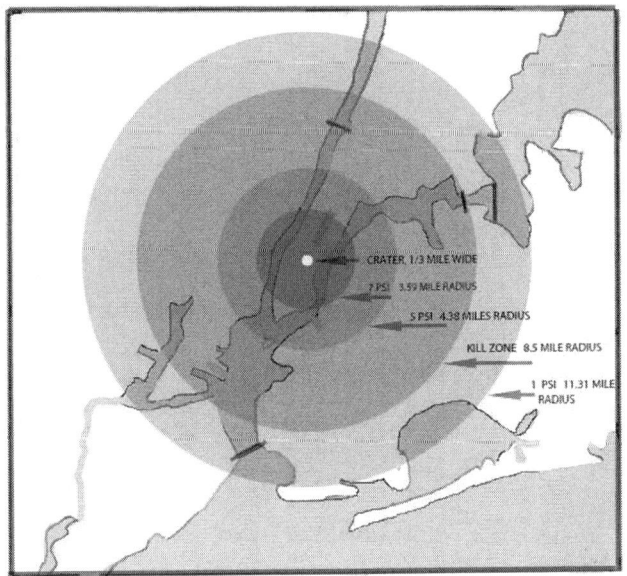

Illustration by author.

Theoretical impact of 3.8 MT weapon, detonated at Empire State Building.

Crater size: one-third mile diameter.

Overpressure Key:

7 psi, radius 3.59 miles. Severe damage to complete destruction of reinforced concrete structures, such as skyscrapers, will occur in this ring.

5 psi, radius 4.38 miles. Severe damage to reinforced concrete structures such as skyscrapers, and complete destruction of ordinary houses will occur in this ring.

8.5 mile radius kill zone per ReVelle. Kill zone of 100% of people in the open.

1 psi, radius 11.31 miles. Light to moderate damage to ordinary houses will occur in this ring.

If we use pure mathematics, one Goldsboro bomb of 3.8 megatons would be about 264 times the destructive power of the Hiroshima bomb.

A much different comparison was reported for a similar weapons test at the 1956 Bikini Atoll test. That was the first airdrop of a live hydrogen bomb and was part of a weapons-testing program named Operation Redwing. The device dropped on May 20 from a B-52 was not a MK-39, it was a TX-15-X1 test device. But it was 3.8-megatons, the same yield as each Goldsboro bomb. It is interesting to note that the experts at the time tended to over estimate when they called the test to be "roughly the equivalent of two thousand bombs the size of the Hiroshima bomb."

Niels Schonbeck has a vivid way of demonstrating the magnitude of nuclear weapons to his classes. Dr. Schonbeck is a college professor of chemistry in Denver, Colorado, and has an ordinary metal trashcan sitting on a table next to a plastic bucket of B Bs, the small copper air rifle pellets. "This is the magnitude of all explosives used in World War Two, including Hiroshima and Nagasaki," he will say, holding up then dropping one B B in the empty metal trashcan, making a tiny sound.

"And this is the magnitude of all nuclear weapons we had on hand in the 1980's." He would then pour in all the other B Bs at one time, making a long, impressive noise.

why whenever a bomber with live nuclear weapons crashed, it was on a 'training mission.'

The Thule Broken Arrow of January 21, 1968 was another apparent milestone: it may have been the last official Broken Arrow. At least the last one known involving an aircraft. There was one involving the US Navy submarine *Scorpion*, and one at a Titan II missile silo in Arkansas. There may have been others, but they have not been released as Broken Arrows by the Department of Defense. There have been suspected Broken Arrows, potential Broken Arrows, and "events" that involved nuclear weapons on test missiles that have gone astray, blown up, or destroyed. But the last, known, aircraft crash official Broken Arrow as of now was in Thule in 1968.

SAC's airborne alert program, which officially began the same week of the Kennedy Inauguration and the crash of *Keep 19*, ended with the last known aircraft Broken Arrow at Thule.

A Broken Arrow at Bunker Hill Air Force Base in Indiana on December 8, 1964, brought to light the susceptibility of the chemicals in secondaries to ignite. A B-58 Hustler, was responding to an ORI, an Operational Readiness Inspection exercise. The sleek four-engine bomber was taxiing behind another B-58 on an icy runway to take off. It turned too close and was blown sideways off the runway by the jet exhaust of the airplane in front. When the landing gear went off the runway in the snow, it collapsed, and the loaded bomber caught fire. Two of the three crewmen escaped, the third ejected but was not carried high enough for his parachute to open. The aircraft had four MK-43 and one BA-53 thermonuclear weapons.

The Goldsboro Broken Arrow – Second Edition

high explosives packed as detonators around the soccer-ball-sized Primary at Faro did not go off.

The *Thule Monitor* was a twenty-four-hour circling mission, primarily to guard the polar route against the Soviets and to alert SAC if a power outage occurred at the Ballistic Missile Early Warning radar station. SAC was concerned that one of the frequent ice storms could knock out communications along with the lights, which might be interpreted as the first strike by the Soviets and thus send us off to war. So a very expensive night watchman, the *Thule Monitor*, a fully armed B-52 walked the beat twenty-four/seven over Thule to let Headquarters SAC know if they had received the first Soviet strike or if the lights had just gone out in another ice storm. General Power put it another way,'' I like to tell the commander at Thule that he will probably be one of the first ones to go if we go to war, but there is one thing I would like to know from him, and that is when he went.''

The Thule crash proved to be the end of SAC's armed airborne alert program, it was the straw that broke the camel's back, so to speak. Apparently the combined risk of carrying functional thermonuclear weapons along with the number of Broken Arrows reached some sort of limit at the highest levels at Washington. Within twenty-four hours of the Thule Broken Arrow on January 21, 1968, the internal memo went out to: ''Terminate the carrying of nuclear weapons aboard airborne alert aircraft indoctrination level missions. No publicity is being given to this fact.'' The phrase ''alert aircraft indoctrination level missions'' was code for ''alert aircraft carrying live nukes.'' SAC was not authorized to carry live nuclear weapons, except for training. If it did, the mission was labeled a training mission. That's

205

which means that when exposed to air as a fine powder it is subject to spontaneous ignition. It should never be stored in water since it could explode, not as a nuclear explosion, but a chemical explosion.

URANIUM. Compared to plutonium, uranium's radioactive hazard is not as great, but the chemical toxicity is higher. If taken internally, it can cause cumulative damage to the kidneys, similar to heavy metal poisoning. When freshly machined, it appears similar to stainless steel, but oxidizes to a golden yellow color, then to black, but at a much slower rate than plutonium. Like plutonium, it is also pyrophoric as a fine powder. It is about one and a half times as heavy as lead.

LITHIUM. It is the lightest of metals, and is a highly flammable silver-white metal, typically stored in mineral oil. It can react with water, causing tissue burns. That is why it is so dangerous to skin, which has moisture. When cut, it shows a metallic luster that quickly turns grey, then black.

According to Sandia Labs in a report to the Air Force on another later accident investigation the thermonuclear weapon secondary was at first thought to be "virtually indestructible." But that would be disproven by the 1968 B-52 crash at Thule, Greenland. The impact forces from that Broken Arrow shattered the bomb secondary and the detonation of high explosives in the weapons scattered the contents. So secondaries were not "virtually indestructible" after all. The secondary at Faro could have been damaged as it broke through the nose of the weapon and penetrated the earth. At least the conventional of plutonium called it the most dangerous substance on earth: less than one-millionth of a gram could cause lung cancer if inhaled.

Between 1944 and 1994, the US created or acquired about 110,000 kilograms of plutonium. About 100,000 kilograms remain in inventory; the difference, about ten thousand kilograms, has been released, usually by atmospheric testing. Airborne soluble chemical compounds of plutonium are considered so dangerous by the Department of Energy that the maximum permissible occupational concentration of air is an infinitesimal thirty-two trillionth of a gram per cubic meter of air. That has been compared to a grain of salt in four cubic yards of soil. Another Los Alamos expert, Dr. George Voelz, says that no known humans have ever died from acute toxicity due to plutonium uptake, but based on animal studies the lethal dose to an average human would be twenty-two milligrams if injected, eighty-eight milligrams if inhaled. Using the benchmark of six hypothetical kilograms the plutonium in one MK-39 Secondary could hypothetically equate to approximately seventy thousand deaths, but only if it was completely, absolutely, and perfectly dissipated as an aerosol, something that is certainly not very likely to happen if it were underground and completely sealed inside the Secondary.

Materials in the Secondary: Their Safety Hazards and Appearance

PLUTONIUM. Very lethal if inhaled, and is both a radiation hazard and a health hazard. When freshly machined, it appears similar to stainless steel, but quickly oxidizes to a dark brown or black when exposed to air. It is almost twice as heavy as lead. It is pyrophoric, second stage, is helpful in estimating the amount of plutonium that is in the Secondary at Faro. Teller found that it would take a shock wave from the primary, traveling through both ends of a cylinder of deuterium, to initiate thermonuclear burning. He realized that a subcritical stick of plutonium at the center axis of the secondary would be the boost to go thermonuclear. He called that stick the *spark plug*. Using that subcritical stick as a starting point in our estimate it would stand to reason that the spark plug of a secondary would have to weigh something less than the minimum necessary for critical mass. A very early definition of critical mass, the Christy Core, was 6.2 kilograms. It was a solid ball plutonium core devised by physicist Robert Christy in 1944. In 2001 the Department of Energy in its report "RDD-7" said that six kilograms of plutonium is enough, hypothetically, to make one nuclear explosive device. The subcritical portion of secondary plutonium would be less than the critical mass of six kilograms.

Plutonium was named after Pluto, the Greek god of Hell, and for good reason. The dangers of plutonium were analyzed early in the Manhattan Project when Dr. Wright Langham, the Los Alamos expert in plutonium, did some experiments on a human body, his own, to determine how much plutonium a human could handle without danger. He actually put small quantities on his skin and drank very small quantities added to water. He determined that sixth tenths of a millionth of a gram, 0.06 microgram, was the limit the body could bear. Later the permissible *body burden* of plutonium was officially set at 0.65 microgram, about ten times Langham's crude estimate, but still a very small amount. Glen Seaborg, the discoverer in Albuquerque. It was seen there by several other people, but is no longer available.

Getting all those explosive lenses of the primary to fire at exactly the same instant was a very tricky problem back at the Manhattan Project. Most of the scientists didn't think it could be solved because no one had ever used explosives to assemble something before; their normal use was blowing things apart. Navy Captain "Deke" Parsons, who was in charge of the explosives research, was skeptical. He said it was like "blowing in a beer can without splattering the beer." Each point of detonation on the sphere created a shock wave that interfered with all the other shock waves. They finally solved it with the study of hydrodynamics—the study of complex, dynamic fluid motions. This problem of this shock wave actually turned out to be a crude safety feature for some types of nuclear weapons—the *one point detonation*. In many future Broken Arrows, a single detonator going off would destroy the weapon without triggering a full nuclear detonation. It would scatter dangerous radiation in many cases, but prevented *the big one from going off*.

An MK-39 Secondary has an estimated total weight of at least two hundred pounds, closer to three hundred, but the true amount of plutonium still in the ground at Faro is not yet known. The material in the Goldsboro secondary component was valued at about $287,000 in 1961, by the General Manager of the Atomic Energy Commission.

Richard Rhodes, a Pulitzer Prize-winning author, wrote the book, *Dark Sun, The Making of the Hydrogen Bomb*. He is a nuclear historian, a type of writer that didn't exist until a few years ago. His account of Edward Teller's work in developing the thermonuclear, or

Teller-Ulam device, such as an MK-39 looked like at that time: a large, high-yield design. The two main components of the bomb were a sphere that was the Primary, and a cylinder, called the Secondary. The primary stage is basically an atomic bomb that explodes first, creating pure energy plasma that flows around the cylinder shape of the secondary stage while at the same time triggering the plutonium *spark-plug* of the secondary. Fusion fuel is supplied in the form of Lithium-6 Deuteride in the secondary.

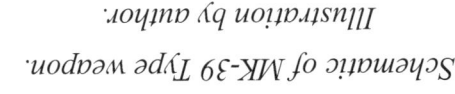

Schematic of MK-39 Type weapon.
Illustration by author.

The exact amounts of plutonium and uranium that were contained in a MK-39 are still classified. What is not classified is other data, including the shape and size of the primary for example. It is about a foot in diameter and has a pattern like a soccer ball around the surface: twenty hexagons and twelve pentagons. This one had ninety-two detonators stuck in explosive lenses all around the surface. When the explosives are fired they compress the plutonium pits inwards creating critical mass. We know that the EOD team removed the primary from Bomb Two—Lieutenant ReVelle carried it out of the hole in his gloved hands. That is the photograph that was in the archives of the National Museum of Nuclear Science and History,

The Goldsboro Broken Arrow – Second Edition

If either Goldsboro bomb had detonated, eastern North Carolina may indeed now have that very large bay that Dr. ReVelle referred to in his interview, or at least a very large man-made lake. After all, the ground surface at Faro is only 108 feet above sea level. In 1977 the Stockholm International Peace Research Institute called the Goldsboro explosion, if it had happened, the "largest man-made disaster in history."

What's In The Ground?

We humans have an inherent fear of the new and unknown, and thermonuclear bombs fit right into both of those two categories. Thermonuclear bombs contain two types of solid radioactive materials, plutonium and uranium. Another material, called tritium, is in gas form. Plutonium, what some consider to be among the world's most toxic poisons, does not readily exist in nature. It can only be created in a nuclear reactor, and is both a poison and a radiation hazard. It was first born about a decade before the Goldsboro crash, but it has a very, very long life. Half-life is the amount of time that radiation will dissipate to half strength. The half-life of Plutonium-239 is over 24,000 years; uranium half-life is approximately 4 billion years.

To help us visualize what's still in the ground at the Bomb Two site at Faro, you have to make some shortcuts through a complex process. The following is based on declassified information and has some very basic assumptions, but hopefully it will help explain what could have happened fifty years ago and what we still have to deal with today. Shown below is a representative drawing of what a typical

It was reported that the fire was extinguished after two hours. The following day when recovery efforts began, the Secondary of one of the MK-43s burst into flames. It had been extinguished but "when this Secondary was moved, it ignited again and was extinguished with sand." It seems secondaries have a way of self-igniting especially when involved in violent activities like crashes.

We may understand more about what awaits us at Faro by some newly declassified information concerning the US submarine *Scorpion* sinking in 1968, and the description of the underwater debris from a nuclear torpedo: "The uranium and plutonium core of these weapons have corroded to a heavy, insoluble mass soon after the sinking and remains close to its original location inside the torpedo room. If the corroded materials were released outside the submarine, their large specific gravity and insolubility would cause them to settle in the sediment."

This complements a similar statement from the Argonne National Lab EVS, where they reported that plutonium has the unique characteristic of not dissolving in water but attaching to and *riding* on grains of sand. Typically one part of plutonium will remain in solution for every two thousand parts in sediment or soil. In wetlands it tends to settle out and adhere strongly to sediment, and will move only when the soil moves. The word sediment is a very good way to describe the deep waterlogged soil of the farmlands of Nahunta Swamp.

Dale Dusenbury, Health Physicist Supervisor of the North Carolina Radiation Protection Service, still takes water samples from a number of shallow water wells in the Faro region. So far all samples are consistent with levels of radiation found naturally. But, he said, "The federal government has never released an accident report to us. We are not sure what is under the soil, or even if it warrants monitoring." When asked to speculate on the chances that any radiation would ever leak into the groundwater, Dusenbury said, "The Air Force has been evaluating this, along with other state agencies. If they clean up a place sufficiently to make it environmentally releasable, or if they can establish that what is there is harmless they will release their ownership. At this time, the Air Force intends to keep its easement because there is still an open question as to whether a hazard exists."

His water samples, however, are from wells in an area where the water table is very near the surface, not from a depth of one hundred eighty feet. In fact, the surface ground elevation of the Bomb Two site is only forty-three feet above the surface water level of the nearby Nahunta Swamp. That puts the buried Secondary component at least 140 feet inside the water table assuming the table is level throughout the area. This underground water, known as the Northern Coastal Plain aquifer system, consists of thick sequences of porous sand beds running to and under the North Carolina coast.

Today's environmental engineers have the expertise to track toxic and dangerous chemicals from municipal waste dumps by measuring their rate of underground flow, or migration. That expertise has apparently never been put to use at Faro. An environmental engineer who reviewed this data said that any underground toxic debris at Faro, if it were fragmented, could be miles downstream after fifty years.

Weapons Testing

Starting around 1951 there was a surge of nuclear testing worldwide and the US was the leader. The following is the total number of nuclear tests worldwide for the period 1951 to 1963:

Year	Tests
1951	18
1952	11
1953	18
1954	16
1955	24
1956	33
1957	55
1958	116
1959	0
1960	3
1961	71
1962	178

(Source: Federation of American Scientists)

On August 21, 1957, something happened that affected the upward trend. President Dwight Eisenhower announced that the United States would suspend testing for two years under certain conditions. The following March the USSR announced a unilateral moratorium, provided the West would also stop testing. For two years there was a gap in the number of world nuclear tests. Between October 31, 1958, and September 14, 1961, the United States conducted no nuclear tests because of this self-imposed moratorium. The world was practically free of nuclear weapons testing. France was the only country to test in 1960 with three detonations in the Sahara Desert of Africa.

On May 1, 1960 Francis Gary Powers was shot down in his CIA U-2 spy plane over Soviet Russia. It was code named "Grand Slam," and was the twenty-fourth such mission.

On January 17, 1961, exactly one week before *Keep 19* crashed, and as the keynote of his farewell address as the thirty-fourth president, former five-star general Dwight Eisenhower warned of a new entity in America—the Military-Industrial Complex: "The immense military establishment that has joined with a large arms industry is new to the American experience.... We must not fail to comprehend its grave implications."

On September 15, 1961, the US resumed nuclear testing. On October 30, 1961, the Russians detonated biggest thermonuclear weapon ever detonated in the world, *Tsar Bomba*. It was in three stages and designed to be one hundred megatons but was reduced to fifty megatons over the Russian's concern of world fallout. Some Russian scientists feared that one hundred megatons would ignite the very upper atmosphere of Earth.

In 1962 Jack ReVelle traveled to Christmas Island in the South Pacific, to be part of the EOD team for Operation Dominic II, a twenty-five-shot nuclear test series.

Chapter 6. The Cause of the Crash

Pushing the Design Envelope

A critical part of the development of any new aircraft is the measuring, in great detail and early on in each prototype phase, of actual flight characteristics discovered compared to the engineering expectations. This is done by the plotting of data points—such as weight, speed, temperature, air density, power settings, etc.—at a number of different configurations. Then in flight testing, pushing beyond those limits, in small increments and recording the responses. This is called pushing the envelope. Many who have done it also call it, "hours and hours of extreme boredom interrupted by moments of sheer terror."

Early aircraft development tended to overbuild by making the aircraft much stronger than necessary but also much safer. A good example is the DC-3, also known in the military as the C-47, a real workhorse, very difficult to overload. There was one fabled incident in the backwaters of the South Pacific where a badly damaged wing and engine of a C-47 was replaced by a much shorter fighter's wing since it was the only way of getting out of the bush. And it flew—with one engine on the good side and a much shorter wing without an engine on the other.

A better-documented example is the Lockheed C-130 Hercules, a cargo plane rated for 92 passengers or 64 airborne troops. In April 1975, a C-130 was loaded up with evacuees and flown out of Saigon's Tan Son Nhut Airport. When it landed, 452 people got out, 32 of them from the flight deck alone.

Later, the art of aircraft development would sometimes push the design *process* envelope. In the design of the G-model, considerable attention was paid to reducing the structural weight of the aircraft in order to carry more fuel, a requirement of the new airborne alert mission. Different materials were used in the construction of the airframe, and the wing structure itself was extensively redesigned. However the most visible difference was in the height of the vertical tail, which was now eight feet shorter… 40 feet 7 inches down from 48 feet 3 inches…making the G-Model forever known as the "Short Tail."

The "G" had the *wet wing*, three metal fuel tanks in each wing that replaced the rubber-bladder types. The new wing required long alloy wing skins so that stiffeners were an integral part of the structure. The 'chord' is the cross section of a wing, the airfoil shape discovered by the Wright brothers that gives the airplane wing its lift. This design of the long wing skins had a minimum of chord-wise joints that, it was hoped, would reduce the possibility of fuel leaks and fatigue. That design of the long wing skins would prove to be a problem in the G model.

The new design of the G-model also saved weight by dispensing with the ailerons, relying entirely on the spoilers for lateral control. This, combined with an aluminum alloy material change in the wing box structure along with the shorter tail permitted a fuel load increase of 41,000 pounds. But overall, the changes made to extend the aircraft's range increased the gross weight from 450,000 pounds up to 488,000 pounds. They got the increase in the fuel capacity, but at a cost. The missing ailerons, along with the shorter rudder, increased the tendency to Dutch roll, and the spoilers caused a slight buffet and tended to cause the nose to pitch up. The original 'Short Tail' G carried more fuel, but with a weaker wing, and lost some of the sensitivity in flight controls.

The wing of previous models of the B-52 had a very pronounced flex in flight: 16 feet up and 16 feet down, a total of 32 feet. With a total wingspan of 185 feet tip to tip, the length of one wing from root to tip would be about 90 feet. That wing moving up and down over one-third of its length would have been dramatic. The G-Model wing was stiffened, but still had vertical movement. Any movement would also mean the linkages inside the wing structure was moving and shifting—machinery like flaps, spoilers, and fuel and hydraulic lines.

Out of the 742 total B-52s built, 193 were the G model, and they were all built between October 1958 and February, 1961 in Wichita, Kansas. Aircraft Number 58-187, which became *"Keep 19,"* was built right in the middle of the second of the three orders for G Models, number AF 33(600)-36470. Based on later events, that must have been about the time Boeing and the Air Force began correlating the fatigue stress fractures of the wing root with the increased weight of the fuel carried, along with the reduced weight of the structure. Low-level flying and the structural strains that occurred during air refueling were expected to speed up fatigue considerably. Aeronautical engineers were becoming worried that the design process envelope may have been pushed too far on this one. That may have been the reason that *Keep 19* was selected to have a VGH recorder installed, a process usually reserved for test aircraft or those undergoing design development. Certainly no one could forecast accurately when wing failure would happen during operations, but it was estimated that under fairly similar circumstances the operating stress placed on this new wing was approximately 60 percent higher than the stress inflicted on the wing of preceding B-52s. The fatigue cracks got so bad that stringent flying restrictions had to be imposed, pending modifications.

It is unknown if the "stringent flying restrictions" were in effect for *Keep 19*. We know a $219 million wing modification was approved in May of 1961, four months after the crash. The retro fit started in 1962 and was completed in 1964. The crash of *Keep 19* in January 1961 may have been the final motivation for the program. Production of the G-Model ended in early 1961, and the last two G-Model B-52s made were delivered to the Air Force in February, 1961 one month after the crash of *Keep 19*.

The relationship with Boeing and the Goldsboro crash was interesting. Major Tulloch was sure that "the experts must have decided that the wing was OK, and our only problem was the fuel leak." A call was made at 11:21 p.m. to Mr. Ed Hensley at Boeing, outlining the problem and requesting assistance. Mr. Hensley advised them to stand by but did not call back until 12:15 a.m., and was discussing the situation with the Command Post when the aircraft crashed. Boeing would take the position later that they had not completed their analysis before the Air Force made the decision to land. There was no need to land immediately, in Boeing's view, because there was plenty of fuel on board.

Today Boeing says that there probably was a failure to detect the metal fatigue crack during inspection or possibly a lack of inspection procedures. However, the Accident Review Board stated, "The aircraft records were minutely examined to determine the adequacy of aircraft maintenance. No discrepancies were found." The Air Force was backing up their crew chiefs: their guys maintained it just the way it was written up by Boeing to be maintained. The Accident Report Findings also reported that the flight manual failed to point out that when a large fuel leak in a wing occurred, some structural damage was *always* associated with it, and the manual had no instructions on how to deal with it.

Item 3 of the Accident Board Findings stated:

> T.O.[Technical Order] 1B-52G-637 (ECP 951-5), requiring depot level compliance, was scheduled for 5 May 1961 during High Stress II modification. Compliance with this technical order would have prevented the failure of the #2 panel of the right wing lower skin.

Here was the classic command dilemma: a fix for a known problem was planned, but the risk of flying with that risk was overridden by current mission pressure. The risk of scheduling a crew to fly an aircraft with a wing defect was overridden by mission pressure in the start-up of Airborne Alerts and Chrome Dome.

It is difficult to evaluate from fifty years after the accident, according to Mr. Michael Lombardi of Boeing Historical Research. He has been very helpful, and reminds us that whatever was learned from this accident has no doubt saved many lives and contributed greatly to the outstanding level of flight safety that we enjoy today.

Most pilots would agree that knowing what we know now, the best thing learned from this accident was to stop making the G Model, immediately. And that actually happened. The last G Model was delivered to the Air Force a month after the crash of *Keep 19*. And then they started fixing the wings.

The Weather Factor of This Crash

Officially, weather was not considered to be a factor in the crash of *Keep 19*. The mission weather portion of AF Form 14 stated at 0100 (1 AM), the time of the crash, Goldsboro weather at ten thousand feet was clear, with unlimited visibility, and winds from the west (270°), at fifty-seven knots. However, the weather dramatically deteriorated during the actual crash sequence. Consider these key points:

Three days before, the unexpected severity of a blizzard almost shut down President Kennedy's inauguration and the rebound front from this giant, circulating low-pressure area was now driving into North Carolina from the west. The front itself had advanced to a position near Raleigh-Durham as of 1 a.m., the time of the crash.

Texas Tower Four, an offshore radar dome about seventy miles east of New Jersey was completely destroyed five days before the inauguration. A "fierce winter storm" collapsed the Air Force installation with a loss of all twenty-eight men. This storm was part of the weather system known as the Gail of 1961. There were no weather satellites at that time.

At the time of the crash the jet stream was "centered over Seymour

Johnson AFB with winds of 160 knots at 40,000 feet; and 110 knots at 29,000 feet." Under these conditions winds at 10,000 feet would at least be considered *dynamic*.

Within forty-eight hours after the crash, freezing rain and snow were severe enough to delay all recovery efforts. For days immediately afterward, snow and ice shut down portions of the state from Manteo to Murphy. Heavy icing stopped road traffic and cars were stranded in many areas. Goldsboro had snow for three days. On Day Three the high was twenty-eight degrees, and the low was ten degrees.

Right after takeoff and during the initial climb, moderate to severe turbulence was reported by *Keep 19*. Normally turbulence of this nature would not be considered a problem for an aircraft weighting about a half million pounds, but it may have been a contributing factor in the sequence of events that followed. We are not sure how the winds aloft and the turbulence affected the aircraft since the VGH Gust Recorder was not sufficiently protected to preserve the recordings, as stated as Item Ten of the Findings. Note this device is not the "black box" of much later commercial aircraft, but a recording device installed by the manufacturer on certain selected aircraft in the fleet or on test aircraft to gather basic data: airspeed, pressure altitude and gusts. This missing information, in light of the varying wind speeds aloft, would have been extremely useful in determining what *Keep 19* was going through right up to the point of disintegration.

The Endorsement

Officer Effectiveness Reports, or OERs, are the key to a career officer's future. This is where an Air Force officer's professional life is writ large, his permanent record. His performance factors, his overall evaluation, and his promotion potential are all spelled out annually in excruciating detail by his immediate commander and endorsed by his boss's boss. The OER record would follow him around from base to base and can either be a star in his crown or an albatross to wear for the rest of his career. It could even end his career.

Scott Tulloch received *excellent* or *exceptional* ratings in all categories throughout his entire career. But the real measure of the man can be read, not in the boxes checked on the form, but in the comments section written by the reporting official. That is where you get the feel for the person. Here are some of the comments written on his OERs throughout Major Tulloch's entire career:

"Completely reliable; has mature judgment. Hard working, competent, constant smile, ready wit. Personal enthusiasm. A good family man. A most pleasing personality and his morals are beyond reproach. His greatest strength lies in his tenacious attitude. Has a keen interest in military history. Active in the community, works with the Boy Scouts. Accomplished writer. Excellent analyzer. He will not give up on a problem until it has been satisfactorily completed."

After a major aircraft accident such as *Keep 19*, the prevailing mind-set of the Air Force is to eventually set blame. With the enormous loss of equipment such as a B-52, and the potential of unfavorable public scrutiny, the unwritten rule of command structure was to find the person or persons responsible for the crash.

From Major Tulloch's OER dated 10 July, 1961, the first Officer Effectiveness Report written after the accident, Wing Commander, Colonel Osce V. Jones, said straight out in his endorsement, "I am pleased to have him in my command." The reporting official was Lieutenant Colonel Colin Hamilton, Commander of the Seventy-Fourth Bomb Squadron, and had written in his comments: "CINCSAC, CG 8AF, and CG 822 AD stated that in effect that Major Tulloch expertly handled the emergency and that this was one of the very few aircraft accidents that crew or supervisory efforts were not in error."

CINCSAC is the Commander In Chief of the Strategic Air Command.

CG 8AF is the Commanding General of the Eighth Air Force.

CG 822 AD is the Commanding General of the 822nd Air Division.

Major Scott Tulloch had the backing and support of the brass all the way up the line from his boss to Commander In Chief, SAC. You don't get any better backing than that.

Part II.
AFTERMATH

Chapter 7. The Tension of Command

There is a frightening scenario of an accidental nuclear detonation being perceived by military leaders in 1961 not as an accident, but as an attack by the Soviets. Would cool heads wait for a confirmation that a terrible accident had just occurred, or would there be enough confusion in the fog of disaster to think of it as the first in a Soviet strike? In the Cold War a B-52 bomber could be used as a show of force, it could go out there and remain on station. If it went to the fail-safe point and did not receive the launch command, the aircraft would turn around and return home unused. But ICBMs were considered operational in 1961, and there was no fail-safe to a missile once launched. A SAC missile officer once told me, "When the missile was sitting in the hole we had control of it. One inch off the pad at launch and that (sucker) was committed. All the way to the target."

Our military analysts were trying to think of and evaluate every conceivable method of attack. Scenarios had the Soviet first strike as occurring inside America with smuggled nuclear devices exploding inside the Soviet Embassy in Washington, DC; near NORAD or SAC headquarters; and in Soviet offices near the United Nations Building in New York. The United States, through it's mighty right arm, SAC, was ready to make an immediate response to any such an event, if it was determined to be a deliberate attack by the Soviets.

If the US made such a response by accident, it would not be the first time that a country would make such a decision. The initial bombing of London in World War II was an accident. Carl Builder, an analyst for RAND wrote: "It happened on the night of August 24, 1940. Flying through the fog and clouds over England, two German bombers were separated from their radar-equipped pathfinder guiding them toward a target in the Midlands north of London. Unable to regroup, they meandered through the sky until they attracted antiaircraft fire from the ground. Knowing that they were hopelessly lost, they jettisoned their bombs and turned for home."

As things happened, the pilots were over London and the bombs did incredible damage. One bomb hit a national monument, one exploded on a church, another killed civilians coming out of a late-night movie, and more. Retaliation was nearly instant. Wrote Leonard Mosley in *The Battle of Britain (World War II)*: "Churchill ordered Bomber Command to attack Berlin as a reprisal, which in turn provoked Hitler to order that London should now become his air force's main target." The bombing of London had begun.

"I believe there has never been a military force more difficult to surprise than SAC. SAC is a jumpy alert-happy force," a CIA officer said. "There is little if any exaggeration in saying that if small fires were to break out simultaneously in the paint lockers of three or four SAC bases in the world, the bombers of the SAC alert force, numbering in the hundreds, bombed up and fully fueled, would within approximately fifteen minutes take off and head out to their assigned targets."

SIOP

There was an amazing plan created in 1960 for the entire nuclear forces of the United States to go to war. It was called SIOP, for Single Integrated Operational Plan, and it was designed as a unified action to effectively destroy all Soviet states including Red China. The need for it was originally Eisenhower's idea, and General Thomas Power was appointed by the Joint Chiefs of Staff as the Director of the Joint Strategic Target Planning Staff. They had the responsibility to design the plan, utilizing a "team of experts" from all military services. There would be revisions to the plan at later times, but the first SIOP was written primarily in Omaha by SAC and Naval officers. It was designated as SIOP-62, after the Fiscal Year 1962 which would start on April 1, 1961.

The working relationship between the officers of the Navy and the officers at SAC during the development of SIOP must have been very interesting. The US Navy had been the most influential military branch during the early part of the war in the Pacific with its massive ships of the line, a proud tradition. Airpower at the beginning of the Pacific war came from the Navy aircraft carriers, not the Army Air Corps. It was only later when Pacific islands were captured by land forces, and the land-based bombers were led by Curtis LeMay, did the strategic power shift away from ships and toward airplanes. A measure of the status of a Naval officer during the war was always known to the other Naval officers by a simple code following his name, as in Adm. Chester Nimitz, NA 05, or Adm. William Halsey, NA 04. The code stood for Naval Academy and the year of graduation.

The Air Force officers did not yet have that sort of tradition. The first class of the Air Force Academy had just graduated in 1959, so the 'pecking order' for Air Force officers was rank and date of rank. Nimitz and Halsey were long gone before the creation of SIOP, of course, but the Navy men trained by them and involved in SIOP were mostly Naval Academy graduates, and they found themselves on an Air Force base on the plains of Nebraska by order of the Joint Chiefs of Staff, writing this SIOP. And if that was not enough to test inter-service relations, they were under the direction of a new four-star Air Force general, Thomas Power, whose greatest educational degree was a high school diploma. General Power as the Director of Joint Strategic Target Planning now had a Naval Vice Admiral, Edwin N. Parker, as his Deputy Director. The number of personnel assigned to his joint planning staff totaled 269: the Navy had 29; the Army had 10; Marines, 3. The rest was Air Force, including 140 SAC officers.

SIOP was to be the largest, most complex war plan ever created, synchronizing the entire nuclear forces of the United States. It was to involve all American nuclear weapons including the Navy's new Polaris submarine the *USS George Washington*, along with the SAC bombers and Atlas missiles, with most of the heavy lifting falling to the SAC bomber fleet. It was developed over a period of several months and revised many times but the overall design would not change in significant ways until the late 1970s. Some of the information is still classified and may never be declassified.

It was presented to President Eisenhower on November 25, 1960, just two months before *Keep 19* took off. It was reported the extent of the plan both "surprised and horrified him." The plan had evolved into "overkill," the ultimate instrument of war. His science advisor George Kistiakowsky said it would "kill four or five times over somebody who is already dead." Ike told his naval aide, "SIOP frightens the devil out of me." Others were also alarmed. The Commandant of the Marine Corps said that SIOP made no difference between Communist countries that were at war with the United States and those that were not. Army and Navy leaders as well as scientists in the White House were concerned that the fallout from the weapons would be a "hazard to ourselves."

The plan was completed and approved just days later in December, 1960, and governed the operations of all American strategic as well as many theater nuclear forces. It was designed to be executed either in retaliation or in a "preemptive measure." If the Soviets struck first, SIOP would call for full US retaliation and deliver 1,706 nuclear weapons against 725 targets. If we stuck first on a preemptive basis, SIOP was much larger, it called for a delivery of 3,200 nuclear weapons onto 1,060 targets in the Soviet Bloc including China and other Communist countries in Asia and Europe. Targets would include Soviet bases and missile sites, government and military command and control centers, and at least one hundred thirty cities in the Soviet Union, China, and their allies.

SIOP was approved by President Eisenhower to be in effect on April 1, 1961. The paperwork would weigh over nine tons. Since it was written essentially under the direction of General Power, he was already planning for it in his command. He had been wearing two hats during this period: Director of Joint Strategic Target Planning, and Commander In Chief, SAC. Since he was heading up both the organization that devised the plan and the organization that would carry most of it out, the pressure from headquarters SAC would be intense, brought down through the numbered air forces. The people at wing level knew what was coming and unofficially referred to SIOP-62 as the 'million-pound shit hammer.' But it had another name, the official code word used by SAC Command Center: "DROPKICK."

This led to a briefcase containing an authorization device to be carried by a military officer who would be near the President at all times. Since the original war plan was known as DROPKICK, of course the briefcase became known as "The Football." Contrary to popular belief, the Football does not contain the Go Codes that fire nuclear weapons. Those codes always remain in military custody at command posts—at SAC, the Pentagon, and other Air Force and Naval alternate sites around the country. The Football contains a device that identifies the President as himself, to those commanders who would order the launching, as well as which options the President was selecting. The Football did not have the Go Codes; it has the equivalent of a PIN number for the Go Codes. And it had numerous responses the President could select for different scenarios.

SIOP-62 required massive effort to be made to get the airplanes manned and the crews trained, ready for maximum response at any time. General Power and his SAC staff had been working hard to get to this point. One can only imagine the intense pressure that the career command pilots of the Strategic Air Command were feeling as they prepared for this upcoming mission change. These would have been men who had been through World War II, and had probably participated in the bombing of Japan from the huge airports at Guam and Tinian. The aircraft commanders such as Major Walter Scott Tulloch would have been using any spare time in the SAC alert facility briefing rooms to the best possible advantage: get his crew to the top of their game.

To meet SIOP requirements, SAC had earlier determined that it would need 24-hour sorties, instead of the usual 10-hours. Only the B-52 with the third pilot sitting in the Instructor Pilot position was physically large enough to provide room for twenty-four hours of continuous flying. The goal was for one-fourth of all B-52s to be on alert by April 1961. They would require more of everything: manpower, engine spares, and POL stores (petroleum, oil, and lubricants). At least 1,000 new bomber crew members, fully trained, were needed; this is why Mattocks had been reassigned from F-86 fighters to B-52s. SAC was having a number of problems in the buildup, some as routine as not getting POL leases fast enough— facilities for holding and transporting the vast quantities of necessary aircraft fuel. The Joint Chiefs of Staff set a goal of SAC to be flying 11.25 sorties per day by April 1961—an enormous effort. The 'step up' level at 1 January 1961, was 9 sorties per day. It was this huge pressure from Headquarters SAC that would lead to the wing commanders making every effort, maximum effort, to get as many B-52 crews qualified to fly the alerts as soon as possible. General Power was cashing in his 'blank check' that he received from Congress.

The Strategic Air Command Airborne Alert, the most powerful, continuously running military operation in history, was officially initiated by General Power on January 19, 1961, one day before the Kennedy inauguration. Airborne alert was the key to SIOP-62.

Chapter 8. The Worst Case

There is a terrible possibility that should at least be considered, now that we have passed beyond this event by a comfortable half century. That is the possibility that a single accidental nuclear explosion in the United States around late 1960 or early 1961, had it occurred, could have evolved into something much more sinister—all due to three critical factors that were already in place in early1961: the enormous build-up of thermonuclear weapons, the unreliable state of communications, and the inclination of commanders who had predeligated authority to go to war.

Critical Factor Number One: The Build-Up of Weapon Systems:

MANPOWER: In 1953, Strategic Air Command made up about sixteen percent of the total manpower of the Air Force, 158,000 out of 978,000. Just eight years later, 1961, it was double: over thirty percent with 254,000 in SAC and 815,000 in the total Air Force. The number of officers being commissioned jumped into the thousands per year just from the Officer Training School, located at Lackland Air Force Base, San Antonio. OTS began in 1960 and was able to turn out "ninety day wonders" as the needs for SAC officers climbed. That one facility at Lackland gave the Air Force the flexibility to quickly meet fluctuating officer requirements, something the two main sources, the Air Force Academy and ROTC (Reserve Officer Training Corps), could not, since they were four-year collages. The peak year for OTS was 1967 when 7,894 brand new second lieutenants were commissioned into the US Air Force as officers and gentlemen.

BUFFs: A total of 742 Boeing B-52s were delivered to the US Air Force. Those deliveries, by Fiscal Year, were as follows:

FY 54	3
FY 55	13
FY 56	41
FY 57	124
FY 58	187
FY 59	129
FY 60	106
FY 61	57
FY 62	68
FY 63	14
Total	742

By the year 1960, more than 88% of all the B-52 that had been made or would ever be made were on the flight lines of the Air Force.

ICBMs: The build up of missiles was just beginning in the 1960s, when the United States was producing them "by the score." At the end of 1963, there were 631 ICBMs in silos.

MEGATONS: Between 1959 and 1961, the US nuclear capabilities had nearly doubled, growing from 11,700 weapons to more than 23,200 in barely two years. The nuclear stockpile would level off at about 32,500 weapons, with the all time high point in explosive yield in 1960. When Eisenhower entered the presidency, there were about 1,000 bombs. When he left office, there were over 20,000 weapons counting nuclear bombs, missiles, mines, and torpedoes. At various times, Ike called the numbers "fantastic," "crazy," and "unconscionable."

If we could imagine a composite graph showing all of these components, manpower, B-52s, ICBMs, and megatonnage, the top of the bell curve would be somewhere around the end of the 1950s to the beginning of the 1960s, about the time when *Keep Nineteen* was becoming a cog in the biggest military machine in history.

Critical Factor Number Two: The State of Communications:

In early 1961, Secretary of Defense Robert McNamera gave a report to newly elected President Kennedy that was as stark and alarming as any president has ever received. It concerned the US strategic command and control, and McNamara reported that the President's chain of command to the strategic forces was "highly vulnerable in almost every way." Communications connecting key military headquarters with each other and with the strategic forces were soft, concentrated, and vulnerable to sudden Soviet attack. In fact, a surprise nuclear attack was now *the* supreme threat to our nation. Our warning system was considered "rudimentary, weak, and fairly inaccurate."

There was another hidden communications problem that would be more thoroughly researched in the coming year. Now that we were in the megaton range, we were just beginning to examine in full and scientific methods the phenomenon called electromagnetic pulse, or EMP, the abrupt burst of invisible electromagnetic radiation. We knew of it's existence. It had been observed from the beginning of nuclear testing, and scientists had seen how it affected electronics in previous experiments. But it was thought of as anomalies or instrument malfunctions. But the true *effects* of EMP upon communications was not closely studied until 1962 STARFISH PRIME. That was the nuclear airborne test carried out in the mid-Pacific a full year after the crash of *Keep 19*. STARFISH PRIME was a nuclear detonation of 1.4 megatons at high altitude, and it's EMP shut off streetlights, burglar alarms, and microwave communications in Hawaii, 900 miles away. A 3.8-megaton detonation at Faro, much larger and 888 miles closer, even at ground level, would have done much more than shut down burglar alarms and street lights at Seymour Johnson. The reality is, we simply did not know the effect of EMP upon our unshielded electronic communication system in 1961. We had an Achilles heel and didn't even realize it.

Just ten months after the Goldsboro crash, another weakness of the communications system was revealed. On November 24, 1961, General Power was called in the middle of the night by SAC's headquarters at Omaha. SAC had just lost all communications with North American Air Defense Command (NORAD) in Colorado

Springs, Colorado, along with multiple radar sites. The complex communications between SAC, NORAD and the warning sites were fully redundant and designed so that there would be no loss of contact due to accident or human error. The SAC duty officers even tried to call NORAD on regular AT&T telephone lines, but all the lines were dead. Planners had always thought that if the Soviets attacked, it would be a surprise attack, and this sudden and total loss of communications with NORAD looked very much like that scenario. General Power signaled B-52 ground alert forces to exercise Coco, where the BUFFs taxied into position, ready to launch. The Klaxon horns sounded, and the crews poured out of the moleholes. The B-52s were ready for 'bust out'—maximum effort with minimum interval takeoff, black smoke pouring out of their exhausts, thermal curtains buttoned up over the cockpit windows as soon as the landing gear came up, just in case nuke flashes went off behind them— the BUFFs would fan out and head off to their Positive Control Points, their 'fail-safe' points. The missile silos were alerted and were standing by. The radar navigators and the 'E-Dubs' on the B-52s were planning ahead, thinking about their lock combinations on the steel secrets box, how to open them and distribute the war order envelopes when told to do so.

But it was the Thule Monitor that saved the day. That fully armed B-52 circling the early warning base in Greenland confirmed to HQ SAC that the arctic base had not been attacked and all was well in Thule. As improbable and as embarrassing as it was—the fully redundant nuclear early warning system had been knocked flat by a minor fire in one telephone junction station somewhere in Colorado. The BUFFs stood down.

The ground alert response time of fifteen minutes for SAC

bombers in 1961 was built around the time for a Soviet missile detection to detonation time. This is ironic, but we should remember it took as long as thirty to forty-five minutes for the Seymour Johnson command post to realize, only by Mattocks' and Rardin's arrival at the main gate, that there had even been a crash. Strategic Air Command's communication system for this nuclear incident had been reduced to two crewmen being driven from the site of the crash, in farmers' trucks and cars, back to Seymour Johnson. Of course had there been an actual detonation, the Seymour Johnson control tower would have certainly witnessed it immediately from only twelve miles away and may have had time to react in some way before communications were knocked out.

The entire phenomenon of the Air Force nuclear delivery system had been built over the previous ten years, during the 1950's, without any overall coordination or plan of the communications system. Bombers had joined the land-based missiles as well as the nuclear-armed submarines, completing the strategic triad. The Air Force had a command post inside the Pentagon, and the Joint Chiefs of Staff had their own command post. Back-up command posts were built. Increasingly sophisticated communications, data processing, and display techniques were introduced into the new centers to maintain control of strike forces. The headquarters of SAC at Offutt Air Force Base, Omaha, Nebraska became the nerve center of the world-wide bomber and missile force. It had its own huge command center, complete with a closed circuit color TV system and an IBM 704 computer. There were big impressive display boards with speakers and lots of lights and moving icons. Twenty years later in 1982, a Joint Chief of Staff study looked back and summarized the state of communications:

"The United States decided in 1953 to build a Distant Early Warning (DEW) System as a precaution against aircraft attacks and the system was competed in 1960. In 1954, construction of the Semi-Automatic Ground Environment (SAGE) computerized system for integrating the entire warning and defense network and begun and, by the end of the latter part of the decade, development of both the Ballistic Missile Early Warning System (BMEWS) and satellite reconnaissance systems were underway. All of these systems of the 1950s were developed without any overall coordination or plan."

The SAC Command Post at Offutt Air Force Base, Omaha, Nebraska.
Photo courtesy USAF.

In the early 1960s, we were insufficient in the way of reliable communications, but we did hold a critically needed asset: the national will and talent to design and deliver. A good example is this: In May 1959, the Air Force asked Western Union to present a proposal for a nationwide nuclear bomb detonation alarm. The alarm would not give any advance notice of impending attack, but would at least determine if a nuclear detonation had indeed occurred. The turn-around for the request was phenomenal. Full plans for the system were presented to the Air Force within thirty days. It is very possible such plans had already been in the works as a potential need; after all, Western Electric had this subsidiary called Sandia. The prototype system was quickly in operation by March of 1960 covering fourteen target areas in the eastern United States. That same year the Western Union Telegraph Company patented the device known as the Western Union Bomb Alarm, Display System 210-A.

The sensor was a simple, rugged apparatus mounted on a telephone pole for operation in all weather conditions. It was a white metal cylinder about ten inches in diameter and eighteen inches high with a glass shield on top. It was an inexpensive and foolproof method of continuously observing more than 100 strategically important target areas and population centers throughout the United States. It was designed to look like a transformer on a utility pole. Its sensors would detect only an explosion from a nuclear bomb, as opposed to lightning. The sensor itself was modern, but its signal was sent not by vulnerable electronic means but by the oldest and most reliable method available: telegraph wire. The system would only do one thing: notify SAC, the Pentagon, and the North American Air Defense Command Headquarters if the signature of a nuclear thermal flash was detected. Simple telegraph wire was thought to be more robust in delivering the signal than some sort of electronic or wireless method. The complete nationwide system was declared fully operational in early 1962 with no false alarms and a performance level of 98.1 percent out of 18,600,000 tests, but it did have a weakness of not being self-powered—it relied on the local electrical grid. Still, it was a marvel of how American ingenuity and resourcefulness could react to a national need and it was a secret in plain sight: it looked like a transformer on a utility pole. We had something we never had before—an automatic alarm system for nuclear detonations.

The bomb alarm prototype was operational in the form of thirty-seven detectors along the eastern seaboard when *Keep 19* crashed in Goldsboro.

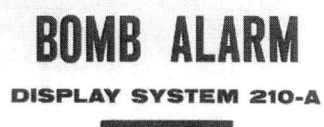
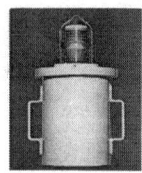

The Western Union Bomb Detector Alarm System
Photos courtesy Alfred LaFrance

It appears that even during this period of worrisome communications, there was at least one area of communications that worked really well: the SIOP execution by SAC. Here's what *Study S-467, The Evolution Of U.S. Strategic Command and Control And Warning* said:

"SIOP EXECUTION

"Emergency command functions and procedures were developed ahead of time and streamlined insofar as possible to permit effective operations even in the degraded communications environment of a nuclear attack. This was especially the case with respect to absolutely critical actions, like directing the execution of the strategic war plan. Assuming the continuity of political authority and a prompt retaliatory decision, the procedures in effect called for transmitting a simple, short prepositioned "go code" to the strike forces, giving them the signal to carry out previously designated assignments to deliver prescribed weapons in a specified manner against preselected targets, all in quasi-automatic fashion that reduced communications and other command requirements to the barest human and technical minimums. This called for a thoroughly developed, clearly understood, and well-rehearsed operational plan that could be implemented with a simple unambiguous decision, almost without further command intervention...The strategic war plan of 1961, basically the Single Integrated Operational Plan (SIOP-62) developed by the Joint Strategic Planning at SAC Headquarters, was as all-inclusive as was possible to make it."

The good news was we had quasi-automated communication methods of transmitting a short, concise "go-code" to the strike force without further command intervention.

The bad news was we had quasi-automated communication methods of transmitting a short, concise "go-code" to the strike force without further command intervention.

Communication problems continued at Goldsboro on the night of January 23-24, for *Keep 19*, both in the air and on the ground. Lieutenant Wilson, the EW officer, tried repeatedly to use the normal high frequency radio on various channels, but it was failed. Command Post radios were sometimes also unable to make contact with the aircraft, so about half the time the wing commander resorted to going outside to the Command Post parking lot using the more reliable radio in his staff car. Also, this was a long in-flight emergency and the tape recorder in the Command Post was frequently turned off to save tape and was not always turned back on before radio transmissions were started. In addition were telephone problems at the Command Post earlier in the evening. Tom Parker was a Marine veteran with a security clearance who worked with Southern Bell Telephone at Goldsboro. He had been summoned to the base command post to check the suspected phone problem with Boeing and was there when *Keep 19* was coming back from the Wilmington area. He saw and heard enough tension in the command post that when he left the base, he quickly gathered up his family and hurried towards Raleigh in the family station wagon. He thought there was a good chance Goldsboro was going to be hit with a nuclear weapon. They were speeding toward Raleigh when he learned over the car radio about the crash of a "big bomber."

If the state of radio and telephone communications in 1961 was so vulnerable and unreliable that a fire in a junction box could cut off NORAD from SAC headquarters, or that a wing commander had to go out to his staff car just to talk to an aircraft in distress, and we still didn't know of the hidden effects of EMP, what would be involved in Seymour Johnson commanders (assuming they were still alive) in convincing Headquarters SAC and the Joint Chiefs of Staff that a huge nuclear detonation at Goldsboro had really been a terrible accident, and not an intentional attack? What if General Power was called in the middle of the night and told that ADC radars, the prototype Bomb Detection Alarms, and other NUDETS sensors indicated there had been a nuclear detonation in North Carolina, that Seymour Johnson was off the network, and the SAC wing there was not answering the phone. He would probably at the very least 'bust out' his B-52s, but would he wait and take the time to find out if it was an accident?

So here we had a mix of different communication systems in various states of development, some reliable, some not so much. We had the Canadian DEW line, up and operating, but BMEWS was still on the drawing board. An unproven Bomb Detection Device prototype was now being installed along the East Coast. Traditional land lines and radios were suspect and "highly vulnerable in almost every way." But the execution system for SIOP-62 was in good shape: reliable and redundant.

There's more. Here is an another part of the S-467 Study, describing what the Kennedy administration faced when they came into Washington on January 20, 1961, three days before *Keep 19*.

> "Once the plan (SIOP-62) was put in motion, it was expected to run it's course. There was, in fact, no way to stop it after an authentic execute order was issued. After

the initial strike list was exhausted and the initial strike weapons were expended, any continuation of strategic operations depended on whatever surviving authorities might be able to improvise with whatever forces remained at their disposal. It was a plan, it was said, oriented toward a 'one-shot war'—not entirely unsuitable, it may be added, for what may well have been at the time a one-shot command, control, and communications system. A strategic command and control system that could only manage a semiautomatic all-out response, if even that, and that required risky split-second reaction on penalty of catastrophic failure, was hardly acceptable to the leaders of this incoming administration. They sought alternatives to a strategic predicament in which at the first signs of attack decision makers were under great compulsion to fire everything at once against the entire target system because it was the only really feasible retaliatory option—'spasm war,' they called it."

It is very important to acknowledge the difference between a Broken Arrow, which does *not* create the risk of nuclear war, and a NUCFLASH, which *does* create the risk of nuclear war. Would an accidental nuclear detonation at Goldsboro be erroneously but intentionally designated as NUCFLASH by command and used as the excuse to go to war?

Critical Factor Number Three: Willingness of the Commanders:

We don't know for certain what LeMay and Power would have done, but we do know what they said they would do. There are some quotes from that time that indicated a leaning toward preemptive nuclear strikes, even without provocation. In 1954, an overflight of the Soviet Union was planned by US Air Force RB-47s from the Ninety-first Strategic Reconnaissance Wing in England with Lieutenant Colonel Hal Austin, commanding. General LeMay told Austin before takeoff, "Well, maybe if we do this overflight right we can get World War III started."

It is not known if he was joking but General LeMay was not well known for his humor.

LeMay never wavered in his thoughts of massive retaliation as being the only workable doctrine against Communist aggression. Naval officers said that LeMay had but one plan: to leave the Soviet Union "a smoking, radioactive ruin in two hours." In a 1957 meeting with Robert Sprague, deputy director of the Gaither Commission, LeMay said, "If I see the Russians massing their planes for an attack, I'm going to knock the shit out of them before they can get off the ground." When Sprague said that was not national policy, LeMay said, "I don't care. It's my policy. That's what I'm going to do."

When General LeMay left SAC in 1957 to become the Vice Chief of Staff, USAF in Washington, he hand-picked his replacement—his trusted subordinate from the Japanese bombing missions launched from the Northern Mariana Islands, General Thomas S. Power. He did not just continue the policies of LeMay, those policies would be hardened. Like his predecessor, General Power believed that SAC was already at war. He once said: "Day and night, I have a certain percentage of my command in the air. The planes are bombed up, and they don't carry bows and arrows." He had but a simple mission in life: to defend American by nuclear deterrence, and convince the American people that the Russian and Chinese Communists were our mortal enemy, and we could only win by overwhelming military superiority.

General Power was Commander In Chief, SAC at the time of the Goldsboro crash and would remain in that position until he retired in 1964.

Much has been written about Curtis LeMay, and he is a very interesting and compelling subject. Officers who served directly under him consider him either an icon or a tyrant, and there is a lot of information on Curtis LeMay. One thing is very clear about him: he was exactly what we were asking for when we needed protection from the Japanese and the Soviets. But Thomas S. Power is difficult to know from fifty years away—primarily the little that has been written about his style and personality was usually by selected sources within the Air Force, by him, or was limited to anecdotes about him.

General Curtis LeMay was considered the father of SAC. He was Commander from 1948 to 1957. He became the youngest general since Ulysses Grant, and was a general for 17 years, longer than any other man in the U.S. military.

Photo courtesy USAF.

General Thomas S. Power was promoted to four star general when he was assigned to the Strategic Air Command after Curtis LeMay. He was commander in chief, SAC, from 1957 to 1964. He was the last US general without a post-secondary education.

Photos courtesy USAF.

Thomas Power was the last US general without a post-secondary education, as reported by Stephen Budiansky in *Air Power: The Men, Machines, and ideas that Revolutionized War, From Kitty Hawk to Gulf War II*. Thomas Power's first two years of high school was at Mamaroneck High School, New York, then he transferred to the Barnard School for Boys in the Bronx. He graduated from Barnard in the class of 1922 with the nickname 'Teetie,' according to the

1922 Barnard Yearbook. After high school, he worked as a clerk for a construction company. He "became hooked" on aviation after a $10 barnstormer's ride in a WWI Jenny at a company picnic.

Power, the son of Iris immigrants, considered the Army Air Force as composed of "the haughty elite." Anyone without two years of college had to earn his way in through an examination he believed was designed to keep him out. Power studied at the public library until he believe he was ready, then passed the exam. He said he considered his studying for the exam the equivalent of a college education. Later, when competing for a regular commission, he outranked most of the college-trained members of his cadet class. He entered the Air Corps Flying School on February 17, 1928, at the age of 23, and was commissioned February 1929.

PREDELEGATION

One very important piece of history which is little known by most Americans is this: At the time of *Keep 19* in 1961, General Power actually held both the authority on his own to start nuclear war and the intense desire to do so. Americans had always been told that only the President, or his immediate successor, could authorize the use of nuclear weapons. In fact, instructions had been given to specified military commanders that could, in certain situations, use nuclear weapons on their own authority. This policy was spelled out in a document entitled *Authorization for the Expenditure of Atomic Weapons in Air Defense* and was signed by President Eisenhower. This authorization was to be used for defense only, not as an offensive measure. The authority was broadened in magnitude on

May 22, 1957, by a document of *predelegation*, which listed the five commanders authorized to launch a retaliatory strike if conditions made it impossible to communicate with the secretary of defense and the Joint Chiefs of Staff. Among the five commanders was CINCSAC, the Commander In Chief, Strategic Air Command. In 1961 that would be General Thomas Power. And SAC was the command with the most nuclear weapons and the systems to deliver them. The other four were the US Commanders in Chief: Atlantic, Europe, Pacific, and Naval Forces.

John S. D. Eisenhower would write in his notes, "[The President] agreed that it is most important that word of any delegation from the President be withheld from our allies. It is in the U.S. interest to maintain the atmosphere that all authority stays with the President without predelegation."

Not only was the document top secret, the knowledge of the existence of the document would be limited to only a very few people and was denied for years by government historians. We as a nation had reached the level of the movie *Animal House's* "double secret probation." It was a secret, and the fact that it was a secret was a secret.

The National Security Archive published the first official documents in 1998 confirming predelegation. In 2001 the archive released a second set of documents that reconfirmed that the authority to launch the nuclear force was in the hands of General Power in 1961. He had the authority, if, in his opinion, America had been attacked by the Soviet Union and his communications with the Join Chiefs of

Staff were cut off. He was authorized to execute SIOP either "as a preemptive measure or in retaliation."

In January, 1961, when Kennedy first took office, National Security Advisor McGeorge Bundy had a meeting with the new president. The meeting had to have occurred within days of the crash of *Keep 19*, since the inauguration was on January 20, the crash was just four days later, and the Bundy meeting happened in the month of January. It is very possible the crash of *Keep 19* was the reason for the conversation. Bundy advised the president of the possibility that "a subordinated commander faced with a substantial Russian military action could start the thermonuclear holocaust on his own initiative if he could not reach you (by failure of communication at either end of the line)."

In a conference with President Kennedy and other generals on September 20 of the same year, General Power told the President "the time of our greatest danger of a Soviet surprise attack is now and during the coming year. If a general atomic war is inevitable, the United States should strike first..." General Power as Commander of Strategic Air Command was telling the President of the United States we needed to make a preemptive nuclear strike. Now.

In a Boston newspaper interview, when asked about restraint in the conduct of nuclear war, General Power said, "Restraint! Why are you so concerned about saving *their* lives? The whole idea is to *kill* the bastards.... Look. At the end of the war, if there are two Americans and one Russian alive, we win!"

Several historians have written that both Presidents Eisenhower and Kennedy held Power in "low regard," and that Power was colder, and in some respects, scarier than LeMay. LeMay, in retirement, acknowledged that Power was "a sadist." Horace Wade, who was one of Power's subordinate commanders agreed: "General Power was demanding; he was mean; he was cruel, unforgiving, and he didn't have the time of day to pass with anyone. A hard, cruel individual.... I would like to say this. I used to worry about General Power. I used to worry that General Power was not stable. I used to worry about the fact that he had control over so many weapons and weapon systems and could, under certain conditions, launch the force. *Back in the days before we had real positive control*, SAC had the power to do a lot of things, and it was in his hands, and he knew it."

Another policy that was in effect at the transfer of the presidency from Eisenhower to Kennedy, was an astonishing concept called FURTHERANCE. It called for an "automatic full nuclear response" in the event the president was killed or "could not be found" (i.e. vaporized) during an attack on the United States. Both the USSR and Red China would be targeted simultaneously, even if the event was conventional or accidental, and regardless of who was responsible. The document creating FURTHERANCE has not yet been released, but we can now measure the size of the US response since there is a document that reduced the scope. On October 14, 1968 President Lyndon Johnson restricted the scope of FURTHERANCE by permitting only a conventional, small-scale response; not a full nuclear response. Also under the LBJ policy change, the response "could go to either country—not both." It would take nine years for the LBJ document to be declassified after the original request under the Freedom Of Information Act. The change document that summarized the original FURTHERANCE and the moderations to it was called *"Notes of the President's Meeting of October 14, 1968, 1:40 PM."* It was marked EYES ONLY FOR THE PRESIDENT. The extent of FURTHERANCE was not known until the 1968 document was posted to the National Security Archives Briefing Book No. 406 on December 12, 2012. The document is shown as Appendix J. It was declassified by a mandatory review of documents from the LBJ Library.

TAKING A DEEP BREATH

By 1961 it became apparent to a great number of people that nuclear proliferation combined with the war powers of military leaders had now grown far out of proportion to the needs of national defense. President Eisenhower had been "alarmed, surprised, and horrified" about SIOP, and said "...it frightens the devil out of me." His science advisor said it would "kill four or five times over somebody who is already dead." With his experience in WWII, Eisenhower was keenly aware of the possibility of 'leadership decapitation,'— one nuclear weapon on Washington effectively wiping out the government of the United States. No other target could offer such high returns from so little expenditure of weapons. To defend against the risk of leadership decapitation, Eisenhower had signed the secret Predeligation Authority in 1957 that gave the five commanders the authority to go to war. Then in January 1961, four days before the end of his administration, he seemed to be deeply concerned about the gravity of the situation. He gave his farewell address that told of the 'military-industrial complex' and warned the nation of the potential of the disastrous rise of misplaced power. Eisenhower was a revered military leader and respected president and this may have been his method of trying to slow down the trend toward a more aggressive nuclear posture of the country.

Kennedy officials became highly concerned about the hair-trigger tensions now in the system, and sought stronger safeguards against war caused by accidental or unauthorized actions, such as human or mechanical error. They wanted to make sure the strategic forces would react not only when duly authorized and directed, but also the forces would *not* initiate action when not so authorized and directed.

It seems we had passed safely through a narrow niche in our history when we were most vulnerable to accidental nuclear war. That window of time where a single commander, authorized by a specified set of circumstances to start such a war, began to close. General Thomas Power had certainly proven that he had the drive and determination to protect America from the mortal enemy of Communist aggression. The window was opened widest in January 1961, due to the sheer volume of functional nuclear weapons on bombers constantly in the air with the beginning of the SAC airborne alert. It began to close shortly afterwards when President Kennedy heard from his National Security Advisor McGeorge Bundy of the possibility that "a subordinated commander faced with a substantial Russian military action could start the thermonuclear holocaust on his own initiative." The year 1961 was the point of increase in instituting better physical safeguards, such as tamper-proof arming switches, better electro-mechanical locks, and PALs, the Permissive Action Links that would be developed to strengthen the physical and administrative controls over nuclear weapons. Starting in 1961, scientists at the Lawrence Radiation Laboratory turned their attention toward a PAL that would permanently disable itself and require the weapon to be disassembled to replace it when attempts were made to operate it by entering multiple codes. Such a device was in effect a pick-proof lock. By 1964, the Category B PAL featured this "lockout" feature in its design.

Yet the window of vulnerability to accidental war may never be fully closed. Future historians may decide that as dangerous as the Goldsboro Broken Arrow was, at least it pointed out the need for our national leaders to regain a sense of reason and logic in the prevention of accidental nuclear war.

Even with the information we now have about the Goldsboro Broken Arrow, we are still not sure what would have happened in the early morning hours of 24 January 1961. We may never know exactly how close we came to a nuclear detonation or even a war. But with what we know now, and judging how both the Kennedy administration and Sandia reacted in making weapons safer after Goldsboro, we would have to say that a nuclear detonation at Faro was at least considered a possibility in some degree and that possibility alone would make it extremely dangerous.

We would like to think that the scientists and engineers who built the weapons at that time did so with the best wisdom—the very best available. But there would be similar scientists and engineers who would also be designing systems later known as Chernobyl and Fukushima. The best we could learn from all three events, and the many others that could be just as serious, is that accidents are just that: accidents, and we should hope to minimize the possibility of disastrous outcomes with careful wisdom. We must remember the statement concerning accidental nuclear detonation made by the MIT physicist, "What isn't forbidden is compulsory. It will eventually happen. If the probability is not zero, it WILL happen." We should also remember that the Lesson will be repeated until it is learned.

There was an intriguing article in the April, 1981 issue of *Mother Jones Magazine* written by Gary Hanauer, where he interviewed Dr. Ralph Lapp, well known atomic scientist and the former Executive Director of the Department of Defense's Atomic Research and Development Board.

Dr. Lapp stated, "There were problems involved at the [Goldsboro bomb] site that I don't feel comfortable talking about."

He was asked about Ellsberg's statement that between the two bombs all six types of safety devices had failed. When asked specifically about the charges, Lapp replied to *Mother Jones*,' "You can't get that out of me."

"Are you denying that this failure is what happened?" Hanauer asked.

"No," he said. "But you won't get anything out of me."

"Then was the problem at the site something else?"

Lapp then paused a moment and said, "I can't tell you."

Grave sites photos by author.

Francis Roger Barnish. Master Sergeant, 97th Bomb Wing, US Air Force. World War II. Buried at Raleigh National Cemetery, 501 Quarry Road, Raleigh, North Carolina, at Section 4, Plot 130. The grave is under a huge oak tree, north of the entrance, near the main gate. The cemetery is now at capacity, and is well maintained by the Salisbury, NC, National Cemetery. Next to Frank's grave is an unmarked grave. Records at Salisbury show that it is of his wife, June.

Decorations are: Air Medal with Two Oak Leaf Clusters, Purple Heart, POW Medal, World War II Victory Medal, and the Korean Service Medal.

Eugene H. Richards. Major, 4241st Strategic Wing, US Air Force, World War II. Buried at Stephens-Memorial Gardens, 3650 Georgia Highway 17/Big A Road, Toccoa, Georgia. Fountain Section 4, Lot E-13, Space 3. Buried with wife Sue who died on 8 Jan. 1966, five years after her husband.

Decorations are: Air Medal With Seven Oak Leaf Clusters, World War II Victory Medal.

Eugene Shelton. Major, 4241st Strategic Wing, US Air Force, World War II. Buried at Fort Sam Houston National Cemetery, 1520 Harry Wurzbach Road, San Antonio, Texas. Section H, Plot 355-A. Next to him was the grave of his wife that was unmarked in 2010. I now understand from family members that her grave is now marked. Eugene Shelton had enlisted at age twenty-two at "Fort Sam," the place where he is now buried.

Decorations: Air Force Commendation Medal.

Chapter 9. After Goldsboro

The Goldsboro accident happened during the long decade when we were starting to look hard at all things nuclear. We invented safety devices for the weapons and began to seriously explore nuclear energy for peace. Just four years before the crash of *Keep 19*, the first nuclear power plant opened at Shippingport, Pennsylvania, operated solely for peaceful use. We were delighted—we thought we had invented something new, but we really only discovered it. It had been there all along since the dawn of creation. After all, the sun is a continuous chain of nuclear explosions, which makes our attempts to mimic it seem puny. We were in a new era. We thought we had the answers to our increasing need for energy. In his book *Future Shock*, Eric Toffler stated that most of the energy ever expended on Earth has been both created and consumed in just one lifetime: our own.

Nationally, we were at the top of our game; we were aware of enemies and knew we had the ability to retaliate against our primary foe, the Soviets, if such a need arose. After all, we had SAC and LeMay. Curtis LeMay had little to do directly with the Manhattan Project in the 1940s, but he was just the right man to take what they had built and use it to create the behemoth that became SAC in the 1960s.

Prior to the Goldsboro crash, actual physical control of nuclear weapons in SAC B-52 bombers resided only within the aircraft itself. It was up to the agreement of three key officers on board: the radar/navigator, the aircraft commander, and the electronics warfare officer. They were the ones who decoded the radio message, agreed to it's intent, then matched it up to the secured tickets from the secrets box, and only then perform the many steps of weapons release. That was the overall purpose of the Human Reliability Program—psychological evaluations to insure those men could be trusted and relied upon at all cost. Other than the receipt of the coded message, there was no external input into weapons release. And once the bomb was released from the aircraft, there was no external signal to force it into a safe mode.

However, there were some very logical devices built into the weapon system to impede accidental release or detonation: Both the pilot's readiness switch and the EW's manual cable lock handle required an external action by crew members. This is known as a strong link—a mechanical device that must be properly activated. The same thing applied to the ARM/SAFE switch, which was controlled by the radar navigator. A *strong link* isolates a weapon's firing set and detonators from all electrical signals. A *weak link* is designed to fail during a fire or accident before the strong link can be utilized. One example of a weak link is a Mylar capacitor in a weapon *fire set*. If the weapon experienced an excessively high temperature, such as in a fuel fire, the Mylar would melt and prevent the weapon firing signal from going to the detonators. A weak link would be any of the other devices that would *fail to dud*. In other words, a failure of this device would not allow a subsequent action to occur.

Even though the crew of *Keep 19* did absolutely nothing to start the arming process at any time during the flight, and those two bombs were in a secured mode when they were flung out of the aircraft, this accident became the tipping point in nuclear weapon safety procedures. President Kennedy, shocked by the close call of Goldsboro, ordered that all weapons safeguards be reexamined to reduce the possibility of an accident. His order led weapons designers to equip weapons with better electronic locks called Permissive Action Links, or PALs, ensuring that only the president's authority could launch a nuclear attack. In the spring of 1961, there were a series of hearings in Congress, where Sandia presented the first prototype. PALS would not be used until early in the Kennedy era. This effectively eliminated the possibility of a single commander of being able to launch the nuclear force on his own.

When single pilot aircraft were equipped with nuclear weapons, they would be locked by PALS, and the pilot would not received the unlock code until en route to the target. The only exception to the policy was in time of war, when an enemy attack was considered imminent, such as the Cuban Missile Crisis of 1962. The urgent need for PALs was never more apparent than in 1958, when single-pilot F-100s, each armed with a nuclear weapon, sitting on runway alerts in Incirlick, Turkey. The aircraft were protected by one Turkish enlisted man with an unloaded sidearm. Any pilot in any such aircraft had the opportunity to take off and release that nuclear weapon on his own. The squadron commander later said, "Nuclear safety was so loose, it jars your imagination. In retrospect, there were some guys you wouldn't trust with a .22 rifle, much less a thermonuclear bomb."

Many of the PALs safety procedures were the brainchild

of Dr. John Foster, a physicist of the Livermore Corporation, in cooperation with Sandia Laboratories and Western Electric. In 1962 after the Goldsboro incident, such procedures designed by Dr. Foster were adopted into the US nuclear arsenal and later NATO. There would be many other generations of PALs and strong-link/weak-link modifications following Goldsboro, all to help strengthen the potential weaknesses of the ARM/SAFE switch as pointed out in the 1998 Sandia Report.

Regardless of all the safety policy procedures, the joint authority for national nuclear activity, the Atomic Energy Commission and the Department of Defense, made clear the reality: "Nuclear weapons are designed with great care to explode only when deliberately armed and fired. Nevertheless, there is always a possibility that, as a result of accidental circumstances, an explosion will take place inadvertently. Although all conceivable precautions are taken to prevent them, such accidents might occur in areas where weapons are assembled and stored, during the course of loading and transportation on the ground, or when actually in the delivery vehicle, e.g., an airplane or a missile." (AEC/DOD, *The Effects of Nuclear Weapons, 1962*).

Robert McNamara said, "We all make mistakes. There *is* a learning period—but there isn't going to be a learning period in nuclear weapons. You make *one mistake,* nations are going to be destroyed."

Two Examples of Mistakes

Here are just two events after Goldsboro that have been declassified, out of several incidents that never made it to the Broken

Arrow category, but which demonstrate how small mistakes could have resulted into something much more serious.

October 25, 1962. Volk Field, Wisconsin. A cautionary tale of the times during the Cuban Missile Crisis. Nuclear-armed F-101s and F-106s had been dispersed to civilian airfields all over the country in a plan to avoid destruction by Russian or Cuban missiles. Some of the airfields were used mainly as auxiliary training landing strips, and were not operational airports. At one airport in California, Siskiyou County Airport, there was "virtually nothing except a runway and a converted dental van that served as a control tower." At Duluth, Minnesota, a guard fired at an intruder coming over the fence, triggering alarms to go off all over the network. At Volk Field, Wisconsin, there was no hangar for the alert planes, no ILS, no Klaxon, and no control tower. The pilots raced to their planes at Volk, each armed with a MB-1 Genie nuclear-tipped missile. The assumption was they would head north to intercept the Soviet Bears and Bisons believed to be swarming over the pole. Lieutenant Dan Barry was taxing into position on the runway in a snowstorm when a Jeep with lights flashing kept coming down the runway straight at his aircraft. A message had come in from Duluth canceling the alert. Since there was no control tower at Volk, the only way to stop the jet was by physically blocking the runway. Back at Duluth guards had found out the fence-climbing intruder was a bear.

June 3 and 6, 1980. A NORAD computer at Colorado Springs, Colorado, registered an alarm indicating a massive Soviet missile attack. One hundred nuclear-armed B-52s were alerted for immediate takeoff. The mistake was caught and the bombers stood down. Three days later the same identical warning was given. Again one hundred SAC bombers were alerted. The problem was traced to an integrated circuit in a computer, which was producing random digits that were reflected as missiles launched. This is reminiscent of the October 5, 1960, incident at Thule. NORAD received a "massive" Soviet ICBM strike approaching the United States. A computer fault removed two zeros in the radar ranging components and was picking up radar returns from the surface of the moon, which was rising for the first time after the system was activated in a certain configuration.

Under the twenty-four-hour airborne alert policy, if a mission had to be cut short for any reason another aircraft would immediately launch to fill the slot, which, in turn, would either move up another mission behind it or stretch out current missions out. Every SAC crew member was very aware of the intense pressure to continue every single mission regardless of problems that turned up in flight, some of which continued into accidents caused by bad decisions.

A good example of mission pressure and bad decisions occurred just seven weeks after the Goldsboro crash when a B-52, flying out of Mather Air Force Base, California, had a series of problems beginning with uncontrollable cabin heat and ending with a crash. While suffering for hours of unstoppable and unbearable 160° F heat in the cockpit, the crew attempted to cool the airplane by depressurizing it in order to continue the mission. Then they decided to go to a lower altitude, below 10,000 feet, to help revive two crew members who had gotten *the bends*. Glass in instruments and windows began to crack from the heat. At times, there was only one pilot on the top deck, trying to give the others relief. After twenty grueling hours, mental miscalculations of fuel used at the lower altitude began to mount up, but still they were making every effort to continue. But they curiously refused at least one offer for a extra tanker downrange, as well as landing at alternative sites. When the critical low-fuel situation was finally recognized for what it was, a rescue launch of a re-fueling tanker aircraft was quickly made in an attempt to meet the low-flying bomber and save it, but the B-52 actually ran out of fuel within sight of the tanker, and crashed near Yuba City, California. Unlike *Keep 19* all eight crew members successfully bailed out while the aircraft was still flying straight and level. The two thermonuclear bombs on board were safely recovered from the crash site.

The above description of the Yuba City crash is a summary of the official accident report. But there was another contributing cause, according to rumors among SAC officers of that era. Impaired judgement of the crew was suspected as been caused by a reaction to 'go-pills,' also known as Dextroamphetamine, or 'little red battle pills.' This was a delicate subject since amphetamine is now considered a Schedule II Substance by the federal government and its use in civil aviation is forbidden. But in the days of Chrome Dome and the twenty-four hour airborne alert, a different war time priority was in effect. 'Go pills' were routinely made available to crew members on a voluntary basis before they launched on long missions where their lives could be at stake. At that time, the pills were considered about the same as strong coffee, or 'No-Doz.' The Air Force approved the 'go-pills' for voluntary use in 1960, according to several retired officers, among them Colonel Rich Graham, a former pilot of the SR-71 'Blackbird.'

The first reported used of Dexedrine was in the airborne alert test called Head Start. That was the third in the series of airborne alert tests, and it was to use bombers loaded with MK-39s or MK-15s and fly them over Greenland and Canada. It would use eight to twelve loaded B-52s in the air for every hour of the day and each bomber would be in the air for twenty-four hours. President Eisenhower authorized the Head Start test on March 9, 1959, and it continued for 29,400 flying hours and had twenty-one hundred aerial refuelings without a serious accident. The flight surgeon monitoring the crews was impressed because "few personnel felt the need for stimulants during the flights."

The official use of such stimulants was not just limited to the military. Ann Whitman, President Eisenhower's secretary, said that the stress from her boss sometimes made the going hard for her, especially during his heart attack period. She admitted to a friend, "I am in one of my I-hate-people moods," and added, "I live on dexamyl, I call them 'jolly pills.'" She was supplied the mood enhancer containing a barbiturate and amphetamine, by Ike's personal physician, Dr. Howard Snyder. He also provided them to staff and reporters, but not to the President.

"Fatigue from sustained operations can place pilots at severe risk from decreased alertness unless effective fatigue-management strategies are used," said Dr. John Caldwell, a scientist with the Air Force Research Laboratory's fatigue countermeasures branch at Brooks City-Base, San Antonio. In a document called *Performance Maintenance During Continuous Flight Operations,* anonymous surveys among pilots who flew in the 1991 Persian Gulf War indicated 60 percent of the pilots said they used Dexedrine. It was found that without performance enhancing drugs, performance by pilots in single-seat aircraft degraded by 60 to 100 percent below fully rested levels. The use of such drugs by the military in life-or-death situations had been done since the Battle of Britain, and continues today. While it was obviously a policy in the 1960s by the US military, there was no official connection with the Yuba City crash. The word in the 1960s was that the 'go pills' were considered as not addictive but helpful, except for the headaches afterwards. Medical literature now indicates that amphetamines can have severe side effects, the worst of which is called "amphetamine psychosis." It causes hallucinations as well as paranoid delusions.

SAC bomber crews that had them available on long flights usually took one pill before the second refueling and again right before landing. It was said that it made the pilots the 'sharpest in the universe.' And we, as a nation, demanded absolute performance perfection in our guardians and protectors.

In the case of the Yuba City crash, the most glaring pilot errors were the decisions to refuse an offered refueling tanker earlier in the mission, to bypass several alternate landing sites, and to descend to any level, much less to 10,000 feet where they would run out of fuel much quicker. At least one very experienced instructor pilot has said that such a descent was not necessary at all, for that was why crew members' helmets came equipped with oxygen masks. Shortly after the Yuba City crash, the little red pills were suddenly no longer readily available from SAC flight surgeons. Then there was another rumor that when CINCSAC (General Power) heard what had happened at Yuba City, he ripped his red phone from the wall and threw it through his office window.

About Classified, Really Classified, and De-Classified

There were four levels of security classification in effect at wing level:

CONFIDENTIAL

SECRET

TOP SECRET

TOP SECRET CRYPTO.

The pilots and navigators were cleared for TOP SECRET CRYPTO. There was another category, TOP SECRET CRYPTO-ESI, which stood for Extra Sensitive Information, to be used on specific missions, usually on a one-time basis. ESI was created as a special category for SIOP material.

Whenever an officer with a TOP SECRET CRYPTO clearance was permanently transferred from a base, a portion of his Personnel out-processing included a peculiar but required security debriefing. This had to be done by a commissioned officer with special authority and it consisted of the officer who was being transferred, in his flight suit and sometimes armed, standing in front of a nervous second lieutenant, signing and swearing a solemn oath that he would promptly forget any TOP SECRET CRYPTO information that he had in his head under penalty of a fine of a bunch of money and years in jail. The lieutenant did not have the foggiest idea of what type information had just been forgotten, neither did he have the need to know, and he certainly would not ask. His job was simply to "debrief" the departing officer.

Jim Oskins and Mike Maggelet are two retired former Air Force specialists who between them have over thirty-five years of experience working in nuclear weapons technology. Everything they report has been declassified. They have completed their second book on Broken Arrows. (*Broken Arrow Volume II, A Disclosure of Significant U.S., Soviet, and British Nuclear Weapon Accidents and Accidents, 1945-2008*). In their first book they set the number of US Broken Arrows at thirty-six, the number announced by the Department of Defense in 1980. Now they are raising the total to around sixty based on recently declassified materials and indicate there may be more, but the declassification process could run for several years. They point out that they have never encountered any efforts by any government agency to cover up or hinder their research. The main problem they ran into was the poor conditions of the historical records and there is no single agency source for requests under the Freedom of Information Act. They also point out that there has never been even a partial, inadvertent US nuclear detonation reported. All detonations involved conventional high explosives only.

They found an interesting document entitled, *Jettisoning Of Nuclear Weapons from DOD Aircraft* that outlines procedures on how to handle press statements to the general public. "If the (jettisoned) weapon lands in circumstances such as to be publicly unobserved, no statement should be indicated." In other words, if nobody in the civilian world saw it, it would not be reported to the press. If no one saw it, it didn't happen.

After *Keep 19* many details surrounding the crash at Goldsboro remained hidden for years behind the cloak of secrecy in accordance with Department Of Defense policy. Now, fifty years later, important records are being declassified. Although normal DOD policy is to neither confirm nor deny the presence of nuclear weapons, recently revised DOD Directive 5230.16, which governs public affairs, allows for confirmation when it is deemed necessary for public safety or it is needed to reduce widespread public alarm. *The Accident Report* itself, (AF Form 14 including *Findings*) has now been declassified and located, as well as the crew's *History Of Flight,* along with the 1998 study by Sandia Corporation entitled *The History of Nuclear Safety Devices. The Explosive Ordnance Disposal Report*, written by First Lieutenant Jack ReVelle, EOD team commander has been discovered. Internal letters with reports from the Atomic Energy Commission are now available. Of course, some words and phrases are still redacted, or blacked out, but by using the details now available plus other reliable sources there are two things now apparent: the collapse of the right wing was caused by the massive fuel loss caused by a design failure; and at least to some degree, we came close to nuclear disaster.

The Lady with the Microphone

In 2011 Adam Mattocks said about the crash: "I feel bad about the crash, the crew did everything they could to save the plane and to protect the community. It was our mission to be ready to deliver that weapon onto the target, wherever that target might be—and to get out of there fast. If we got out, we knew we probably would not survive getting back into our own country, for our own country would be so much on the defensive that we would probably get shot down by our own people, that is, even if we got out of Russia. All of the targets were deep inside Russia and we would have a lot of mainland to go over, a long way to go to get out. We knew we would have to go to a neutral country, and either land there or bail out there if we ran out of fuel."

When Adam Mattocks was talking about getting shot down by our own forces after a nuclear bombing mission, he was referring to the concern called "Safe Passage." It was a problem SAC was trying to work out. Outbound SAC bombers might be identified as enemy and shot down by the Nike Hercules air defense missiles with forty-kiloton nuclear warheads. Likewise, inbound bombers would be in the chaos of the attack and could be hit by European allies armed with the same missile. The only solution at the time was to increase the number of safe-passage corridors and to train crews about them and hope for the best.

Adam was standing out in a field next to Big Daddy's Road at the site of the crash half a century after it all happened. It was a bright, chilly day, a lot like that day in 1961, and it was very windy. A cold front was coming through just like then. A pretty lady was interviewing him with a microphone in her hand, a television cameraman behind her, recording Adam for the night's news. We were standing with Dr. Jack ReVelle, who had carried the core of an atomic bomb in his hands up a ladder at that very spot in that field fifty years ago. Shortly before, Jack and I were hunkered over a GPS receiver, finding a coordinate. This was the spot. We looked up and saw a caravan of cars, SUVs, and TV satellite trucks pulling off the road on to the dirt lane where we were. "What is this, the *Field Of Dreams?*" asked Jack. The vehicles were strung out along the dirt road in the field. People were arriving for the memorial dinner at the Faro Fire Department, and wanted to see the actual spot of the buried bomb component.

271

I was watching the lady with the microphone as she asked Adam and Jack the important questions, thinking ahead, guiding the interview to cover all the important points. She was so caught up in the story that she began to lose focus a little bit. And at some point, just for a few minutes, she stopped being the reporter; she became someone who was fascinated by what she heard, just listening to the real history of that place told by two men who had never met before, and who had not been back to this place in fifty years. The cameraman behind her asked Adam a question, not to get the interview back on track but because he, the cameraman, wanted to hear more about the details of the place where he was standing. He, too, was caught up in the history. Adam paused, gathering his thoughts. He spoke in careful, measured words. He looked away to the west, toward the sun, like he was trying to peer through the mists of time. He turned around as if to fix himself at the correct spot on Earth. Maybe he was remembering his prayers of that night, and measuring himself against those promises made. Something very important to all of us was going on here.

"Every member of that crew should be honored in some way. Some gave their lives... ."

Fifty years ago both of these men arrived at that same spot, a few hours apart, by jet aircraft: Adam Mattocks by jumping out of a disintegrating B-52, Jack ReVelle by a T-33, a special delivery from Wright-Patterson Air Force Base to Seymour Johnson Air Force Base.

Historical Marker at Eureka

Over a year later, on June 29, 2012, and under a cloudless Carolina blue sky and heat of around 100 degrees, there was a public gathering at the only intersection in Eureka, North Carolina. Over 200 people gathered there for the dedication of North Carolina Highway Historical Marker Number F-70 to commemorate the crash of *Keep 19*. This spot is about three miles west of the Faro Volunteer Fire Station, and is the closest point that meets the traffic standards of the Commission. The ceremony began at noon with an invocation by the Chaplain of the Wayne County Veterans Coalition, and the US flag was presented by the color guard of the same organization. The approval and placement of the highway marker was the result of a long personal effort by Goldsboro attorney Mr. Tommy Jarrett, who was assisted by Lieutenant Colonel Wilton Strickland, USAF (Retired), and the author. After introductions and comments by the appropriate dignitaries, the marker was unveiled by Adam Mattocks, assisted by Tommy Jarrett. Then Dr. Jack ReVelle, from California, gave a short talk and introduced three members of his original Explosive Ordnance Team who worked the 1961 Broken Arrow. They were Larry Lack, from Georgia, Mel Baker, from Arkansas, and Larry Cato, from Michigan. The fourth surviving member of his team, Robert Collins, was unable to attend due to health reasons. This was the first time in fifty years these men have been back together.

Adam Mattocks, the only surviving member of the B-52 bomber crew, not only spoke to the crowd from the outdoor podium, he gave numerous interviews to newspapers and TV news stations, he signed his autograph in books, and posed for photos with a great many people who thanked him profusely.

Immediately after that ceremony, the crowd moved three miles east to the Faro Volunteer Fire Station where a stainless steel plaque was unveiled on the outside wall. The plaque was to honor the first responders and the members of the bomber crew, and it was unveiled by Earl and Mary Lancaster. Mary was one of the original eyewitnesses to the crash and her husband Earl was the first fireman responding to the crash site.

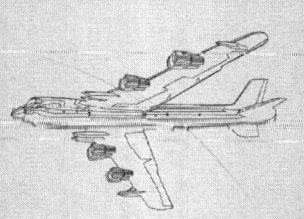

The Volunteer Firemen of Faro, North Carolina

On 24 January 1961, volunteers from this fire station were the

First to Respond

To a deadly B-52 crash 1.6 miles south, when the aircraft suffered a structural wing failure in mid-air. Three crew members died and two thermonuclear (hydrogen) bombs fell from the disintegrating aircraft. Both bombs were safely recovered by the EOD (Explosive Ordnance Disposal) Detachment from Wright Patterson Air Force Base, Dayton, Ohio, led by Lieutenant Jack B. ReVelle. A non-explosive bomb component remains buried near the B-52 crash site.
This accident is known as the "Goldsboro Broken Arrow."

Based at Seymour Johnson AFB, Crew R-10, members of
the Strategic Air Command, USAF were:

Major Walter Scott Tulloch, Pilot
Captain Richard Rardin, Co-Pilot
Lieutenant Adam Mattocks, 3rd Pilot
Major Gene Shelton, Radar/Navigator (did not survive)
Captain Paul Brown, Navigator
Lieutenant William Wilson, EWO
Sergeant Frank Barnish, Gunner (did not survive)
Major Eugene Richards, EWO Instructor (did not survive)

Plaque honoring the first responders and the B-52 crew, on the Faro Volunteer Fire Station.

This plaque was dedicated on June 29, 2012.

Photo by author.

Then the group moved out of the baking summer heat to a nearby air-conditioned church where a meal of classic North Carolina barbecue, cooked all night by Billy Reeves, was served up to the entire group. A Major from the Salvation Army presented Jack ReVelle and the other EOD team members with personalized Salvation Army coffee mugs, in remembrance of that cold night in the mud where Jack first learned to drink coffee. Official letters of appreciation to each of the team members was presented by the Wayne County Commissioners. There were more talks, a lot of hugs, great food, and then the playing of Taps, to remember the three crew members who died.

The people of Faro and surrounding Wayne County have never had an opportunity to thank the people involved in this tragedy and their heroic efforts from a half century ago. Most of the people did not even know of the presence or duties of the EOD team at that time. The team just came there and did that very important job. One lady went up to one of the team members, Larry Lack, and thanked him for allowing her to grow up.

Larry had to excuse himself for a few minutes and step outside.

The firemen of the Faro Volunteer Fire Department received a hand-written thank-you note from Betty Tulloch, of Del Mar, California. It now hangs in the fire station. She is the widow of Lieutenant Colonel Walter Scott Tulloch, the aircraft commander of *Keep 19*.

The members of the original EOD team shared stories of their visit of fifty years ago. They said they were very well treated by the people at Seymour Johnson, given whatever uniforms and personal effects they needed. They said they were welcomed at the Non-Commissioned Officers Club on base in their time off. One night they played bingo with other NCOs at the club, and won the pot, which was "pretty big." They donated the entire winnings to the widow of their fellow NCO, Frank Barnish, the gunner.

Crash Prevention

At some point the question has to be asked: could some sort of crew intervention have prevented the crash of *Keep 19*? The short answer is no. The fact is, there was no way the crew could have kept the wing on that aircraft. They did nothing to cause or exacerbate the situation. They had no knowledge of the extensive damage of the lateral wing controls, and that kept them from making different decisions early on that might have possibly limited the loss of life. The experts on the ground had told them that the only problem they had was the fuel leak and that was already resolved. There was no mention of the wing design problem that was then known only at the higher command levels. They were completely unaware of the growing problem inside their own right wing. The crew knew that Boeing had been contacted by the command post, but they didn't know that Boeing had not yet called back with any helpful information.

There is the question of why didn't Major Tulloch use up more fuel before attempting a landing? They answer is, he wanted to: he wanted more orbits out over the ocean east of Wilmington to burn fuel, and said so in his narrative, but he was overruled by the wing commander who ordered him to return to Seymour Johnson. Apparently the wing commander was very worried about the electrical, fuel pump, and other problems that were going wrong with that flight and he wanted them back at the base quickly. It is not known if he knew of the history of structural collapse of the G model wing. But the mission pressure of Chrome Dome was extremely important, more important and bigger than anything SAC had ever handed him before, and he was walking that fine hard line called command decision.

If the crew could somehow have known everything about what was about to happen, they might have gone for a no-flaps landing. But even that is a huge gamble with two engines out, the possibility of fire, and the risk of leaking more fuel. Major Tulloch even made the comment in his narrative, "In combat the rule had been to never lower the flaps if you had a damaged wing." They didn't know if the wing was damaged or even if the flaps would work at all, that's why the Command Post wanted a flaps test at a higher altitude. When Tulloch started the flaps test, Approach Control had them begin the intercepting turn to the airport.

It was known that the B-52 was not stressed for negative g-forces and was limited to sixty degrees of bank, which meant it had to be flown strictly by the charts in the pilot manual. Exceeding sixty degrees of bank could lead to a stall and the wings to fail—that was already known to have happened.

Another B-52 pilot said, "If you had a choice, and could get the guys on the bottom out, and if things turned to [bad word] during the final approach, better to have only the guys with the upwards seats." Major Tulloch said that he wanted to bail out everyone but himself and the co-pilot but he needed the navigators to guide them around populated areas in the dark. There was no way for the extras to bail out without the navigator ejecting.

Major Tulloch said, "I'd flown many a bombing raid at night and those folks sleeping down there [in North Carolina] were depending on us to defend them, not rain flaming death and destruction on them in the middle of the night." And Major Walter Scott Tulloch was completely successful in that goal. He did not rain flaming death and destruction on the people of Faro. It may have been strictly a matter of chance, or perhaps divine intervention, but not a single person on the ground was killed or hurt in any way.

To quote a former pilot, when pressed for some Monday morning quarterbacking: "So without knowing what transpired with the guys on the ground and the discussions with Boeing, I would hesitate to second-guess the guys on the sharp end. I just can't judge the guy in charge. Especially if he's no longer around to defend himself. But there was no way he could have prevented that crash. Just no way."

The Danger Today

There are three apparent dangers at Faro today:

The biggest danger is the presence of any toxic materials from the Secondary in the ground between 72 and 180 feet down, just north of the old cemetery on Big Daddy's Road. The 72-foot depth was based on the EOD's maximum 50-foot probe of the hole of travel of the Secondary, which was done from the 22-foot level of the dig. The 180-foot depth, plus or minus 10 feet, was based on the University of North Carolina study. Although the exact depth is not known, the geographical location of that danger from the Secondary is known:

it is beneath the 400-foot circle easement that is listed in public land records. That is, unless fragmented materials have migrated downstream in the underground aquifer. See BOMB LOCATIONS in the attached Appendix F.

The second greatest danger is any souvenir .50 caliber bullet sitting in someone's closet. Fifty caliber bullets are very powerful and these would be either incendiary, explosive, or armor piercing, designed to shoot down enemy aircraft and missiles. If any were still around today, fifty years later, they would be very unstable and extremely dangerous. If someone banged one around it could go off and either burn the house down, explode, or shoot through their house. It would be a supreme tragedy if the only Faro casualty from the Goldsboro Broken Arrow was the death or injury of someone's grandchild, or great-grandchild, years after the crash of *Keep 19*. The chief of the Faro Fire department has agreed to handle any reported shells with the explosive ordnance disposal flight commander at Seymour Johnson Air Force Base. That announcement has been made at every event where the author speaks about the Goldsboro Broken Arrow. There were about twenty-four hundred bullets in the four tail guns of *Keep 19*. We do not know how many shells have been recovered and turned in.

The third potential danger could be whatever is in those fifty-five gallon metal drums buried in a deep hole north of bomb site two. They probably contain oil- or fuel-soaked dirt. Protection of the environment was not an important issue in the 1960s, like it is today. That location is unknown, but it is somewhere north of the cemetery on Big Daddy's Road.

In a report by the Los Alamos Laboratory, which was obtained in 2004, the protocol for making the Faro site safe concluded: "After the aircraft debris was removed, the bomb crater was filled, the impact area was purchased, a concrete slab poured over the area, the area fenced, and notices posted prohibiting digging."

As Scott Hardy said in his thesis, "All the measures seem reasonable and responsible to secure the site. Sadly, in the above statement, 'The bomb crater was filled' seems to be the only true portion. The others, based on testimony of witnesses and the landowner, are falsehoods. The area was never purchased by the government, never had a concrete slab poured over the top, has never been fenced in, and the only signs that have been put in the area have been posted for the purpose of hunting."

"The question must be asked," Hardy continued, "Why would the United States Government produce a classified document for the use of scientists at Los Alamos that contains obvious fabrications of procedures to insure the public safety? The only rational conclusion is that the statements in the document are what should have been done to secure the site. But it appears the only procedures ever initiated by the government were those in the statement on the easement agreed to by Charles Davis. When Mr. Davis read the document, he laughed and said, 'None of this is true.' Sadly, Davis is right. The site is clearly visible from the road. None of the measurements laid out in the Los Alamos document seem to have ever been implemented."

The cost of locating and recovering the Secondary at Faro was quoted at the time to be $500,000 in 1961 dollars. Today that would equal around $3.6 billion. The plutonium is probably still contained within the metal cylinder—that is, if it was not damaged on impact or during its 180-foot foot travel down through the soft, wet earth of the Nahunta Swamp. There was no trace of radiation down to as far as they could dig, around 45 feet, so it was probably OK that far. But we don't know what happened from that point on down. The long-term danger of just leaving it alone is a question yet to be answered.

A message from Los Alamos Laboratories the Atomic Energy Commission on 4 April 1961, stated that the uranium compound will be absorbed in the soil within a few feet of the "object" and that they can foresee no hazard unless someone drilled a well immediately adjacent to it. A dilution in one and a half million gallons of water would reduce the concentration below tolerance levels. "Nevertheless we recommend that a sample of the water be analyzed to determine the natural uranium background for the record so that if in the future traces of uranium are found in the ground water, this object will not be blamed for more than its actual contribution.….In this case, all that is necessary to assure future safety is to prevent drinking the ground water obtained within say one hundred feet of the hole for a year or so.….In any case it is the considered advice of the LASL that some water samples be taken for analysis and the hole be filled up and forgotten."

We should keep Faro in mind as we watch how the world wrestles with two new ongoing Level Seven nuclear accidents. We should also count the costs of those accidents as they add up.

PART III.
DE-BRIEF

Chapter 10. Comparison With Chernobyl and Fukushima

The $3.6 billion cost of recovery from the Faro nuclear accident is minuscule compared to two others—the 2011 Japanese disaster and the 1986 Chernobyl disaster. There was horrible radiation poisoning at both sites, none at Goldsboro. At Chernobyl, a new two billion dollar shield is now being planned for the Russian reactor, to replace the crumbling steel and concrete sarcophagus currently surrounding it. When the sarcophagus was built in the 1990s it was thought that it could contain the escaping radiation from the reactor fire. It was designed "like a house of cards," said Eric Schmieman of the Battele Memorial Institute. It was just pieces of metal leaning against one another and hooked together. "There are no welded joints or bolted joints—it wouldn't take much of a seismic event to knock it down." The roof of the Chernobyl containment building is now starting to collapse due to snowfall, as of February 2013. "But there is no danger of radiation," so said Ukrainian officials.

We have found that radiation does unusual things to steel and concrete, and we don't have a lot of experience in measuring radiation effects on huge masses of steel and concrete. That falls under the category of "things we are now learning the hard way."

The new containment device will be a half-dome built on rails beside the wreckage and then rolled over it. When it is finished the shield will be the largest movable structure in the world, taller than the Statue of Liberty at its highest point, and will weigh twenty thousand tons. Supposedly it was designed to last for one hundred years, hopefully long enough for workers to get inside to dismantle the reactor site. It will also have three remotely controlled cranes inside to assist. So far the Russians have agreed to pay only one percent of the cost. They say it happened in the Ukraine, which is now no longer part of Russia. The project remains unfunded. European Union nations have promised to pay for half the cost. The accident happened almost thirty years ago, and it will probably take another twenty to build the shield after the funding is found.

When Chernobyl happened it was reported as the worst nuclear disaster in history, a Level Seven on the International Nuclear Event Scale. Japanese officials now say the Fukushima disaster has skipped from Level Five (Accident with Wider Consequences), right over Level Six (Serious), straight to Level Seven, a Major Accident. Now there have been two Level Seven nuclear accidents in the world, Chernobyl and Fukushima. Both on our watch.

The costs estimates of Chernobyl so far are:

18 billion rubles, about 12 billion US dollars, as estimated by the Russians

350,000 people relocated

500,000 workers involved in the cleanup

31 deaths of emergency workers at the time, could reach 4,000

or 985,000 deaths, as estimated by Russian publication, *Chernobyl*, between 1986-2004.

But that cost is only about five percent of a later 2011 estimate. Roubini Global Economics estimated that the total cost of Chernobyl to be around $235 billion and predicts the cost of Chernobyl will increase. A Wall Street Journal article in 1990 estimated the contaminated land to be a total loss for at least two generations, and concluded that "The total bill suggests that the Soviet Union may have been better off if they had never begun building nuclear reactors in the first place."

The costs of Fukushima so far are: 13,000 dead, with 13,000 missing. Other costs: to be determined.

Goldsboro compares to these two nuclear accidents only in *potential* destruction. But what is also comparable are the root causes. All three accidents began with the idea that we knew just about everything there was to know about consequences. In reality we are pretty pompous creatures. We tended to have a great deal of faith in ourselves in the fields of nuclear physics, aeronautics, natural, and other sciences. What we did not have, at least in the 1950s and 1960s, was a lot of experience in combining possible future anomalies and in estimating the results of those combinations.

For example: People had a good idea that television was going to be invented years before it actually was. They did not know all the properties of television transmission, but could foresee that it would, someday, be invented. Also, before man first walked on the moon a lot of people thought there was a good chance of that event happening at some point. They didn't know *how* or *when* it would

287

happen but they could visualize man on the moon years before it actually occurred. What few people could grasp, right up to shortly before it occurred, was the idea that billions of people on earth would be able to see the first man from Planet Earth walk on the moon via television. It was the connection of the two different concepts that was the surprise, relatively speaking.

To reduce the causes of these three accidents down to the basic points:

Chernobyl happened because of a combination of poor reactor design plus a bad management decision to run a test with inexperienced people and incorrectly calibrated Geiger counters. Then the tipping point occurred: another power plant on the same circuit unexpectedly shut down, which threw additional electrical demand onto Chernobyl. The crew did not know of the developing danger when the second unexpected power surge started the chain of events. The chain of *causes* was relatively slow and unimpressive, occurring over many years, but the conclusion was fast and dramatic.

Fukushima Daiichi happened because of a poorly designed reactor placed in the wrong location, combined with lax government oversight. The electrical generating plant, powered by nuclear energy, was built in the 1960s using the latest engineering and scientific methods at the time. It was designed to withstand a 7.9 magnitude earthquake, bigger than practically anyone could possibly imagine at that time. The unexpected 9.0 earthquake was *ten times bigger* than 7.9, and it caused a ten-meter tsunami to wash over a six-meter seawall and flood the cooling pumps, which started the chain of events. Again, the chain of *causes* was relatively slow, beginning with the design and placement decision half a century ago, but the conclusion was fast and dramatic when another element was added, the totally unexpected earthquake/tsunami tipping point.

The Goldsboro Broken Arrow happened because the G model B-52 wing structure was well designed for the aircraft's original mission, but was now inadequate for the new mission with the need for more fuel capacity. When the B-52 was designed in the 1940s and '50s, no one could visualize the need for a continuous twenty-four hour flight involving heavy-weight aerial refuelings. Then a fuel leak caused more pressure on a cracked wing panel than it could stand. The unexpected wing collapse was the final event of the aircraft catastrophe, not the beginning. Again: A slow chain of causes, with a fast tipping point.

This comparison is not intended to minimize any of the three events, but to point out that modern disasters usually do not have one cause; they have multiple causes. Usually, each cause is not beyond the realm of possibility in itself but can be very surprising and extremely unpredictable when combined with more unexpected events. With the compression of time and the increased level of seriousness, results can be catastrophic, and the costs of this new type of catastrophe, a nuclear catastrophe, can accumulate for a very long time. One could say it has a very long half-life.

At the beginning of this book I wrote that nature has a simple rule: The Lesson will be repeated until it is learned. Dr. Kenichi Ohmae of MIT agrees with that thought. He wrote for the Christian Science Monitor on April 5, 2012, that Fukushima's most important lesson is this: The probability theory (that nuclear disaster is unlikely) has failed us. If you have made assumptions, you are not prepared. Nuclear power plants should have multiple, reliable ways to cool reactors. Any nuclear plant that doesn't heed this lesson is inviting disaster. He said his investigation showed that the Fukushima accident could have been avoided if the plant had the capacity for electrical generation of any form along with the appropriate heat sink—a gravity-fed supply of water to cool down the reactor rods. No matter what happens, any reactor must have the ability to be brought to cold shutdown, which requires electricity and heat sinks. It is a pretty simple principle.

All the nuclear reactors in the world have been designed by the same set of probability assumptions. The Nuclear Regulatory Commission produced a memo entitled, "Probabilities That The Next Major Accident Occurs Within Prescribed Intervals." The memorandum states that the probability is less than 50/50 that the next (i.e., the first) major accident would occur within the next 400 reactor years.

That was on March 9, 1979. Less than three weeks later, the Unit 2 reactor at Three Mile Island suffered a meltdown of the radioactive fuel in the reactor core.

The Far Future

"Six weeks ago, when I first heard about the reactor damage at the Fukushima Daiichi plant in Japan, I knew the prognosis: if any of the containment vessels or fuel pools exploded, it would mean millions of new cases of cancer in the Northern Hemisphere." So said Dr. Helen Caldicott, a prominent physician known worldwide as a cofounder of Physicians for Social Responsibility. She says that we are decades away from seeing the full effects from the radioactive emissions from Chernobyl in 1986, and it will be the same for Fukushima. That wasn't the stance of some commentators who asserted that there were relatively low risks of another type of worry: genetic abnormalities in survivors' offspring.

"This is dangerously ill-informed and shortsighted; if anyone knows better, it's doctors like me. There's great debate about the number of fatalities following Chernobyl; the International Atomic Energy Agency has predicted that there will be only about four thousand deaths from cancer, but a 2009 report published by the New York Academy of Sciences says that almost one million people have already perished from cancer and other diseases. The high dose of radiation caused so many miscarriages that we will never know the number of genetically damaged fetuses that did not come to term. And both Belarus and Ukraine have group homes full of deformed children.

"As we know from Hiroshima and Nagasaki, it takes years to get cancer. Leukemia takes only five to ten years to emerge, but solid cancers take fifteen to sixty. Furthermore, most radiation-induced mutations are recessive; it can take many generations for two recessive genes to combine to form a child with a particular disease, like my specialty, cystic fibrosis. We can't possibly imagine how many cancers and other diseases will be caused in the far future by the radioactive isotopes emitted by Chernobyl and Fukushima."

Dr. Caldicott is in a controlled rage. She is furious, among other things, because radiation is so slow—if it were much faster everyone could see more easily the dangers it holds. She says doctors must do more than just treat cancer, they must enter the nuclear debate. Doctors know that there is no such thing as a safe dose of radiation, that radiation is cumulative, and that we all carry several hundred genes for disease. There are now more than twenty-six hundred genetic diseases on record and any one of which may be caused by radiation-induced mutation. At the beginning we had no sense about radiation-induced cancer. Marie Curie and her daughter didn't know that the radioactive materials they handled would kill them. They could not conceive of the need for their research notes and papers to be later stored in lead boxes. But it didn't take long for the early nuclear physicists, like Dr. Wright Langham in the Manhattan Project, to recognize the toxicity of radioactive elements. Dr. Caldicott says she knew many of those physicists well; she says physicists had the knowledge to begin the nuclear age, and that physicians have the credibility and legitimacy to end it.

She is also very explicit in describing the power that lobbyists have in the US Congress in giving attention to those in her own profession: "For many years now, physicists employed by the nuclear industry have been outperforming doctors, at least in politics and the news media. Since the Manhattan Project in the 1940s, physicists have had easy access to Congress. They had harnessed the energy inside the center of the sun, and later physicists, whether lobbying for nuclear weapons or nuclear energy, had the same power. They walk into Congress and Congress virtually prostrates itself. Their technological advancements are there for all to see: the harm will become apparent only decades later.

"Doctors, by contrast, have fewer dates with Congress, and much less access on nuclear issues. We don't typically go around discussing the latent period of carcinogenesis and the amazing advances made in understanding radiology. But as a result, we do an inadequate job of explaining the long-term dangers of radiation to policymakers and the public."

Pipe Cleaning

"In the fall of 2007, workers at the Byron nuclear power plant in Illinois were using a wire brush to clean a badly corroded steel pipe—one in a series that circulate cooling water to essential emergency equipment—when something unexpected happened: the brush poked through. The resulting leak caused a twelve-day shutdown of the two reactors for repairs. The plant's owner, the Exclon Corporation had long known that corrosion was thinning most of the pipes. But rather than fix them, it repeatedly lowered the minimum thickness it deemed safe. By the time the pipe broke, Exelon had declared that pipe walls just three-hundredths of an inch thick—less than one-tenth the original minimum thickness—would be good enough.... No documented inspections of the pipe was made by anyone for the NRC for at least the last eight years preceding the leak, and the agency also failed to notice that Exelon kept lowering the acceptable standard."

New York Times, Sunday, May 8, 2011

Tornado

On April 29, 2011 the worst tornado outbreak in forty years ripped through seven southern states killing over 360 people. Tuscaloosa,

Alabama, "looks like Hiroshima" after a mile-wide tornado struck that town. TVA's Browns Ferry nuclear plant thirty miles west of Huntsville, went off-line due to the storm. Emergency generators kept the water pumps going, keeping the reactor cores covered.

Browns Ferry also happens to be the source of the worst, but not widely reported, nuclear accident in America, at least until Three Mile Island occurred four years later. On March 22, 1975, two electricians at the Browns Ferry plant were down under the control room checking for air leaks in the wiring tunnel that ran between reactors. They were using strips of spongy material to seal the leaks, at arm's length in a wiring chase, a tight utility tunnel. They were testing for airflow from the leaks by using a lighted candle and watching the direction of the flame. The material they were using to fill the cracks was extremely flammable polyurethane foam.

The insulation sparked when a gust pulled the candle flame into a gap in the wiring chase. A major fire resulted and a combination of events almost led to a nuclear core meltdown. The fire severed control, communications, and the telemetry and data links between the control room and the reactor core. Other problems were soon discovered: the plant's emergency phone numbers were incorrect, fire control devices were somehow sealed off and not available, air breathing units were unusable, fire hose connections were mismatched. When the control room lost the entire electrical system, warning systems became inoperative and the water level in the core dropped from two hundred inches to a dangerous forty-eight inches. The fire burned out of control for six hours while makeshift pumping kept the fuel rods covered enough. "Meltdown was averted by a thin margin."

Ironically, it was discovered that just two days before, a similar fire had started the exact same way but had been extinguished successfully. After the first fire, the shift engineers and assistant shift engineers met. According to one of them, "We discussed among the group the procedures for using lighted candles for checking for air leaks. Our conclusion was that the procedure should be stopped."

Except for one news release written March 27, 1975, the Nuclear Regulatory Commission in Washington, DC, has remained silent about Browns Ferry. The cost of correcting the design flaw of wiring tunnels for all reactors was estimated to be between seven and twelve billion dollars.

It took thirty years for the Nuclear Regulatory Commission to get effective fireproofing installed in nuclear reactors. During those thirty years, according to two internal agency investigations, the NRC approved a whole string of ineffective fire barrier materials. Even after the materials were installed in dozens of plants, the materials did not work as advertised. One of those materials was a product called Thermo-Lag, which the commission approved on what was later determined to be fraudulent lab tests submitted by an obscure company. "No inspector ever checked out the lab or to question the results," said George Mulley, a former investigator with the Inspector General's office. "There were good fire barrier materials on the market from 3M and other companies that people knew and trusted," he said. "But these plant operators kept complaining that they were too expensive. So some company that no one has ever heard of comes along, with tests from a lab that no one has ever heard of, for a material that's cheaper than anything else on the market, and the NRC says, 'Perfect! Use this!'"

Critics of the NRC say the agency's failures are especially disturbing because the very creation of the agency by Congress in the 1970s was to separate the government's roles as safety regulator and promoter of nuclear energy—an inherent conflict of interest. The same conflict that was present under its predecessor the Atomic Energy Commission.

"It wasn't much of a change," said Peter Bradford, a former NRC commissioner who now teaches at Vermont Law School. "The NRC inherited the regulatory staff and adopted the rules and regulations of the AEC intact."

In 1985 the Tennessee Valley Authority shut down all of its reactors because of a variety of safety problems that industry experts say mostly boiled down to bad management. The others reopened, but Browns Ferry Unit One stayed closed for twenty-two years.

The NRC finally declared the fire barrier Thermo-Lag "inoperable" in 1992 after independent fire tests revealed that the barrier was as combustible as "treated plywood," and required utilities to have hourly fire patrols. But it has not ordered the inoperable fire barriers to be removed and replaced.

Drop by Drop

The attitude of the NRC also brought the Davis-Besse nuclear plant in Ohio to the brink, again, to the worst American nuclear accident *since* Three Mile Island. On August 3, 2001, the commission asked twelve nuclear plants to conduct inspections of the control nozzles that penetrate the vessel heads of most reactors. The commission had evidence of potentially dangerous cracks and leaks in those nozzles. The agreement was to wait until the end of the calendar year to comply. FirstEnergy Corp., owner of Davis-Beese, said it would comply, but not until March of the following year. On March 6 workers started on the inspection. To their horror, they found that corrosion had eaten through six inches of carbon steel on top of the six-and-a-half-inch reactor pressure vessel. Less than half-an-inch of stainless steel liner remained, keeping the pressurized internal radioactive environment contained. The liner was bulging outward under the pressure but had not yet ruptured. Reactor cooling water, which contains boron, had leaked around the control rod mechanism to drip and crystallize on the surface of the reactor head. Over time, the boric acid in the water ate through the carbon steel, creating a crater four-by-five-by six inches. The plant then closed for two years for emergency repairs, two FirstEnergy engineers were convicted for lying to investigators and the company paid more than $33.5 million in civil and criminal penalties.

"They should have just shut them down," said George Mulley, who investigated the case. "But the attitude at NRC was always, 'You can't shut them down, they'll fight us in court!'"

A Cup of Coffee (My Opinion)

We are more than lucky that we are not comparing Goldsboro with Chernobyl and Fukushima today—that we did not have a National Fiftieth Anniversary Memorial of a tragedy in North Carolina. Goldsboro was not "the worst man-made catastrophe in the world" as feared by the International Peace Institute, mainly because that ARM/SAFE switch worked. It was beat up by ground impact and the outside indicator was twisted to show ARM, but the internal component was on SAFE. We are now at a place in history where we can look back with the accumulated knowledge from half a century and with access to previously classified documents now available under the Freedom of Information Act. With those documents along with the benefit of interviews with those involved, and with the analyses of others concerning the Goldsboro Broken Arrow, we can gain insight into what this crew faced during this time of peril in 1961. This was a tragic aircraft accident with the loss of three brave, professional airmen. It could have been so much worse: a nuclear explosion on American soil, hundreds of times bigger than Hiroshima. And that could have turned into something far more sinister, all because of the unique combination of events and people at that time in history.

To summarize the aircraft accident: this crew, flying a heavy aircraft with an unknown structural weakness, fighting the controls during exhausting refuelings in changing weather, and after three hours of crisis, faced a chain of progressive problems that was unknowingly still growing. During a night approach to landing, while slowing from 220 to 180 knots, the aircraft made a sixty-degree turn to the left into freshly gusting headwinds, with landing gear already down, two engines out on the right side, and going to full flaps. This condition is known to pilots as a 'dirty' airplane—not aerodynamically clean. These flight stresses alone would never have been even remote factors in a crash, certainly not enough to break the wing off a B-52. But it is now apparent that during the flap extension something reached the breaking point inside that right wing. Obviously, this aircraft had more compounding stresses on a damaged wing than it could abide; structural damage to the wing combined with an attempt to stop a barrel roll to the right with only two engines on the far right side was too much. The pilots ran out of airspeed and control at the same time. When the control surfaces jammed and the airplane continued the turn until it rolled, the right wing cracked, folded upward, and the big aircraft came apart.

We constantly worry about nuclear materials in the hands of terrorists but we have forgotten about some dangerous dust in the back of our own closet: that Secondary buried at Faro. Our descendants are probably going to have to clean it up someday. Perhaps they will have both the money and the desire to do so, if only someone will remember where we left it buried. That's one of the reasons to write this story down now.

Few people thought about terrorists in 1961, but Adam Mattocks later said the crew realized if they had to bail out over the ocean at least they would let the aircraft go down and be in water deep enough so no enemy would find the bombs.

Maybe that was the thinking of the Air Force in leaving the Secondary alone. Maybe they thought that 180 feet down in the wet earth at Faro was just as impossible to retrieve as a nuclear weapon in deep ocean water. But today, fifty years later, bridge and tunnel builders go to far greater depths. We can cap an oil well a mile under water, and pluck Chilean miners from a depth twelve times the depth of the Secondary at Faro. We have the equipment and the knowledge on how to locate and remove hazardous waste from 180 feet beneath the farming fields of Faro, North Carolina.

We have a distinct advantage in analyzing the thought process of the nuclear weapons scientists and engineers. Being able to read their own words, written over a period of decades, is a unique window into the minds and souls of those patriotic Americans who so desperately wanted to protect their homeland. They did their absolute best they knew how to achieve these national goals, and it is interesting to witness from afar their worries, doubts, and concerns about working through the quest to create the perfect weapon—never before seen on Earth—that at the same time could be a horrible monster of unknown capabilities that might devour us all in our beds. In all three incidents (Goldsboro, Chernobyl and Fukushima) the best and brightest minds of the 1950s and 1960s created a newer version of two old needs: weapons and power sources. But they created each to use a piece of the sun: nuclear energy. Engineers have been building both weapons and power sources for centuries. But it was the degree of newness of these inventions or maybe the repercussions and consequences of any slight errors in judgment that was so disproportionate. Hopefully, we can learn from those events of the time and the current events we read about today.

All the ingredients for spontaneous combustion of nuclear war were on hand by the time the wheels of *Keep 19* left the ground on that Monday morning, January 23, 1961. We had the world's largest standing army of strategic bombers, brim full of weapons that were hundreds of times more destructive than any weapon ever used in war. The weapons were carefully designed to perform most efficiently; they were made from rare and magical materials created in the forges of nuclear reactors. Our most intelligent and gifted people built the weapons using the best and safest devices they knew of, but they were just that—devices built by men. We trained our sons and fathers to be brave and skilled professional warriors with faith in their country, a country that had just saved the world once from despots, and we were certainly ready to do it again. These men and women had the dedication and perseverance of our forefathers—it was in their DNA. We put them in the finest flying machine ever invented for all those purposes—the two-hundred-ton Boeing B-52. The unstoppable momentum of this new force—the combination of science, industry, hubris, and pride—brought together all that equipment, manpower, and expertise. Then we built a massive pyramid controlled by the spoken word, communications from the conscience of man. There are people today who firmly believe that if just one of those *best devices made by man* had failed in either one of the bombs at Faro, logic would *not* have prevailed, we would *not* be thinking clearly; we could have thought we had been attacked, and would have launched the force and delivered the fire, and we would have witnessed the horrors of nuclear winter.

Final Thoughts

Fifty-eight years before the Goldsboro crash, and 128 miles away, the Wright brothers successfully launched their flimsy aircraft at Kitty Hawk, North Carolina. Millions visit the Wright Brothers National Memorial now, and the massive 60-foot monument on top of a 90-foot hill is very impressive. It is made from than 1,200 tons of granite; it took years to build and was dedicated in 1932.

However, pilots are more impressed by standing at the spot nearby where the first flight actually took place, which is marked by a simple 6-foot high boulder marked with a bronze plaque. Leading away to the north like runway markers is a series of four more smaller stones, at 120 feet, 175 feet, 200 feet, and 852 feet, each marking a landing spot of those four flights on December 17, 1903.

During a recent trip to the beach, I was out at that boulder and I asked a park ranger who was walking by, "How do you know this was the spot, the exact spot where the first flight left the ground?" I pointed toward the iron launch rail beside the stone and looked around the acres of sand. "This is a big area. Why is the rock right here, and not over there, for example?"

"Because Orville said this was the spot," was the reply. "When this marker was dedicated in 1928... before *that* monument was even planned," he gestured over his shoulder at the big stone colossus on the hill, "Orville came back to Kitty Hawk, was welcomed by various committees, and then he walked around a bit, followed by the crowd. Then he said something that was very important. The group gathered around to make sure they heard it all. What he said was, 'Yep, this is the spot.'"

It was obvious to the ranger that the real Wright Brothers monument was this simple 6-foot high boulder. That was really the spot where *man first left Planet Earth*. Right there.

In 2011, I drove Jack ReVelle to the spot on Shackelford Road near Faro where the reports and the eyewitnesses said the bomb was caught up in the trees, the first bomb that fell, caught by the parachute. He walked straight to a unique shaped gum tree beside a ditch, about a hundred feet north of the road, looked around, and said, "This is it." Right there was where he had disarmed a 3.8-megaton MK-39 thermonuclear weapon on the misty morning of January 24, 1961.

We now are over fifty years on this side of the Goldsboro Broken Arrow, just as the Wright brothers were fifty-eight years on the other side. We should be awed at how much aeronautical science and skill mankind has learned on both sides of that one point in time. If we measure anything we are pretty good at—for example, speed—we can chart the growth. In just two centuries we have gone from how fast man can travel: first on horseback, then behind a steam locomotive, and later, at the speed of spacecraft. Likewise, weapons have gone from swords to bullets to *Hell in a bucket*. We should remember how close we came to nuclear winter back in 1961. We should also remember this event and try to learn the lesson so that we don't repeat it.

Here is an old saying from the area where this all happened: We drink water from wells we did not dig. We eat food from fields we did not plow. We worship in churches we did not build, and we enjoy freedoms we did not earn. Let us remember those who came before us. We should feel grateful for these men who put themselves in harm's way for the security of generations yet to come.

Joel Dobson

2013

The return to Bomb One site, fifty years later in 2011. Dr. Jack ReVelle was the Explosive Ordnance Disposal officer who 'rendered safe' the 3.8 megaton thermonuclear bomb in 1961.

Left photo by author, Right photo courtesy USAF.

AFTERWORD
BY WILTON W. STRICKLAND,
LT. COL, USAF, (RETIRED)

For more than forty years after World War II and until the collapse of the Soviet Union in 1991, there was a period known as The Cold War, The United States and the Soviet Union, figuratively, held a very sharp-pointed *spear* to each other's throats. Those spears were in the form of very large nuclear arsenals capable of inflicting unimaginable holocaust and were guided by a policy of Mutually Assured Destruction (MAD)—an attack by one on the other would result in complete destruction of both.

For nearly sixteen years, during the period from February, 1957, through October, 1981, I lived on the very point of that American spear as a member of the US Air Force Strategic Air Command—first, for nearly three years as a maintenance crew chief on B-47 long-range nuclear bombers and later, for thirteen years, as an aircrew navigator and a radar navigator/bombardier on B-52s, the very long-range, heavy bombers that have been the mainstay of the nation's nuclear deterrent force for more than fifty-five years, along with land-based and submarine-launched intercontinental ballistic missiles. During most of my time in B-52s, I spent about every third week on ground alert, ready to take off at a moment's notice, and deliver nuclear weapons to targets in the Soviet Union. During my five thousand hours in flight on B-52s, I also flew several airborne alert (Chrome Dome) missions into the north polar and Mediterranean areas armed with nuclear weapons and, again, ready to quickly turn and strike targets in the Soviet Union.

This book is the tragic story of eight other men who were also on the point of that spear— plus their aircraft and its cargo - the men of crew R-10 and *Keep 19*, the ill-fated B-52 from Seymour Johnson AFB, NC, that broke apart on approach to landing at Seymour Johnson on the cold, very early morning of January 24, 1961, which caused the two H-bombs aboard to separate from the aircraft as if they had been deliberately released, and raining possible massive destruction onto the small farming community of Faro, NC.

I vaguely remember hearing about the accident soon after it happened in 1961, but I never delved into the details of it until the Air Force brought me to the B-52 unit at Seymour Johnson in 1979. Since then I've read many articles about the accident, too often including much misinformation and sensationalism. This book is the most comprehensive and complete work on the subject that I have seen. It also dispels much of the misleading sensationalism that has prevailed over the last fifty years. The author's open-mindedness, his search for the truth, and the recent declassification of certain government documents has resulted in this outstanding historical account of the incident.

APPENDIX A
CREW MEMBERS INFORMATION

Role	Name	Rank	Age	Serial #		Location
Pilot	Walter Scott Tulloch	Major	46	AO726513		*San Diego, CA*
				born	15 Aug 1915	*Phoenix, Arizona*
				died	9 May 1992	*San Diego, CA*
				spouse	Elizabeth C.	
Co-Pilot	Richard William Rardin	Captain	33	AO1856099		*San Antonio, TX*
				born	10 Mar 1927	*Hamilton Co, Ohio*
				died	5 Jul, 1981	*San Francisco, CA*
				spouse	Charlie Belle Gainer	
EW	William R. Wilson	1/Lt	27	AO3054755		*(Somerville, NJ,*
				born 1933 +/- 1		*or Temple, TX*
						both are listed)
Nav	Paul Edward Brown, (Jr)	Captain	37	AO759891		*Beardstown, IL*
				born	27 April, 1923	IL
				died	29	April, 1988
Nav/Bomb	Eugene Shelton	Major	41	AO724231		*San Antonio, TX*

309

					born	15 May, 1919	Bexar Co. TX
					died	24 Jan, 1961	Goldsboro, NC
					spouse	Coloma M., "Rusty"	
Gunner	Francis Roger E. Barnish	TSgt	35	AF31415124			*Greenfield, MA*
					born	30 June, 1925	Mass
					died	24 Jan, 1961	Goldsboro, NC
					spouse	June F.	
EW	Eugene Holcombe Richards	Major	42	AO804873			*Toccoa, GA*
					born	18 June, 1918	Fla.
					died	24 Jan, 1961	Goldsboro, NC
					spouse	Sue C.	
3rd Pilot	Adam Columbus Mattocks	1/Lt	27	AO3072164			*Maysville, NC*
					born 1	9 Aug, 1933	Onslow Co, NC
					spouse	Anne	

(Rank, age, and *hometown of record* at time of crash, 1961)

APPENDIX B
"THIS IS WHAT IT WAS LIKE," MAJOR TULLOCH'S NARRATIVE, WRITTEN 1961

A few months ago we were flying this big jet bomber, a B52G, out over the Atlantic Ocean one night, and she developed trouble, which finally progressed to the point where an explosion shattered a wing. Most of us got out of her OK, but so many of my friends, even people who have flown for years during all sorts of conditions of war and peace, have asked me what it was like, that I would like to tell it as best I can in my own unskilled words. Many have endured much more harrowing experiences and real adventures have written hair-raising tales of happenings which leave us breathless. But to me, the real drama is the terse account by some ordinary Joe who was just doing his job and suddenly came to grips with real terror.

Frank, the gunner, had been shot down over Germany in WW II, been made a prisoner, but escaped to the American lines. Paul, the navigator, had survived two crashes during the same war. Dick, the co-pilot, was an ex-fighter jockey and test pilot who had survived three flamed out jets, which nearly took him with him. He did not talk about it much, but he was gray in his thirties. All the rest of us, except the very youngest had survived hundreds of hours of combat flying. What I'm trying to say is we were just a bunch of guys doing our job, and the last thing we wanted was for that plane to come "unglued" (strikethrough: sic) dump us out like dice out of a cup.

We were flying one of those exercises to train for the "Airborne Alert" posture. The airplane was loaded and ready to go to war by the simple procedure of turning her nose in the direction of the enemy and throwing a multitude of switches that cocked her bombs and weapons. You are up there for twenty-four hours tooling around in range of potential customers, and occasionally one of the jet tankers will come up and pump a few tons of fuel into the bomber just to keep her able to cover a good share of the earth's surface. Because of the long hours we had a third pilot along to take a turn at the controls, this bird can get out of hand in seconds and requires an alert eye. This young Lt. was not in a seat that would eject, and was to experience an escape that was little short of miraculous. Back in the defense section, a Major from Wing staff was also occupying one of those deadly spare seats that are not equipped with an ejection mechanism. He was an electronics warfare officer of wide experience and had volunteered to go along to help our defense team smooth out their operation. He was not lucky.

The first hint of trouble, like that first puff of smoke that proceeds a forest fire, was when we were completing an in-flight refueling with one of our tanker aircraft. We had backed off to get set to take on the final few thousands of pounds of fuel that would top our tanks when the "boomer" on the tanker (often called Casey, because he lowers the refueling boom from the tanker into the receptacle on the bomber) called us and told us that we were losing a great deal of fuel out of the bottom of our right wing, just aft of one of the jet pods. There is a tremendous vent near the end of each wing to take care of over flow in case a valve should fail, but for a lot of fuel to be pouring out into the exhaust of the two jets was quite another matter. A quick check revealed that one of our main tanks was indeed losing thousands of gallons of fuel. Evidently it had split, or an inspection plate had come loose. Fuel pouring out into the open air at that altitude is scarcely combustible and most large aircraft are equipped to dump fuel in an emergency to lighten the load, so it did not appear to pose an immediate danger. Were were rapidly approaching our home base, so I had the co-pilot call them and explain our difficulties, advise them that I intended to remain at altitude out over the ocean, in case anything happened, and that at dawn I wanted a chase plane to come up and check us over before we tried to land. In the meantime, I wanted our tanker to drop down below us and try to see what was wrong, but it was dark, and it is dangerous for a big plane to get too close, so he could not see much. The way the wing is swept back on the B-52, we could see nothing. It seemed a good idea to shut down the two jets adjacent to the leak, even though the tank was nearly drained by now. One of the rules of war is to be prepared for the worst, so I warned the crew to be ready to leave in an instant in case we found ourselves in what is known as an "untenable position."

Down in our Wing Headquarters things really came alive. Every Wing has a Command Post, manned by some very keen personnel who have telephone, Teletype, and radio contact with everyone up and down the whole SAC chain of command. In a few moments I was talking to our Wing Commander who was in his staff car, hurrying down to see that we got every bit of assistance possible, even to calling the people who built the airplane to get their views on what was wrong. The SAC Wing Commanders in my experience have, to a man, resembled tough football coaches faced with a crucial game. They can be as relaxed and charming as any other big executive on rare occasions but there are no seasons in the deadly game we are playing and the safety of our nation and the free world is at stake, so you had better know what you are doing and saying when your are around one of these gentlemen, or you won't be around long. Our Colonel is no exception, and I know that he had plenty of experts around him to make sure that we did not overlook anything. Our crew were all expert also, or we wouldn't have been trusted with a multimillion dollar aircraft loaded with more destructive power than most Generals commanded in by-gone wars, but I wanted any help they had to offer. It was my own lonely responsibility, and all decisions were up to me, as Aircraft Commander, but the Good Book says, "with good advice, make war," and under the complexities of modern operations, this is truer than ever. I particularly wanted to hear from the chief of our Standardization Crew. His job is similar to that of an Air Line's Chief Pilot. He had checked us out in these machines when we had reported to this base, and all of the other pilots shared my own high esteem of him. This was not because he was lenient, for he resembled nothing so much as a lean hard-boiled sheriff in the old frontier towns, who would drink beer with the boys, but shoot them down if they got out of line. We knew we had trouble, which was like a crouching tiger— soon it would spring.

 Many pilots were like hypochondriacs about their airplanes. They are careful to the point of being fearful. They always look on the dark side. Caution has its merits, but carried too far, it has been responsible for people abandoning aircraft that could have been easily saved. We have always looked on the bright side. Besides, this bomber cost millions of dollars. In the Air Force we are intensely conscious of waste, and every officer is graded on what he can do to save the taxpayer dollar. It would have been a simple thing to just point the stricken plane's nose out to sea, and bail out before things got too tense, but we were determined to try to save her. However, she was getting worse each minute, for now the next big fuel tank had sprung a leak and was rapidly pouring its fuel out into the slipstream. The Wing Commander decided we should land as soon as possible even though the plane was still very heavy from the recent refueling and it was night. His wishes were revealed to us by a coastal radar sight, as we were circling out over the ocean, a safe distance from where the citizens slumbered peacefully in their beds. I concurred with the decision to land for I had studied a recent report of another bomber who had made it safely down under similar circumstances, but it had burst into flames on the runway, so I warned the crew to be ready to "make tracks" as soon as we could land and get stopped. Our main problem was to try to land without flying over anyone on the ground. Those folks down there were depending on us to defend them, not rain flaming death and destruction down on them in the middle of the night. I wanted to bail everyone out but the co-pilot and I, but we needed the navigators to guide us around the cities and towns on our way in. This was to cost the radar operator his life.

We lowered the ten wheels that comprise our landing gear while we were in the thin air of high altitude as there is much less chance of explosion there. Then we started down, and back to the base, threading our way cautiously around the cities, towns, and villages—I'd flown many a night bombing raid, and I never want to see that happen to an American city. When we got down to ten thousand feet they called us to check the airplane with full flaps down at that altitude, before landing it. In combat the rule had been to never lower the flaps if you had a damaged wing, so the experts must have decided that the wing was OK, and our only problem was the fuel leak. This did not seem too serious, as both tanks had drained themselves long before we started down. At our heavy weight without flaps we would have been landing at a terrific speed, so if the wing would stand it, it would be much better to make a normal landing with the flaps down, so we started them down. Had we put the flaps down at low altitude, as usual, it would have destroyed us all, for it triggered immediate, insurmountable trouble.

I'd told the co-pilot to tell them that the airplane seemed to handle OK with full flaps when there was a loud noise down under her like we had struck something and she started a violent roll to the left. We had no sooner got her out of that, and back on an even keel then there was an even worse noise, and she started trying to roll over to the right, and though fighting desperately we could not hold her. I ordered the crew to bail out. In this B-52 G, only the pilots can see out—the others have no way of knowing what is going on, so someone called me back on intercom and said, "Did you say 'bail out'?" It is amazing that anyone would stop to double check at a time like this, but people had ejected by mistake before and our boys were tuned to a much higher state of discipline—not by me, but themselves. So I shouted into the intercom, "Yes! Bail Out!" There were a lot of muffled explosions which I at first thought were more trouble, but when, finally, the co-pilot ejected and the shell which fires the seat out went off, I realized that this was a good sound—the lads were firing their seats off, and were safely away. I was putting up the fight of my life, using every trick I had been taught or learned in thousands of hours of flying and many trips over enemy targets, trying to hold the big beast from rolling over on her back, until the extra crew members could dive out the holes left in the bottom of the aircraft when the navigators on the lower deck had ejected. It was in vain, for the big ship got up into a vertical bank, and started plunging toward the earth. This had all happened in seconds, but now, all was lost—regretfully I let go of the controls and fired my seat.

The aircraft was inverted, and I was hanging in my seat belt, which I had neglected to pull real tight, so the seat got a couple of inches start and hit my behind with a terrible jolt and I found myself tumbling through the blast, pummeled and wrenched in all directions. It was like when you catch one of those big breakers at the beach: it overpowers you and finally flings you stunned and gasping up on the beach. My crash helmet and oxygen mask were torn off, but the automatic devices opened the seat belt and the seat fell away, and the parachute opened smoothly. I was surrounded by flaming pieces of wreckage which the plane had shed in its mad plunge and in danger of dropping into the holocaust on the ground where it had struck, but the feeling of floating down in an open chute is among the finest physical sensations I have ever enjoyed, I can see why people do it for sport, and it was made doubly enjoyable when I viewed the flaming death I had so narrowly escaped. Surely the boys had all made it out safely. I had heard their seats fire, and it would take just a second for the extra crew members to dive out after the navigators ejected. I could see someone now, floating down in his parachute, and I shouted to him hoping we could get together on the ground, but he hung there like a rag doll, and did not answer. Much later I found that this was

317

the radar navigator. He had ejected safely but something had struck him in the head and killed him. The reason he did not answer was that he was already on his way to a better world.

Suddenly I found myself plunging into treetops and arranged my arms and legs to protect myself. It seemed a shame that such a delightful ride should end with such a rude jolt, but there I was safely on the ground. My own most deadly peril was to come much later.

I made the usual check for broken parts, unbuckled my chute, took a sighting on the North Star, hung up my chute where I could find it should I need it again, and set out to find a farm with a telephone where I could phone to report in and find out if everyone was down safely. As I tried one direction after another only to fall into pools of freezing water, I was surprised to find myself lying with my face in the mud. I had blacked out. Obviously I was in the middle of a swamp and exhausting myself in my struggles. It was freezing cold, and my teeth were chattering, so I made my way back to my chute and rolled up in it to get warm. When the rescue helicopters started coming over, I got up and made a feeble attempt to signal them by waving the chute, as I had lost my flashlight and matches when the trees ripped my flying suit on the way down through them. I soon gave up, for I knew I could get out as soon as it grew light, and I was starting to black out again. I rolled up in that good old chute again and soon felt better physically, but my anxiety about the others was mounting. If someone were really hurt, and in a swamp like I was, it might be hard to find him.

At the first light of dawn, I made my way out to a road, got a ride to a farmhouse with a phone, called the Wing Command Post to report in, and find out if the rest of the boys were all OK. The spare pilot was my main worry, for he had been up on the flight deck helping us with circuit breakers we could not reach, and I was not sure that he had got down to the lower deck in time to dive out after the navigator. It developed that he had still been on the flight deck, and when the plane went over on her back he dove out the topside after I ejected. Ordinarily, the fin and rudder would have hit him, but it had snapped off so he was saved, and landed right in a farm yard and did not even have to walk. They assured me that the others would soon turn up, now that it was light. I was to get a ride over to the crash scene where our Commander was, and he would get me back to the base. I phoned my wife, who wept with relief. No words can express what the girls go through at a time like this. As I write these words, a crew I flew with for months has vanished over the North Atlantic without a trace. To watch the young wives wait with waning hope while trying to comfort their small children is heartbreaking.

The crash scene was ghastly, but my heart welled with gratitude that, although there were farmhouses in the area, no person or stick of property had been destroyed. The kindly farmer who let me use his phone, and gave me a ride over there had an expression of shock on his face as he viewed the terrible destruction, and considered that his own small house was only a mile away. I reported to our Wing Commander, who tried to reassure me about the rest of the crew, and had me hustled off to the hospital. I must have been in worse shape than I suspected. My real ordeal stall lay before me.

In the hospital I blacked out three more times, and crashed to the floor before the corpsmen could catch me. They were glad to get me into a bed where they set up a round-the-clock watch, until the

Doctors were sure I was out of danger. I was told that the others were being collected and were in a room down the hall. I even thought I heard some of them outside my door. Relief and exhaustion helped me to drift off into sleep. Next morning, when I kept insisting that I wanted to see them I was told the grim truth—three of them had perished.

The next night, I was alone with my grief. This loss sorely afflicted me. The radar operator was a burly Texan, with a fine crop of three boys and a little daughter, and devoted wife. The Major from the Wing Staff was one of the most popular officers in Wing. Something had delayed his dive out to safety, and when the airplane got over on its back, he was doomed. His wife and son can hardly bare their loss. Frank, the gunner, who had survived so much had started to fire his seat, and had blown the escape hatch off, but then something had gone wrong. The few seconds' delay had been fatal. He left three children and a sick wife.

I was stricken with remorse. The beating I had taken, coupled with this news, destroyed an equanimity that had carried me through a life of hardship. Why had I tried to save that cursed plane? According to the newspapers few seem to worry much about a few million dollars of government money. And I had lost, not only the airplane, but also three men I loved like brothers. Black despair dragged me down to the depths, and waves of grief swept over me. As a lad, my Sunday School teacher had been a retired General, and he had inoculated me with the highest ideals about life and military service. I could see him standing trim and erect as though he was addressing his troops, and I could almost hear him saying, "The Captain should go down with his ship." I'd thought I was the last one out, but I had survived, and three had been lost. The ancient scripture I had learned in my youth came ringing through my troubled mind—"Greater love hath no man than to lay down his life for his friends." But my friends were gone, and I was safe. Feebly I struggled in the grip of despair that could bring on a shattered mind. I knew I needed help from the angels and one was right down the hall—I rang for the nurse.

My angel was a little slip of a girl who looked like someone's kid sister, and when she saw my face, she looked scared. I begged for something that would knock me out and help me escape my horrible thoughts, but the doctor was off delivering a baby and orders were that I could be given nothing 'till some tests they were running were finished. She looked troubled, and finally said brightly, "I'll give you a back rub, perhaps that will get you to sleep." Anything was better than being left alone in this hell of despair so I eagerly acquiesced. Gradually my troubled mind returned to normal, and I drifted into a healing sleep.

Now, when I roll our big bomber out on the runway for takeoff, just before I reach out my hand to advance the eight throttles that will send her rushing off into the night, I think of all those other hands that helped me back to a useful life. Tender hands in the hospital, hands at home that were clasped in prayer through a long night, comradely hands on the flight line that welcomed me back to duty, the hands of superiors that gave me a reassuring slap on the back and put me back in a cockpit where I loved to be. And all the hands across our nation, working to build a better life for all Americans, and yet have enough left over for all the empty hands in the world. It steadies my own hand.

WST

Lieutenant Colonel Walter Scott Tulloch continued to fly the BUFF until he retired, on February 27, 1967. His last currency flight was January 18, 1967, one month before his retirement. He had over 26 years of service with 6,740 flying hours, 458 of them in combat. He was awarded the Distinguished Flying Cross and the Air Medal with Three Oak Leaf Clusters. He died of cancer on May 9, 1992 in San Diego, California, where his widow, Betty still lives. She is eighty-six years old.

APPENDIX C
FINDINGS OF OFFICIAL ACCIDENT BOARD [*WITH DESCRIPTIVE NOTES*]

AF FORM 14, B-52G 58-187

1. The primary cause of this accident was materiel failure in that a fatigue crack in the #2 panel of the lower wing skin occurred at wing station 556 of the right wing, causing a major fuel leak in the #3 and #4 fuel tanks.

2. A contributing cause factor was also material failure in that the already weakened right wing separated from the aircraft following flap extension.

3. T.O.[*Technical Order*] 1B-52G-637 (ECP 951-5), requiring depot level compliance, was scheduled for 5 May 1961 during High Stress II modification. Compliance with this technical order would have prevented the failure of the #2 panel of the right wing lower skin.

4. The fact that a B-52G wing had experienced a similar failure during cyclic testing was not known at the operating level.

5. The present flight manual does not provide adequate guidance for major fuel leaks and fails to point out the fact that some

structural damage is always associated with a large wing tank fuel leak.

6. The aircraft was directed into landing configuration because of concern over fire hazard accompanied by lateral control considerations, prior to detailed analysis of the emergency being completed by Boeing Airplane Company and while several hours of fuel remained aboard the aircraft.

7. In order to maintain near normal lateral balance for landing, the recommended fuel usage procedures contained in T.O. 1B-52G-1 were not followed.

8. The UHF radio in the Command Post was unsatisfactory during a major portion of the emergency.

9. Information recorded on the Command Post tape was of limited value in establishing sequence of events, in that it was turned off during portions of the emergency and the time was not periodically recorded.

10. The VGH Gust Recorder in the aircraft was not sufficiently protected to conserve the information.

11. The Staff EWO [*Major Richards*], occupying the IN seat [*Instructor Navigator seat, at the back of The Hole*], was unable to reach either of the two downward hatches.

12. The gunner [*Technical Sergeant Barnish*] was unable to find and/or pull the catapult trigger to complete his ejection sequence.

13. The Radar-Navigator [**Major Shelton**] was jerked against his

ejection seat when the parachute inflated and after his helmet was lost, resulting in fatal injury.

14. Surviving crew members did not pull down their helmet visors and did not have chin straps tightly fastened.

15. Two survival kit life rafts were inflated inadvertently and could have resulted in unsatisfactory parachute opening or a fatal injury.

APPENDIX D
TABLE OF COMPONENT BEHAVIOR, FUSING AND FIRING SYSTEM

(Speer Report, Feb 16, 1961)

MIC No.	Component	Bomb #1	Bomb #2
	Arming Wires	Pulled	Pulled
845	Pulse Generator	Actuated	Actuated
543	Timer	Ran Down (deleted)	Ran 12-15 Sec.
832	Differential Pressure Switch	All Contacts Closed	2 Contacts Closed
640	Low Voltage Thermal Battery	Actuated	Actuated
772	Arm-Safe Switch	Safe	(See Sect 5)
1-A	Tritium Reservoir	Full	Full
641	High Voltage Thermal Battery	Actuated	Not Actuated
788	Rotary Safing Switch	Not Operated	Destroyed
730	X Unit	Not Charged	Not Charged
615	Nose Crystals	Crushed	Crushed

(End of Report)

APPENDIX E
LIST OF KNOWN BROKEN ARROWS
(DECLASSIFIED AS OF 1980)

In addition to the Goldsboro Broken Arrow there are thirty-five known other accidents that involved nuclear weapons that were released by the Department of Defense and Department of Energy in 1983. Here are the thirty-six as reported by Maggelet and Oskins in their book, *Broken Arrow, The Declassified History of U. S. Nuclear Weapons Accidents.*

February, 13, 1950	B-36	Pacific Ocean
April 11, 1950	B-29	Manzano Base, New Mexico
July 13, 1950	B-50	Lebanon, Ohio
August 5, 1950	B-29	Fairfield-Suisun AFB, California
November 10, 1950	B-50	Outside US, St. Lawrence River
March 10, 1956	B-47	Mediterranean Sea
July 27, 1956	B-47	Overseas Base

Date	Aircraft/Item	Location
May 27, 1957	B-36	Kirtland AFB, New Mexico
July 28, 1957	C-124	Atlantic Ocean
October 11, 1957	B-47	Homestead AFB, Florida
January 31, 1958	B-47	Overseas Base
February 5, 1958	B-47	Savannah River, Georgia
March 11, 1958	B-47	Florence, South Carolina
November 4, 1958	B-47	Dyess AFB, Texas
November 26, 1958	B-47	Chennault AFB, Louisiana
January 18, 1959	F-100	Pacific Base
July 6, 1959	C-124	Barksdale AFB, Louisiana
September 25, 1959	P-5M	Off Whidbey Island, Washington
October 15, 1959	B-52, KC-135	Hardinsburg, Kentucky
June 7, 1960	Bomarc	McGuire AFB, New Jersey
January 24, 1961	B-52	Goldsboro, North Carolina
March 14, 1961	B-52	Yuba City, California
November 13, 1963	Storage Igloo	Medina Base, Texas
January 13, 1964	B-52	Cumberland, Maryland
December 5, 1964	ICBM	Ellsworth AFB, SD
December 8, 1964	B-58	Bunker Hill AFB, Indiana

October 11, 1965	C-124	Wright-Patterson AFB, Ohio
December 5, 1965	A-4	At Sea, Pacific Ocean
January 17, 1966	B-52/KC-135	Palomares, Spain
January 21, 1968	B-52	Thule, Greenland
Spring, 1968	Submarine	At Sea, Atlantic Ocean
September 19, 1980	Titan II ICBM	Damascus, Arkansas

In 1962, there were four Thor IRBM explosions involving nuclear warheads on Johnston Island, Pacific Ocean:

June 3	Thor-Bluegill
June 20	Thor-Starfish
July 25	Thor-Bluegill Prime
Oct 15	Thor-Bluegill Double Prime

APPENDIX F
BOMB LOCATIONS AT FARO:

Bomb No. 1, the "bomb in the trees" was on Shackelford Road, SR 1616, .67 miles east of intersection with Big Daddy's Road, Faro.

35° 29.526 N 77° 50.808 W

Location is based on eyewitnesses, including the original Explosive Ordnance Disposal Officer, Dr. Jack ReVelle; as well as the coordination of Jes Hales, former BUFF pilot, whose family still owns the land.

Bomb No. 2, the "buried bomb." on Big Daddy's Road, SR 1532, .4 miles south of intersection with Shackelford Road, Faro.

35° 29.628 N 77° 51.497 W

Location is based on eyewitnesses and the legal deed description of the 400 foot wide circle (200 ft radius) easement, which is now owned by US Government. The site is not fenced or marked, and is 420 feet NE (320° magnetic) from centerline of Big Daddy Road.

If you go there, please do not trespass. This is active farming land. The good folks of Faro have had enough damage done to their land.

HOW I LOCATED THE 'LOST' BOMB OF GOLDSBORO.

The site is not marked or fenced. As of 2011, there is nothing there but a cultivated field with a small overgrown cemetery near the center. By using a software such as Google Earth to measure distance, one would need a GPS receiver, maybe a compass, and the following information:

The legal easement for the 200 ft radius circle is recorded on the deed books in the Wayne County Courthouse (Book 581, pp 589-91, State of NC, County of Wayne, 13 October, 1962) as follows:

> *"All of that area in the form of a circle, having a radius of 200 feet, with the center point of radius located through the following traverse: From a common corner to the lands of heirs of Charles T. Davis, Sr. and land of J. A. Edmundson, located on the centerline of N. C. State Road 1534 and approximately 2,135 feet northeasterly from the centerline of Nahunta Swamp; thence along the centerline of N. C. State Road 1534, N 49 degrees 28' E, 835.56 feet; thence leaving the centerline of N.C. State Road 1534, N 40 degrees 32' W, 420 feet to the center point of radius, and containing 2.88 acres, more or less."*

Here's how to use that somewhat bewildering information:

1. (For "Centerline of the swamp," see the following graphic.) Start at the the Nahunta Swamp where it is crossed by NC State Route 1534 (Big Daddy's Road). The concrete bridge is about two miles southwest of Faro, NC. The legal description

of the swamp where this road crosses it, actually starts at the northern end of the bridge and extends northeast only about 700 feet. You will have to estimate the centerline of the swamp, most of it is wetland, then go 2,135 feet northeasterly (toward Faro) on Big Daddy's Road. That will bring you to:

2. The common corner of the Davis and Edmundson land as it was in 1961.

3. From that point, continue northeast for another 835.6 feet along the centerline of the road, (49° magnetic). You just passed the white abandoned farmhouse and the spot where the main wreckage lay in the middle of the road. That was where Fred Johnson found the remains of Frank Barnish, under his unused ejection seat.

4. Look northwest, 90° relative to the road. You will be looking on a magnetic heading of 320 degrees.

(Or, in the wording of surveyors: N 40 degrees 32' W. This actually means 40 and 1/2 degrees WEST of magnetic NORTH, which makes it 320 ° by compass.) Four hundred twenty feet along that line of sight from the center of the road is the center of the circular easement.

Stare at the horizon for a minute, the way the guys in the hole did in 1961.

The GPS coordinates of the spot on the edge of the road are:

35° 29.579 N 77° 51.440 W.

5. From here, if you could hit a reasonably good 420 feet, or 140 yard golf shot, (a six iron for me), you would (maybe) hit the approximate center of the easement circle. That's where Bomb Number 2 hit that night, and where the core is now: 180 feet down. Under the circle of "2.88 acres, more or less."

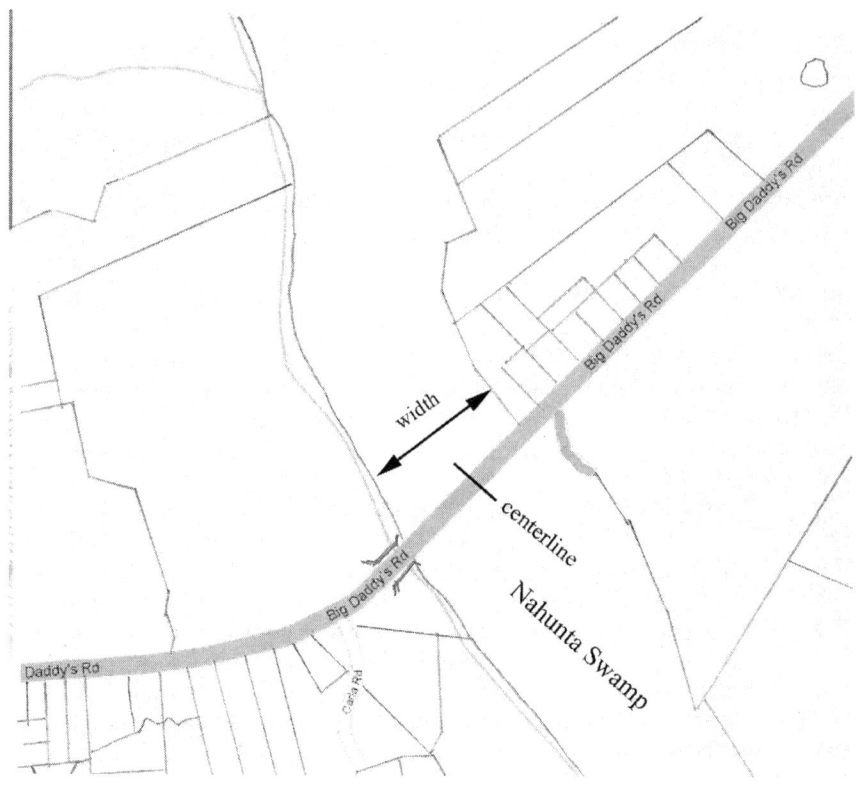

Nahunta Swamp Bridge, is at the lower left. The government's 400 circular easement of Bomb Two site is at upper right.

Illustration by author.

APPENDIX G
WHERE DID THE *KEEP 19* CREW MEMBERS LAND?

According to crew statements, the order of bailout was determined to be:

1. Paul Brown, Navigator
2. Bill Wilson, EW
3. Gene Shelton, Radar/Navigator
4. Dick Rardin, Co-Pilot
5. Scott Tulloch, Pilot.
6. Adam Mattocks, Third Pilot

We know that the bodies of Frank Barnish and Eugene Richards were found in the crushed fuselage on Big Daddy's Road. We know the actual landing location of only two of the other crew members who bailed out—Shelton and Rardin—but we do have some clues where we can approximate the landing spots of the remaining four.

If we look backwards from the main aircraft crash site on Big Daddy's Road along the direction of flight, and looking at the debris field, it is obvious that the aircraft broke up in midair about one-half mile southeast of the fuselage crash site. That breakup point would also be the general area of the bailout, at 9,000 feet. We know there was a strong west wing, (270 degrees, at 57 knots, or 65 MPH)—at the 10,000 feet altitude. We know where Dick Rardin's helmet was found: in the field near Bomb One, just east of the point of the midair breakup. A helmet would probably drop very near the spot where centrifugal forces would pull it off the crewman. On a direct down-wind line 2.3 miles due east of that helmet was the tree where Co-pilot Dick Rardin landed and left his parachute harness hanging near Bull Head Bridge. We know it was Rardin's parachute by elimination of the others:

-It was not Tulloch's because it was on a slight, dry slope, not in a swamp;

-It was not Wilson's because it was not in a muddy area containing a cow;

-It was not Brown's because it was not near a cemetery.

Gene Selton's body was found in a tree about a quarter mile north of the Rardin spot. Tulloch and Shelton were relatively close to each other during the descent, since Major Tulloch said he called out, but got no response from "the lifeless body." It would seem reasonable those two would land relatively near each other. There is only one swampy area near the Rardin and Shelton sites. It is just west of the Bull Head Bridge and is very probably the place where Major Tulloch landed.

This cluster of five would have been close together since they ejected within split seconds of each other. Brown and Wilson might have traveled slightly further east than the others since they left the aircraft first. Paul Brown would have been the very first, since that was his job: to open the lower hatch. Bill Wilson said he did not question the bailout order, so he was soon behind. Brown said he landed "east of an old cemetery," and a Mr. & Mrs. Singleton drove him to the base. There is a scattering of several cemeteries along Wayne Memorial Drive east of Bull Head Bridge, what is now called Fort Run Road, but no other cemeteries within several miles. That had to be the area where Brown and Wilson landed. I believe this cluster of five men landed within a half-mile radius of each other, possibly closer, after being blown three miles east of their bailout point.

The departure of Mattocks from the aircraft was definitely later than the other five, since he had the terrible problems just getting to and through the pilot's hatch. He stated that when he got outside, the forward airspeed was practically zero, having been stopped by the vertical position of the remaining left wing. The fuselage would have then plunged essentially straight down from that point. He thought he would fall into the resulting fire, so that would be the starting point of his travel by parachute: over the main crash site on Big Daddy's Road, moving eastward by the wind.

Mattocks had a much quicker descent than the others because to these clues:

A) The Accident Report said Bomb 2 left the aircraft between 2000 and 5000 feet, and went straight in since it had no parachute. It hit very near the fuselage wreckage that was the same fire that Adam had to avoid. That would mean Adam departed the aircraft somewhere in the same vicinity as the bomb, and it would also mean near the same altitude, where winds were not as great at 10,000 feet. Seymour Johnson reported ground wind speed at that time as 5 knots, compared to 57 knots at 10,000 feet. Being at a lower altitude and at lower wind speeds, he would not have traveled nearly as far as the others, who were subject to much stronger winds for a longer period of time.

B) His parachute deployment was also delayed by his three-second manual count, and was not the practically instantaneous deployment as in the automatic ejection seat system.

C) His descent speed would be much faster during a short period of time when his chute was collapsed by the explosion. That would put him closer to the ground, quicker.

All of these factors resulted in a shorter descent time for Mattocks in a westerly wind that was not as strong as the others experienced. That would cause him to land much closer to the crash site than the other five at Bull Head Bridge—probably by a factor of at least half, or about one and a half miles from the crash site instead of three miles. And it would be due east of the main crash site, and not near the actual crash since the people on the porch were looking at the flames in the distance, not surrounded by flames.

There are no current homes, only burnt ruins of several old houses in the area one-and-a-half miles due east of the crash site. Abandoned houses were routinely intentionally burned in later years as fire department controlled training burns. The remains of only one house that closely resembles Mattock's description of "a house in two parts with a walkway between" is on the west side of Lanetown Road just north of the intersection with Shackleford Road. That house is the most logical spot for Mattock's landing.

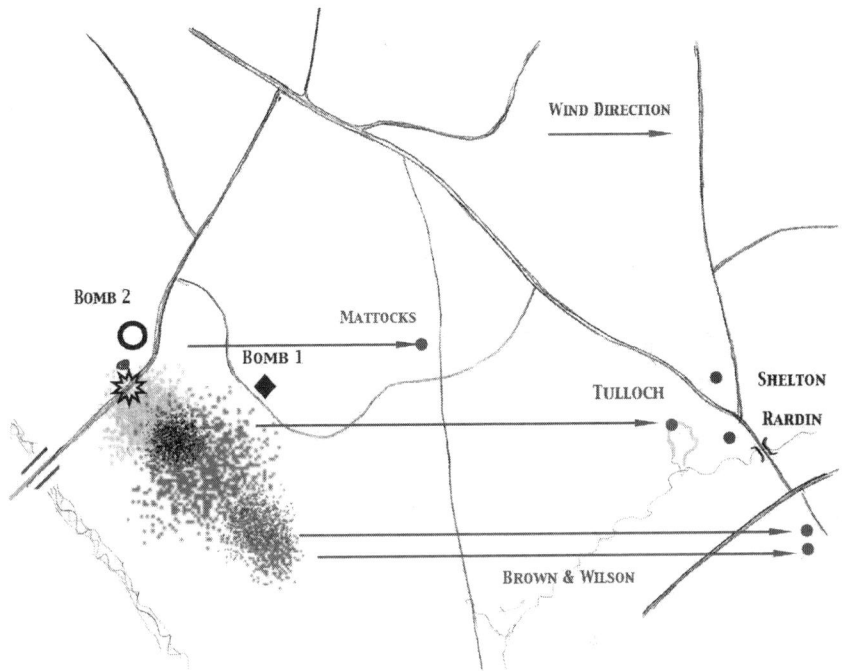

Estimated landing spots of each of the crew members, based on wind speed, anticipated bailout points, and ground landmarks.

APPENDIX H.
HAND WRITTEN "RANDOM NOTES AT GOLDSBORO," BY SCOLMAN AND SMITH

1. The upward pressure from the Artesian well situated at the 72' level is about 6 psi.
2. Surface water is no problem.
3. Underground water veins at 12, 23-25 and 40-46 feet
4. Rainfall averages 4 to 7" except Oct which has 2.7" avg
5. Maximum depth of the excavation is 42" with average at the bottom of about 30 x 30 feet.
6. Sunk 14 wells about 50 feet apart on the edge of the excavation pumping 7000 gph since 15 Feb.
7. There has been no lowering of the water table. Readings taken 4 times a day at five sounding points.
8. DELETED
9. Earth indexes checked to assure unit not inadvertently moved.
10. North Carolina Public Health Service makes a monthly check

of local water supply. Check is for radiological contamination and a state wide program has been in effect.

11. DELETED

12. If excavation was closed now the total cost would be about $66,000.

13. No firm estimate of owner's claim but it will be in the neighborhood of $50,000.

14. Cofferdam and $200,000 no longer feasible since underground water flow is not as originally thought.

15. Caisson is only solution for about $150,000 for 1. Four caissons of about 30' diameter - $500,000.

16. Unit has been identified to the public as "a small portion of a weapon."

17. Little or no public interest now.

18. NC Public health authorities consider it no problem.

19. Breaking through of the clay layer might disrupt the local water supply.

20. If we restrict well drilling we would by inference admit that there was a hazard.

21. DELETED.

CLASSIFIED SECRET US DOE ARCHIVES, RG 326 AEC

Collection 1188, Box 1, Folder 4 Goldsboro, 1/24/61

Declassified, 5/25/11

APPENDIX I.
THE FIRST TEN YEARS OF BROKEN ARROWS.

The following is a list of notes on the first decade of Broken Arrows, accumulated from a number of sources, from Mike Maggelet and Jim Oskin's excellent book, *"Broken Arrow, The Declassified History of U.S. Nuclear Weapons Accidents,"* some information from Doug Keeney's, *"15 Minutes,"* Chuck Hansen's *Swords of Armageddon Vol VIII*, and others collected over the years. This list stops at Goldsboro, which would begin the second decade of Broken Arrows. I selected to list only the first ten years to show what was had already occurred before Goldsboro.

B-36, Pacific Ocean, Canada

The first known Broken Arrow occurred February 13, 1950, when a huge B-36, a six-engine bomber with a crew of fifteen, was flying a simulated combat mission from Alaska to Texas. They were to fly to Southern California and make a simulated bomb run on San Francisco to test air defense along the Pacific coast. Before takeoff from Eielson Air Force Base, Alaska, they could not get de-icing due to the extreme cold, so they had to keep the engines running at all times. If they stopped, the oil would freeze. They were carrying a 10,000 pound Mark IV atomic bomb, without the nuclear capsule. During the flight, the crew experienced a series of mechanical problems, mostly associated with the deep cold of minus 40 degrees Fahrenheit. They flew on in the dark through hail, freezing fog, then lost a total of three of the engines, half their total power plant, due to fuel system and engine icing. They were steadily loosing altitude because of this loss of power. Having no other choice, they decided on their own, since they were out range of any radio station, to jettison the very heavy weapon at sea. They turned toward the Pacific and set the weapon to air burst at 3,000 feet to prevent the Russians from finding it. This would not be a nuclear detonation since the capsule was not in the weapon. They made up the procedures for doing this as they went along. The weapon was successfully jettisoned, and the detonation of the 5,000 pounds of the conventional high explosives caused a big flash, and they saw the shock wave. They turned eastward, and when they knew by radar that they were over land, they bailed out. They were in the vicinity of Princess Royal Island, British Columbia. Five of the fifteen aboard were never found. There were rumors that the weapons officer stayed aboard and attempted to land at a remote landing strip, but that was never confirmed. It would be three years before the wreckage was found on Mount Kologet in British Columbia, Canada. There was also the rumor that the same officer was seen before bailout putting his life preserver over, instead of under, his parachute harness. That would have prevented the parachute from opening properly.

B-29, Manzano, New Mexico

The second known Broken Arrow occurred April 11, 1950, at Manzano Base, New Mexico. This is the huge complex that comprises Kirtland Air Force Base, Sandia National Laboratory, and the 2,880-acre Manzano Base Weapons Storage Area. Eight to ten miles due east of Kirtland's Runway 8 is Manzano Mountain with an elevation of 8,000 feet. The B-29 from Walker Air Force Base New Mexico had arrived earlier in the day to pick up and ferry a Mark IV bomb back to Walker. At 9 p.m. the aircraft was ready to depart and requested taxi instructions. The Kirtland tower instructed the aircraft to take-off on Runway 8, which heads due east, and has a field elevation of 5,350 feet. On two occasions the aircraft was advised that between eight and ten miles east of the field the ground rises to an altitude of 8,000 feet, and was instructed to turn right immediately after take-off. The message was acknowledged and the aircraft took off. People who were watching noticed that the aircraft did not turn right but continued straight ahead at a low height until the lights of the aircraft could not be discerned. The people in the tower saw a thin line of fire in the foothills of the mountain, then, in about five seconds, a huge billow of flame. There were no survivors of the thirteen aboard. For a pilot starting a take-off roll on Runway 8 at night in 1950, he would be looking at a black void: the mountain was not lighted and there were no street lights or houses since it is part of the large weapons storage area. There have been at least two additional crashes within the confines of the Weapons Storage Area: an F-100C in 1957 and a EC-135 'Looking Glass' in 1977. The F100 pilot ejected safely, the Looking Glass lost all twenty aboard. The tower briefing for

Runway 8 was changed to "Ground to the East rising gradually to 7,000 feet within seven miles and higher peaks beyond." It was also recommended that B-29s and similar aircraft not be allowed to use Kirtland Runway 8 for night or weather take-offs.

B-50, Lebanon, Ohio, July 13, 1950

This is a Broken Arrow where the cause of the aircraft accident was never determined, primarily due to the urgency of a local undertaker to embalm crew remains before autopsy. A B-50 from Biggs Air Force Base, Texas, was bound for England with twelve people aboard, and carrying one Mark IV nuclear weapon without the capsule. A few days before, North Korea had invaded South Korea, and President Truman was very concerned that the Soviet Union would use that as a smoke screen to invade some European country. The Joint Chiefs of Staff as well as the British politicians had already decided that a total of ninety atomic bombs should be based in England and this one was among the first. The B-50, in clear skies and no known mechanical problem, spun nose first into Ohio farmland from 8,000 feet. The 5,000 pounds of conventional explosives detonated upon impact. The lack of autopsies meant that no tests for carbon monoxide poisoning or anoxia were possible. Due to the almost complete destruction of the entire aircraft, no usable evidence was obtainable.

B-29, Fairfield-Suisan Air Force Base, California

Another reaction to the North Korea invasion was to transfer ten Mark IV weapons to Anderson Air Force Base, Guam. Ten B-29s from the 9th Bomb Wing were to ferry the bombs and the mission would be under the command of Brigadier General Robert Travis, an old friend of General LeMay. At 10 p.m. on the night of August 5, 1950, a B-29 with General Travis aboard as passenger, along with a total of 19 other crew members and passengers, took off from Fairfield-Suisan Air Force Base. One Mark IV without nuclear capsule was aboard. Two runaway propellers on take-off prevented the aircraft from gaining sufficient airspeed. The pilot barely got it off the ground, then attempted to return to base, but crashed near a trailer court where the aircraft broke into several pieces and caught fire. The crash was not known to the tower until the Officer Of The Day received a telephone call from civilian authorities and drove to the flight line to report it. Twelve of the people aboard, including General Travis, received fatal injuries. The other eight escaped with minor injuries. But the biggest impact was yet to come.

"About twenty minutes after the crash occurred, the 5,000 pounds of high explosives in the bomb casing ignited. The blast was felt and heard over 30 miles away, and caused severe damage to the nearby trailer park on base. In addition to those (twelve crew members) killed in the initial crash, as a result in large part to the explosion that occurred shortly after the crash, 180 military, civilian, and dependents were killed or injured.... Seven were killed, forty-nine were admitted to the hospital and 124 others received superficial injuries." The fire was visible for 65 miles. The Air Force reported that the explosion after the crash was caused by "ten to twelve 500 lb. bombs" reportedly aboard the plane.

Among the seven rescue workers killed were two military volunteers: Sergeant Ramoneda, an Air Force baker, and John Boyles, an transient Army Private, just passing through, who offered assistance to remove people from the plane when the bomb exploded.

One year later, in 1951, the base where the crash occurred was renamed Travis Air Force Base, in honor of General Robert F. Travis.

The other nine atomic bombs remained on Guam and in April 1951, when the Soviets were making warning noises to America about Korea, the Joint Chiefs asked Truman for the release of nine nuclear capsules. They got them. Truman released the bombs personally to Air Force Chief of Staff General Hoyt Vandenberg, who was formally designated a "personal representative of the President." (Keeney, p. 76)

B-50, Over water, Canada

The fifth Broken Arrow, also in the year of 1950, also involved a Mark IV weapon without the nuclear core, was jettisoned from a B-50. It occurred November 10, 1950, over the St. Lawrence River near St. Alexendre-de-Kamouraska, Canada. The aircraft was returning home to Davis-Monthan Air Force Base, Arizona, from Goose Bay, Labrador. The reason for the jettisoning was not known, and was possibly not reported to the general public under the Department Of Defense rule that if a jettisoning was not observed by the public, it was not necessary for the Air Force to issue a press release. The high explosive in the weapon was seen to detonate on impact near the middle of the 12-mile wide river. Pale yellow smoke rose to 3,000 feet and windows rattled 25 miles away. The Air Force said that three 500 lb. conventional bombs had detonated after jettisoning.

The first year for SAC bombers just starting to carry nuclear weapons, 1950 was not a good year. The learning curve to meet Soviet threats all over the world was definitely costly. In just this first year, there were four aircraft accidents, each with multiple fatalities. They totaled 54 dead crew members, and hundreds of other military and civilian injured. Then there was one unexplained jettison of an atomic weapon that was not recovered. All of the accidents appear to have occurred in the rush of that one year, 1950, to build Strategic Air Command. At least for the next five years there would be no known further aircraft accidents involving a loss of a weapon. There was one accident on March 10, 1956, where a B-47 from MacDill Air Force Base, Florida, with two nuclear capsules (but no weapons,) simply disappeared in poor visibility over the Mediterranean Sea. No trace of the aircraft or crew was ever found.

July 27, 1956. England

A B-47 with no weapons aboard had completed a training mission and was conducting touch-and-go landings at Lakenheath RAF Station, England, about twenty miles from Cambridge. The aircraft had just made its fourth landing when it veered off the runway and into a storage igloo. Inside the igloo were three Mark 6 fission weapons. No nuclear capsules were involved but each weapon had approximately five thousand pounds of high explosive. The bombs did not detonate or burn and there was no radiation contamination. The four airmen aboard the B-47 were killed. "Without a nuclear capsule the Mark 6 contained only natural uranium and a one-point detonation would not have turned the eastern part of England into a desert as has been stated by other sources." (Maggelet and Oskins, *Broken Arrow Vol. 1*).

May 22, 1957, Kirtland AFB, New Mexico

On May 22 1957, at 10:30 a.m. a B-36 took off from Biggs Air Force Base, El Paso, Texas. It was ferrying a MK-17, weighing 42,000 pounds, the largest weapon in our nuclear inventory. It was going to Kirtland Air Force Base, New Mexico, where the bomb would be demilitarized at the adjacent Sandia Labs. There were only two hundred MK-17 bombs made, and the 24 foot long weapon was so big and heavy that only the B-36 could carry it. At a yield of 10 to 15 megatons, it was the most powerful weapon in our nuclear stockpile at the time. As B-47 and B-52 bombers came into the Air Force inventory, the slower B-36 soon became obsolete. And as the phase out of the B-36 began, so did the big bombs it carried. There was no other bomber big enough. The 95th Bomb Wing of Biggs Air Force Base at El Paso, Texas, began to prep for shipment the MK-17s it had on base. They were all going to the Sandia Labs, for 'retirement'.

One hour and twenty minutes after take-off, the B-36 was approaching Kirtland for landing and was flying the downwind leg for Runway 26, the west runway. A crewman went back to the bomb bay to remove the locking pin from the release mechanism. That was the procedure before any take-off or landing with this extremely heavy weapon to allow an emergency jettison if necessary. But before the pin could be removed, the bomb dropped from the rack, tore off the bomb bay doors, and impacted the ground just .3 miles from the west side of the Sandia Base Reservation.

The 300 pounds of high explosive in the weapon detonated, completely destroying it and leaving a crater about 25 feet in diameter and 12 feet deep. Since the nuclear capsule was not inserted, there was no possibility of nuclear detonation. A small amount of radiation was cleaned up at the lip of the crater and there were no other health or safety problems. There were no injuries or further damages, other than the dry cleaning bill for the B-36 crewman who was in the bomb bay.

Unofficially, it was thought to have been caused by the flight jacket worn by one of the observers that caught in the cable that released the pin. Officially, the cause of this incident is unknown. It was ironic that the biggest bomb in the world almost fell directly on the birthplace of most US nuclear weapons.

July 28, 1957, Off Atlantic City, New Jersey

The first known aircraft Broken Arrow that did not involve a SAC aircraft. A C-124 from Dover Air Force Base, Delaware, was ferrying three nuclear weapons and one nuclear capsule, in ferry configuration, bound for Sidi Slimane Air Base, French Morroco. After experiencing loss of power in two engines, the aircraft jettisoned two of the weapons, turned back, and landed at Atlantic City, New Jersey. The depth of the water off the Jersey shore varies, but the weapons have never been recovered and requests for documents through the Freedom Of Information Act have not been acted upon. Chuck Hansen indicated the accident report said the impact area was 100 miles S/E of Naval Air Station Pomona, New Jersey; just outside the Delaware Bay east of Rehoboth Beach, Delaware; and south of

Wildwood and Cape May, New Jersey. One weapon was jettisoned 75 miles off the coast of New Jersey, the other 50 miles. The search lasted three months and the two weapons no weapon or debris was located. No public announcement was made at the time.

October 11, 1957. At Homestead AFB, Florida, a B-47, with a Mark 6 nuclear weapon aboard was number one for takeoff when the tower called and advised that an outrigger tire appeared to be blown. This would be a situation that should immediately abort the mission. The tower for some reason must have been trying to be diplomatic and the aircraft was told to hold and Maintenance would check the tire. Inexplicably, a few seconds later, the aircraft started the takeoff roll and the pilot transmitted that he wanted to see how it felt while rolling. At the six-thousand-foot mark on the runway the tower advised the aircraft that the outrigger landing gear was now on fire. The aircraft reduced power then reapplied power in a futile attempt to get off the ground, taking off with the nose high, right wing low. The airplane could not fly in this stall condition. It crashed and burned for four hours. All four crewmen died. The weapon and a nuclear capsule and its carrying case known as the "birdcage" were recovered intact.

January 31, 1958, Sidi Slimane, French Morocco

The first known Broken Arrow involving a complete weapons system (i.e., with the nuclear capsule inserted or the sealed-pit version), that happened on foreign soil. The base was Sidi Slimane, one of the most active SAC bases overseas. The weapon was the Mark 36 thermonuclear bomb, larger in all respects compared to the Goldsboro bomb. The Mark 36 was 12.5 feet long, 17,500 pounds, and 9 megatons. The Goldsboro Mark 39 was about a foot shorter, one third the weight, and 3.8 megatons. This Mark 36 was aboard a B-47 making a simulated alert takeoff, which involved taxing down the runway at 30 knots in full strike configuration. A wheel casing on the rear landing gear failed, dropping the aircraft down, and the combined weight of weapon and aircraft broke the aircraft in two. Spilt fuel ignited and both the aircraft and weapon caught fire. The firemen were allotted ten minutes time to fight the fire based on the explosive potential, then were pulled back and the aircraft and weapon were allowed to burn for seven hours. The entire base was evacuated and radiation monitors were set up two miles downwind. As the fire was subsiding on its own the monitors were pulled closer. After the area finally cooled off, the EOD team used jackhammers to break out and remove components of the weapon imbedded in the 8,000 pounds of slag. The rest of the aircraft wreckage and contaminated material was buried beside the runway. Then a large portion of the runway itself was dug up and buried deep in place.

Savannah River, February 5, 1958

A B-47 with a MK 15 aboard was involved in a mid-air collision with an F-86 that was doing a simulated radar night interception near Savannah, Georgia. Here's the way Lt. Col Derek Duke told Fred Dungan in the book, "Chasing Loose Nukes," about the F-86 pilot: (used by permission.)

"Meanwhile, both wings having been torn from the F-86 jet fighter, Lieutenant Clarence Stewart (from the 444th Fighter Interceptor Squadron, Charleston, SC) has ejected from 35,000 feet.

The ejection system is designed to open his parachute at about 12,000 feet, but Stewart's automatically opens right away and suffers a 22 mile long, very cold ride east across the Savannah River where he comes down in a small clearing in the largest swamp in South Carolina. Amazingly, his sole injury was a severe case of frostbitten fingers suffered during the six mile parachute to earth under sub-zero atmospheric conditions.

"According to the Air Force accident report, the temperature is 35 degrees, just above freezing. Stewart wraps himself in his parachute, inflates his life raft, turns it upside down and lays down beneath it. Several hours later, he hears an aircraft and fires the flare gun in his survival kit. His frozen fingers fumble and the flare barely misses his toes before tearing into the parachute. Evidently, the pilot of the plane failed to spot this interesting fiasco, but it does set a dog to barking. In due course forest ranger Andy Walker comes along, convinced he's caught a poacher. By sunrise Stewart is wrapped in a blanket next to a wood stove, drinking some fine, untaxed South Carolina whiskey."

Meanwhile, above the Savannah River, the B-47 crew had their hands full. They had serious damage to the right wing and the Number Six engine was dangling down at a 45 degree angle. After contacting SAC, they jettisoned the MK-15 bomb somewhere along the southern shore of Little Tybee Island, just east of Savannah, Georgia. Landing a B-47 with an engine dangling just inches above the runway is a feat deserving of a Distinguished Flying Cross, which the pilot, Colonel Howard Richardson received. The lost bomb has never been located, despite the long-going efforts of Lieutenant Colonel Derek Duke, USAF (Retired.)

March 11, 1958, Florence, North Carolina

The problem of a very heavy weapon requiring a release pin removal, like the B-36 at Kirtland, continued. Take what happened on the morning of March 11, 1958, at Hunter Air Force Base outside Savannah, Georgia. A bomb-loading crew was hurrying through the process of loading a thirty-kiloton MK-6 nuclear weapon onto a B-47, scheduled for a flight to England. The B-47 did not have a way to dump fuel, so the crews needed a fast way of safely jettisoning the heavy, unarmed bomb in the event of power loss on takeoff. The co-pilot, who sat in tandem right behind the pilot, had this job. He would remotely remove the steel safety pin from the bomb's release mechanism for takeoff, in order to allow an emergency jettison if needed. He would then replace the pin when safely airborne.

That morning, the bomb-loading team had a tight safety pin, and they encouraged its seating by use of a big hammer. The unofficial name for the person who would do this type of technical operation was 'hammer mechanic.' They did not have time to go through the engage/disengage cycle of removing the pin. They were running out of time, and if they missed the stated finish bomb-load time, they would lose points. Someone decided to skip the engage/disengage cycle check.

Before takeoff, co-pilot Captain Charles Woodruff removed the pin as required and they had an on-time takeoff. At five thousand feet, Captain Woodruff attempted to reengage the pin, but it would not insert. They could not continue the mission with the pin out. He tried many times but it just would not engage. Captain Earl Koehler, the pilot, instructed the navigator/bombardier, Captain Bruce Kulka, to go back to the bomb bay and try to "fix the problem." Captain Kulka removed his parachute in order to fit through the opening in the bomb bay. He crawled in the bomb bay, but since he was a small man, could not see over the roundness of the huge bomb, five feet wide and ten feet long, filling the bomb bay. He jumped up, spreading his body over the bomb, feeling around in the tight space above the bomb. What he grabbed was the bomb release cable.

The bomb, with Captain Kulka spread out on top, released and fell a few inches against the bomb bay doors. Stunned, Kulka grabbed hold of something in the airplane. The doors flipped open under the weight of the 7,600-pound bomb and it fell toward Mars Bluff, South Carolina, with Captain Kulka hanging on to the aircraft as if his life depended on it. It did.

The crew circled and watched a shock wave radiate out from the concussion when the high explosives in the bomb went off. It did not have the nuclear capsule installed, so there was no danger of nuclear detonation. It did have several hundred pounds of high explosive.

They could not raise Hunter Air Force Base on the radio, so they had to ask—broadcasting in the clear—that nearby Florence Municipal Airport call the Air Force base at Savannah and tell them they had just dropped a nuclear weapon accidentally. No, they did not know the telephone number. Florence had to get Information to call collect. While they circled to burn off fuel, ponder their career choices, and watch the three thousand foot plume of smoke, the only thing Captain Kulka would say was, "We would be better off going to Brazil."

He became known in the Air Force as the Nuclear Navigator.

After Vietnam, he would move to Thailand, and not answer his mail.

No one on the ground was killed but three were injured. Walter Gregg, the farmer who was bombed, settled with the Air Force for $54,000, for the total destruction of the house, contents, trucks, and "six to fourteen" chickens. The Air Force couldn't determine the exact number of chickens because they were vaporized.

The bomb crater is still there, on Crater Road, at Mars Bluff, South Carolina just east of Florence. Chunks of the bomb are on display in the Florence Museum.

November 4, 1958, Dyess Air Force Base, Abilene, Texas. Here's a case where a pilot and co-pilot knew they were in serious trouble and that they were probably going to crash while they were still on the ground, and could do nothing about it. A B-47 with either a Mark 15 or Mark 39 was standing ready for an alert test requiring takeoff. At 9:20 a.m. the Klaxon sounded, and the aircraft taxied out and began the takeoff roll using the jet assisted take-off bottles, which are a group of rockets temporarily affixed to the aircraft, to assist in proving take-off power. When they are ignited, they burn until the solid fuel in them is exhausted. There is no way to turn them off. After take-off the metal bottles are used up and they are jettisoned. While accelerating down the runway, something went wrong this time—at least one of the bottles malfunctioned and kicked sideways, its flames hitting the fuselage like a giant blowtorch. The aircraft caught fire on takeoff, shedding multiple pieces of aircraft and burning furiously. The only thing they could possibly do was gain as much altitude as possible and try to bail out. The aircraft commander made a conscious effort to get the airplane to five hundred feet in altitude so the downward ejecting navigator could bail out. Any lower, and the navigator's ejection seat would slam him into the terrain before his parachute could open. The navigator ejected successfully while the pilot was turning thirty degrees in an effort to avoid populated areas. The three crewmen with ejection seats safely bailed out, but the crew chief without an ejection seat died in the crash. The resulting detonation from high explosive created a crater thirty-five feet wide and six feet deep.

The accident investigation findings are intriguing. The primary cause was a defective weld in the ATO bottle and the rack that held it on to the aircraft. That finding was expected and to the point. What is intriguing are the thirteen other deficiencies, which, while not considered direct causes, did require immediate attention. First of all, the pilot and co-pilot did not have their helmet chin straps fastened. Then, they forgot to pull the bailout bottle "Green Apple" prior to bailout or during their (approximately two second) descent. The Green Apple supplies oxygen in high altitude bailouts. Maybe the fact that they were looking at the ground at the time might have distracted them somewhat. "Item (H): The SAC Manual 400-8 and SAC Manual 50-5 Requirements for Mobility Gear and Arctic Clothing, on USCM and EWO Missions, is not realistic in light of space available in the B-47 cockpit." Those are just three of the thirteen items requiring immediate attention and corrective action. And every one of these thirteen items would soon be part of every pre-mission briefing in SAC, and eventually be part of every ORI, Operational Readiness Inspection.

This points out one thing, not the pettiness of accident investigation findings, because there is absolutely nothing petty about any aircraft accident, but the intense concentration on *every single thing* that could possibly go wrong in an operation where *every single thing is extremely important*. And the mission of SAC required and insisted that intense concentration be given to *every single thing*.

November 26, 1958. Chennault Air Force Base, Louisiana.

On the day before Thanksgiving, a B-47 was being given a pre-flight inspection when the JATO bottles fired up for some still unknown reason and pushed the unmanned aircraft off the runway and into a tow vehicle. The aircraft, its unknown type weapon and the tow vehicle were destroyed by fire. There were no injuries. Since a "Tritium Bottle" was mentioned in the Airmunitions letter, it was a "sealed pit" weapon, probably a MK-15 or a MK-39 like the one at Goldsboro.

January 18, 1959. Pacific Base

An F-100 loaded with weapon, probably a MK-7 without the capsule installed, was destroyed by fire on the ground during a practice alert. No injuries.

July 6, 1959, Barksdale AFB, Louisiana

A C124 Globemaster ferrying one unknown type weapon to Little Rock Air Force Base, Arkansas, developed engine trouble on take-off, and crashed off the end of the runway and burned. No deaths or injuries. "One hundred eighty feet of barbed wire and six fence posts were torn up by the crash."

September 25, 1959, Whidbey Island, Washington

A US Navy flying boat, a Martin P-5 aircraft, crashed into Puget Sound after a series of mechanical problems. It was carrying an unarmed nuclear anti-submarine weapon that was not recovered. All ten crew members were rescued after twelve hours in life rafts by the Coast Guard Cutter Yacona, from Station Astoria, Oregon.

October 14, 1959, Hardinsberg, Kentucky

A B-52 F, from Columbus Air Force Base, Mississippi, collided with a KC-135 refueling tanker at night, and crashed near Hadinsberg, Kentucky, with a loss of five of the nine member bomber crew. There were two tankers and two B-52s involved in the mission, and due to radar malfunctions, changes to the refueling sequence were made. The Instructor Pilot was in the right seat, taking the place of the co-pilot. "Approximately at the contact position, it became apparent to the pilot and the Instructor Pilot that the speed differential was too great and the B-52 would overrun the tanker. Indicated airspeed was approximately five knots above the briefed refueling speed. Realizing he was going to overrun the B-52 pilot retarded the throttles to idle." As the two aircraft were separating a crunching sound was heard, all interior lights in the B-52 went out, and there was a rapid decompression. As the aircraft rolled to the left, the Instructor Pilot grabbed the controls, but they were not connected to anything. The Instructor Pilot called out the bailout command, but realized he was getting no sidetone on the interphone. The Abandon lights did not illuminate. The Instructor Pilot ejected first, then the pilot, then the EWO, in that order. The navigator's ejection seat would not work, so the radar navigator ejected next. Those were the only four to survive. The co-pilot, who was in the IP seat (Lt. Mattocks' position), did not get out of the aircraft. Neither did the navigator, whose seat did not work, or the "extra" on the lower deck. The tail gunner did not jettison the turret and was found nearby. The four crewmen on the tanker did not survive. The two "sealed pit" weapons were recovered. They were not identified by type. At least one of the EOD team that worked on this accident also worked on the Goldsboro crash 15 months later.

A final note was added to the History of Flight by the Commander of the 2705th Airmunitions Wing:

"Successful accomplishment of this mission can be attributed to the fact that the Explosive Ordnance Disposal personnel called to the scene were well trained, able to apply their training to an actual situation and well disciplined in the requirement for teamwork."

June 7, 1960 BOMARC Missile, McGuire Air Force Base, New Jersey

This was the last Broken Arrow in the decade before the crash of *Keep 19,* and it has the connection of having the same Explosive Ordnance Commander, Lieutenant Jack ReVelle. The BOMARC missile is an anti-aircraft, nuclear tipped missile, armed with a 7 to 10 kiloton warhead. This is not quite as big as the 13 KT Hiroshima bomb, but it is worrisome that the BOMARC's effective range is about

363

as far as either New York city or Washington, DC, from McGuire. Imagine a nuclear weapon, almost as big as the Hiroshima bomb, detonating over either of those cities in order to destroy an enemy aircraft. The missiles were in their 'ready storage' facility, which forms their launching pad at McGuire Air Force Base. The roof of the shelter slides back, and it is ready to launch within two minutes of getting the signal from the SAGE program. The missile in Shelter 204 caught fire after a high pressure helium tank exploded and broke open the missile's fuel tank. A fire resulted and the W-40 warhead was consumed by fire, although the conventional explosive did not detonate. The biggest danger was the huge amount of contaminated water runoff from the fire fighting. After the fire was put out, EOD personnel could not enter the shelter for several days due to the high radiation readings, and had to wait until paint was was applied inside and outside the structure with brooms. The runoff was contained and the area was sealed off with concrete. In 2002, a two-mile long connecting road was paved to the Lakehurst Naval Air Station, the closest railhead, and the concrete was dug up and trucked out. From there, the radioactive material was sent to an unknown western site for proper disposal. The area at McGuire remains closed to the public.

APPENDIX J.
PRESIDENTIAL MEMO ON "FURTHERANCE"

EYES ONLY FOR THE PRESIDENT

NOTES OF THE PRESIDENT'S MEETING WITH:

SECRETARY OF DEFENSE CLARK CLIFFORD WALT ROSTOW
SECRETARY OF STATE DEAN RUSK GEORGE CHRISTIAN
GENERAL EARLE WHEELER TOM JOHNSON
ADMIRAL THOMAS MOORER
GENERAL LEONARD CHAPMAN JOINING THE MEETING:
GENERAL JOHN McCONNELL
GENERAL BRUCE PALMER SENATOR RICHARD RUSSELL
BROMLEY SMITH GENERAL WILLIAM WESTMORE-
  LAND

OCTOBER 14, 1968
Cabinet Room
1:40 pm

SECRETARY CLIFFORD: There have been instructions issued on authority to release nuclear weapons in the event the President has been killed or cannot be found. This is to prevent a breakdown in the chain of command.

The project's code-name is "Futherance."

We recommend three major changes:

(1) Under the former orders, a full nuclear response against both the Soviet Union and China was ordered if we were attacked. Under the change, the response could go to either country -- not both. There could be a small-scale or accidental attack. We do not recommend full attack at all times. This would permit a limited response.

(2) Instructions on the response to a conventional attack would be conventional, not nuclear as is now in the plan.

(3) There was only one document of instructions beforehand. Now there would be two documents.

We all recommend this.

WALT ROSTOW: We think it is an essential change. This was dangerous. We recommend going forward.

GENERAL WHEELER: All the Joint Chiefs of Staff and commanders have been consulted. We recommend approval.

GENERAL McCONNELL: I concur, Sir.

GENERAL CHAPMAN: I concur.

ADMIRAL MOORER: I concur.

# # #

EYES ONLY FOR THE PRESIDENT

ACKNOWLEDGMENTS

Billy Reeves, one of the eyewitnesses who was closest to the main crash site, shared a great deal of information about Faro, North Carolina. He has been a great help in providing contacts and stories; and his off-road, guided tour of the area was especially appreciated. Billy worked tirelessly in setting up the Memorial Dinner at the Faro Volunteer Fire Station on February 8, 2011, which was fifty years, two weeks, and one mile away from the crash. Attending the dinner were: Pilot, Adam Mattocks and his wife Anne, from Jacksonville, NC; Jack ReVelle, PhD, the explosive ordnance disposal (EOD) officer who deactivated the bombs, from Orange, California; Cliff Nelson, Web site originator; Earl Lancaster, who was assistant fire chief at the time, with his wife, Mary; Rudolph Tyndall, whose parent's house was right beside the main crash; C.T. Davis, who owned the land where the main crash occurred; Brent Tyndall, who farms the land; Roy Heidicker, PhD, and Historian of the 4th Fighter Wing at Seymour Johnson Air Force Base; Doc was there with his wife, Judine; Wilton Strickland, retired USAF Lt. Col, with wife Alice; Guy Altizer, former nuclear weapons technician at SJAFB; Andy Tulloch, son of the B-52 aircraft commander; and Randy Gray, Chief of the Faro VFD, host of the dinner, along with current members of the Faro and Eureka Volunteer Fire Stations. A meeting like that has never occurred before, and, (we thought,) would probably never happen again. But it would, in July 2012.

B-52 Veterans: Lieutenant Colonel Wilton Strickland, a retired B-52 radar navigator, was stationed at Robins AFB in Georgia, and Kincheloe AFB in Michigan, where he was the wing standardization officer. That is the official who decided who was qualified to be on the front line as a SAC radar navigator in the Cold War. He was also at Seymour Johnson AFB, where he was the chief of the Bombing and Navigation Division about ten years after the crash of *Keep 19*. He was awarded three Distinguished Flying Crosses, three Meritorious Service Medals, five Air Medals, and he retired in 1981 with twenty-two years of active service. Wilton provided me with the keen insight of a professional airman and has been a true mentor.

Mike Meager, was a B-52 crew chief at Ramey, Anderson, and Mather Air Force Bases in the 1960s and 1970s. He was awarded the SAC Master Crew Chief Badge in 1971. He was very helpful in my understanding of the innards of the G Model.

Pete Seberger, former BUF pilot, retired flight instructor, and organic farmer, gave assistance through a labyrinth of aircraft procedures. His learning experiences helped me understand some things about flying the B-52. He made the definition of compression stalls an explicit experience—frightening, but very explicit.

Lieutenant Colonel Earl (Mac) McGill, USAF (Retired,) a formal aircraft commander and instructor pilot in both the B-47 and B-52. He is author of the excellent books, *Jet Age Man, SAC B-47 and B-52 Operations in the Early Cold War,* and *Black Tuesday Over Namsi.*

I have really appreciated the help and guidance of all these gentlemen throughout this project.

BUF was the original derisive term used by fighter pilots in Vietnam who were upset by their losses in Operation Rolling Thunder, and the "F" was definitely not for the word "Fellow." In 1965 a second "F" was added by correspondents for a sanitized version: "Fat Fellow," making the acronym BUFF, for Big Ugly Fat Fellow.

Walter Scott Tulloch died May 9, 1992 in San Diego, California, and I made contact with his widow, Betty. She told me that he retired from the Air Force as Lieutenant Colonel in 1967. Betty provided the Colonel's actual Pilot Individual Flight Records: his flight log covering his entire flying career. He had 6,740 hours of flying time, 458 of in it in combat. To put this in perspective, he had twice as many combat hours that I had to have in total flying time to qualify for a commercial pilot's license. Scott Tulloch's military records were sealed, possibly at the officer's request. Betty Tulloch, as next of kin, requested and received the records as per regulations. Betty has shared those records with me.

A fire in 1973 damaged a large area of the Records Center in St. Louis destroying the records of some surnames, among them the officer records of Major Richards. A helpful archives technician called me with his available enlisted data. The Center has no record at all for Lieutenant Bill Wilson apparently due to the 1973 fire at the Record Center.

Four students at the University of North Carolina at Chapel Hill started a Web site as part of a class requirement. The site team leader,

Cliff Nelson, had interviewed several interesting people, such as Ralph Lapp, Daniel Ellsberg, and Chuck Hansen.

Over the subsequent fifty years since the Goldsboro incident different people using the Freedom Of Information Act (FOIA), have obtained various pieces of information and thus some key government reports were now being released. Some of the reports have redacted words or lines, which means portions are blacked out, but they still made for intriguing reading. I began to assemble the bits and pieces and began to dig into the details of the crash. A thirty-day road trip around the western part of the country included places like the SAC Museum in Ashland, Nebraska; STRATCOM (Strategic Command), formerly SAC headquarters in Omaha; the B-52 museum sites in Denver, Colorado, and Big Springs, Texas; and Los Alamos and Santa Fe, New Mexico, where the Manhattan Project was formed. My wife and I also visited three specific grave sites along the way.

Adam Mattocks accredits his survival to one source: the prayers of all his kinfolk to God for his safety. Adam and his wife Anne are enjoying their children, their eleven grandchildren, and their five great-grandchildren in North Carolina. He is the only remaining survivor of *Keep 19*. The photograph of Adam as a very young student pilot was one of only two of the period. All other photos were lost in a home fire in the 1970s.

Some of the information on nuclear bombs came from the book *Broken Arrow: The Declassified History of U.S. Nuclear Weapons Accidents* (2007), by Jim Oskins and Mike Maggelet, two retired experts in this field. They were both very helpful via e-mail discussions and challenged me on several points, resulting in much further research.

When they did not feel comfortable discussing certain declassified but still sensitive data, they steered me to other available published sources. They never comment on classified material. Some historical events were recorded on the DVD *No Easy Days*, produced by Doug Keeney. Doug is a Cold War historian, and provided me with copies of various documents, things that he obtained over the years through the Freedom Of Information Act. He searched his personal files to find a critical missing page of the history of the 1961 accident. Information on actions during the in-flight emergency came from the unredacted (not blacked out) portions of the *AF Form 14, History of Flight*. That document was provided by Louie Alley, the FOIA Manager at Kirtland AFB, New Mexico. Thanks also to Staff Sergeant Michael Thomas of the Egress section of the 372 TRS Training Squadron, Seymour Johnson Air Force Base, for his detailed analysis of ejection seats and survival kits. Information and access to the G model B-52 at STRATCOM HQ was provided by Ryan Hansen of the Fifty-fifth Wing Public Affairs Office, Offutt, Air Force Base, Nebraska. STRATCOM formerly was known as Headquarters, SAC. Archivist Marilyn Chang of the Wings Over The Rockies Air & Space Museum, Denver, Colorado, was very helpful in letting me review large boxes of B-52 flight manuals and other data from the museum's reference files. The museum is on the site of the original Air Force Academy in Denver when it was first started. Rebecca Sims, Director of the Thomas S. Power Library, at Offutt Air Force Base, Nebraska, and Nichole Dittrich, of the Special Collections Research Center, Syracuse University Library, were very helpful in defining the early years of General Thomas Power.

Family member Jerry Barnish provided information and photographs of his cousin, Frank, the gunner. Bob Shelton provided the only clear photo of a young Gene Shelton, in arctic gear. And thanks goes to Bernetiae Reed for photographing, taping, and guiding me through the fine art of recording for digital posterity; also thanks to Lt. Col. Derek Duke who encouraged me to keep digging; to Jerry Smith, of the T. A. Loving Company of Goldsboro, whose company did the digging at Site Two; Goldsboro historian Evan Keel, and Goldsboro attorney Tommy Jarrett.

I found a very important clue in a report by the EOD team commander for the Goldsboro event. That was among several declassified 1961 documents that were provided by Jim Oskins. The signature on the report was that of First Lieutenant Jack B. ReVelle. Jack has been exceptionally supportive and helpful in providing an indispensable first person account of the locations, recovery, and safing of the two thermonuclear devices. Goldsboro was his second Broken Arrow. The first was the 1960 Bomarc explosion and fire in storage at McGuire AFB, New Jersey. He later participated in twenty-five nuclear tests at Christmas Island and was involved in government work in Washington, D.C. He is extremely knowledgable and I am honored to count Jack ReVelle as a friend.

Special thanks goes to my wife, Judy, who put up with me while I chased the details. Also for putting up with me in general for the past fifty years.

Also, thanks to two other people: Bob Claxton, for the necessary fact checks, gut checks and all-round guidance and support. Information also came from another friend, John Crowder, who helped find the mysterious centerline of the Nahunta Swamp. He works in biology and environmental science and, fortunately for all of us, he is not so well known for his work in the field of 'the coefficient of retrograde phase specificity in Cholmondely's Grillage Factor.'

NOTES AND SOURCES

Prologue

MK-39. Chuck Hansen, the late civilian nuclear historian, was the first to identify the bomb in the trees as the MK-39 based on published photographs. According to SAC weapons archive, the MK-39 would produce a minimum of two and a maximum of four megatons. The bombs at Goldsboro turned out to be 3.8 megatons each, according to information given to Dr. Jack ReVelle at the time.

Notes to Chapter 1. The Crew and Their Plane

Launch On Warning: The Development of U.S. Capabilities 1959-1979. Found at National Security Council Study, 14 July 1960, *"U.S. Policy on Continental Defense,"* at the National Security Archive, George Washington University website www.gwu.edu

"NUDETS (nuclear detection system), from Howard Simons, Washington Post, October 21, 1962.

Information on Readiness Crew R-10 came from *AF-14, Report of Aircraft Accident,* obtained through FOIA, October, 2010 by the author.

Information on SAC as specified command under JCS from: Wainstein, L. (project leader), "Study S-467, The Evolution of U.S. Strategic Command and Control and Warning 1945-1972 (U)," Study for the Institute for Defense Analyses International and Social Studies Division, Arlington, VA, June 1975, p. 155.

Notes on ability to spy on Russia: "*Spy In The Sky,*" American Experience, PBS.

Curtis LeMay was not so impressed with the U-2. From Thomas, *"Ike's Bluff,"* p. 148.

The goal of one third of SAC bombers to be on alert by the end of 1960: Keeney, *15 Minutes*, p. 205.

The Airplane

B-52 as workhorse: Details of the aircraft and it's performance came from Colonel Walter Boyne's Boeing *B-52- A Documentary History*, and the *History of the B-52 Stratofortress* at Web site globalsecurity.org.

Comments on two B-52s, in two hours monitoring 140,000 square miles of ocean surface came from *Air Force Print News, 50th Anniversary of B-52 Delivery,* June 30, 2005, by J. Manny Guendulay.

Details about SAC's performance in the Cuban Crisis came from *SAC Operations In The Cuban Crisis of 1962. Historical Study No. 90, Vol 1,* 48, and personal experience.

Ground alert, also known as pad alert, began in 1957, from Bob Harder's *Flying From the Black Hole,* p. 172.

Comparison of SAC to Standard Oil: came from Doug Keeney's *15 Minutes, General Curtis LeMay and the Countdown to Nuclear Annihilation,* 116.

The Men

Information on Major Tulloch came from his wife Betty, who was very appreciative of the people of Seymour Johnson and the community of the Faro and Wayne County area. When we had the commemorative dinner at the Faro Fire Department, she sent a gracious note of appreciation thanking the volunteer firemen, then and now, who put their lives on the line without pay to protect their community. That framed note now hangs in the Faro Volunteer Fire Department, the first emergency unit to respond to the 1961 crash.

Other information and photos comes from area newspapers, *AF-Form 14,* and the individual crew members' interviews and records obtained from the National Military Personnel Records Center in St. Louis.

Information on Anne and Adam Mattocks came from interviews in 2011, 2012, and 2013.

Frank Barnish's POW experience came from the Kassel Mission Web site: Kasselmission.com, and from Frank's cousin, Jerry Barnish. Major Tulloch indicated in his Narrative that Frank escaped from the POW camp, but I can find no official record of an escape.

The 445th Bomb Group took off from Tibenham, England as part of a massive bombing raid on Kassel, Germany, on Sept 27, 1944. This was the original bomb group of movie star Jimmy Steward, who was on active duty during the war and flew every type bomber the Air Corps. He was not on this mission. The 39 B-25 bombers of the 445th was separated from the rest of the others when the lead navigator made a grievous error and turned too soon at the initial point. They lost their fighter escort and found themselves 100 miles behind the rest of the division. They were attacked by over one hundred German FW-190 and ME-109 fighters, heavily armed with 20mm and 30mm cannons, who attacked in waves of three abreast.

The air battle lasted only a few minutes, and 31 of the 35 bombers were lost. Of the 235 men aboard, 117 were killed in action.

"This was the greatest single loss of any group in the 8th Air Force," wrote Roger Freeman, in *"The Mighty Eighth."*

In 1986, Lt. Col. John Woolnough, a former B-25 pilot and founder of the 8th Air Force Historical Society, wrote, "One would have thought that with a battle of this magnitude more would have been written about it. Aside from a paragraph in Roger Freeman's book, it received no other publicity. This is understandable, since this was a failed raid, and a big defeat for our side. It is possible that everyone was trying to forget it. But it was certainly not forgotten by those who survived it, nor by anyone who happened to be at Tibenham that day, nor by the next of kin of those who perished."

In August of 1990, groups of families of the former enemies came together and dedicated the German-American Memorial in Ludwigsau, Germany, on the site where the lead aircraft, piloted by Captain John Chilton, crashed. A total of 49 planes went down that day in 1944 within fifteen miles of each other. A total of 136 soldiers from both sides died.

Frank Barnish was one of the survivors.

Information on the tail guns increasing air speed came from Jesman Hales, former B-52 instructor pilot at Seymour Johnson, who also happened to live at Faro.

Bomb Drop

Details of the Radar Navigator's Duties came from interviews with Lt. Col. Wilton Strickland, USAF, (Retired).

Human Reliability

Information on the "two-man" policy came from personal experience and *One Minute to Midnight: Kennedy, Khrushchev, and Castro on the Brink of Nuclear War* by Michael Dobbs (excerpted below). (New York: Alfred A. Knopf, 2008.)

There were other military situations within the Department of Defense where the two-man policy was modified. That was the situation a year after the *Keep 19* crash, during the Cuban Missile Crisis. Here are two of many examples. The Commander In Chief of NORAD wanted F-106 fighter-intercepter jets loaded and dispersed to municipal airports all over the country, ready to intercept Soviet bombers and not be sitting ducks. The jets were equipped with 1.5-kiloton "Genie" air-to-air missiles, which was considered by some to be the "dumbest weapons system ever purchased." It wasn't designed to hit a target, just put it near an enemy aircraft, and it would blow up whatever was in the vicinity through the sheer force of the blast. Some of the F-106s went to municipal airports that lacked adequate nuclear storage facilities. One crash-landed with the nuclear missile aboard at Terre Haute, Indiana, when the drag chute failed to deploy.

Also during the Cuban Missile Crisis the 613th Tactical Fighter Squadron stationed in Incirlik, Turkey, was permitted to load thermonuclear bombs into F-100 Super Sabre fighter-bombers, which were not yet secured by electronic locking systems. The aircraft were responsible for covering thirty-seven high priority Soviet bloc targets, mostly East German airfields. The squadron commander later said, "Nuclear safety was so loose, it jars your imagination. In retrospect, there were some guys you wouldn't trust with a .22 rifle, much less a thermonuclear bomb."

Michael Dobbs, "One Minute To Midnight," p. 251.

There were situations during the Cuban crisis where nuclear bombers and their crews were dispersed to civilian airports around the country—and they lacked the cash to pay their room and board. Most of the time they bunked with the airport fire departments and ate where ever they could. The author is aware of one payroll officer, in civilian clothes and with a suitcase stuffed with cash, flying around commercially to different airports, dispensing per diem money. He also was equipped with a sidearm and credentials to the commercial flight crews about what he was carrying—the sidearm, not the money. The problem of how to announce an alert scramble to the crews if they were in civilian airport terminals was also handled. It was to be a public address announcement along the lines of, "Doctor Duckworth, call your office."

There were two single-seat aircraft Broken Arrows reported in the

1980 DOD release as reported by *Broken Arrows, Vol II* by Maggelet and Oskins (lulu.com 2010) Excerpt below.

In 1959, a parked F-100 at a "Pacific base" caught fire with a MK-7 attached.

In 1965, an A-4 with a MK-43 accidentally rolled off an elevator on the carrier USS Tikonderoga in the Pacific Ocean. The aircraft, weapon, and pilot were lost.

"Maintaining Peace Is Our Profession,"…as an mistake by a sign painter, came from *Winged Shield, Winged Sword*, p. 76.

"…going 390 knots with our hair on fire…" is an excerpt from *15 Minutes: General Curtis LeMay and the Countdown to Nuclear Annihilation* by Douglas Keeney. (New York: St. Martin's Press, 2011.)

Water use on B-52 takeoff came from an interview with Pete Seberger.

The description of spoiler controls came from interviews with BUFF Master Crew Chief Mike Meacher, in 2011.

The description of refueling techniques came from interviews with BUFF pilot Lt. Col. Earl McGill in 2013.

"The spoilers took some getting used to." The quote is excerpted from *"The Dawn of Discipline"* by Colonel Walter Boyne. *(Air & Space/Smithsonian, July 2009.)*

The story of Eisenhower and his first phone call came from Evan Thomas' *Ike's Bluff*, p. 5 .

Notes to Chapter 2. The Mission.

Details of the mission came from *AF Form 14, History of Flight, 24 Jan. 1961*, interviews with Adam Mattocks, and from Major Tulloch's narrative.

Information on Curtis LeMay came from the Strategic Air Command official Web site, http//www.StrategicAirCommand.com

Power's report on Japan, "…..Large fires observed…" from Moran's "The Day We Lost the H-Bomb," p. 12.

The Wright Field Training Exercise: From *Winged Shield, Winged Sword, A History of the United States Air Force,* Vol II, edited by Bernard Nalty

Information on LeMay's 'show-and-tell' at the Maxwell AFB Conference on 6 December, 1948, came from *Young's USAF Oral History Program,*

"…SAC alone…underwrite 100% destruction of DGZs…." from LeMay's *"The Operational Side of Air Offense.* p.104.

LeMay's 'bombs on base.' There are several sources for this policy, but the most interesting one is the general's own words, from Kohn and Harahan's interviews, *Strategic Air Warfare,* p. 92:

"I might add something about atomic bombs at the time: the military services didn't own a single one. These bombs were too horrible and too dangerous to entrust to the military. They were under lock and key of the Atomic Energy Commission. I didn't have them, and that worried me a little bit to start with. So I finally sent somebody to see the guy who had the key. We were guarding them, but we didn't own them...... I remember sending somebody out—I don't know whether it was Monty (Maj. Gen. John B. Montgomery) or somebody else—to have a talk with this guy with the key."

LeMay achieving bombs-on-base from Keeney's *"15 Minutes,"* p. 115.

Information on the Gaither Commission from Evan Thomas' *Ike's Bluff,* p. 274

"...looking into the abyss..." Harkin, *Councils of War*, p.116, as reported by Thomas, *Ike's Bluff,* p. 273.

Atlas probability of successful launch: Zero. Keeney, p. 239.

"...will (the missiles) work?" From *Strategic Air Warfare*, Interviews by Kohn and Harahan

The Bombers

The B-47

SAC B-47 inventory from 1,100 to none in 1966. From Wainstein, "Study S-467," p. 323.

"When it was first wheeled onstage, the B-47.........And when she had killed so many of us, we condemned her to an early grave." is from *Jet Age Man, SAC B-47 and B-52 Operations in the Early Cold War*, used by kind permission of Helion & Company and Lt. Col USAF (Ret.) Earl J. McGill.

The Air Force and Boeing learned from the hard lessons of the B-47. For starters, they learned that if you wanted a long range bomber, you should make enough room for at least six crew members, not the three on the B-47. Simply put, three men could not do the complex work that was required in a strategic bomber. Another lesson was that pilots needed to be side-by-side, not the tandem configuration of the B-47. While the pilot in front of the B-47 had an excellent view of his surroundings, the back-seat co-pilot had to deal with the visual distortion of the canopy reflections when making landings or refueling, particularly troubling when he had to look around the helmet of the man in front. He also could not observe the actions of the man in front, what he was doing. He had the dual controls and instruments of the front man, but could not readily observe some of his actions in the B-47. This was the biggest problem with tandem seating compared to side-by-side seating. In normal side-by-side seating they can visually double check each other. And in the world of checklists and complex machines, the checklist is golden. It is normal for the co-pilot to read a checklist item and the pilot would respond exactly as written on the printed card. The co-pilot could observe the pilot's actions and immediately correct any difference from what is written by repeating the correct response. And that was why Curtis LeMay told Boeing about the seating arrangement in the early developmental stage of the B-52, "Put the seats side-by-side and I'll buy a bunch of the damn things."

"The ICBMs were not designed to ride out a strike." Keeney, p. 174.

"...full pipeline philosophy" on communications from Wainstein's "Study S-467", p. 160

Other branches of the military wanted in on the alternate command post program. Wainstein's "Study S-467", p. 234

LeMay's surprise visits to wing commanders, from Warren Kozak's *LeMay*, p. 213.

The story of Helen LeMay being asked for ID is from *Winged Shield, Winged Sword*, p. 78.

TRAINING MISSIONS

Information on training missions: From HQ SAC paper *"Alert Operations and The Strategic Air Command, 1957-1991,"* dated 7 December 1991.

General Twining's answer that we have no airborne alert aircraft with nuclear weapons... from Kenney, p. 219.

Information on General Power's 1960 talk in New York about airborne alert and the "blank check," from the General's book, *Design for Survival,* p. 162.

"On 18 January, 1961, SAC finally obtained permission to publicly announce B-52 bombers were conducting airborne operations..... but as indoctrination training," from SAC Historical report, *Alert Operations,* 1957-1991, p. 8.

Notes on The Last Three Hours and Six Minutes of *Keep 19*.

Information about the accident came from interviews with Adam Mattocks and the *AF Form 14,* "Accident Report." All quotes by Major Tulloch are from his personal flight records, as loaned by his wife, Betty Tulloch in 2010, and from his personal narrative about the crash, which is attached as Appendix B. Mattocks' quotes and experiences came from personal interviews. (2010, 2011, and 2012.)

Information on refueling history and techniques came for interviews with members of the *Order of the Daedalians*, Kitty Hawk Flight, Seymour Johnson Air Force Base, Goldsboro, North Carolina, during a presentation by the author on May 12, 2011.

"... refuelings at the rate of 6.8 minutes every day." From the "Evolution of U.S. Strategic Command and Control and Warning," p. 169.

"...They were now having to use excessive trim." Is an excerpt from the *"Official Observer's Report."*

ARAC 58 radio was inoperative, fatigue crack, and repair depot info. Is an excerpt from *AF Form 14,* "Accident Report."

Information on "Fuel Gushers," came from the Global Security Web site, http//**www.GlobalSecurity.org/wmd/systems/b-52.htm**

"Fuel Clamp Failure." The Marman clamp was invented by Herbert Marx, better known as Zeppo, one of the original five Marx Brothers. He was in seven of the Marx Brothers movies, including *Monkey Business, Horse Feathers, and Duck Soup.* He was the founder of Marman Aerospace Products of Inglewood, California. This tidbit was found in column, "Oldies and Oddities: Zeppo's Gizmo," by N. D'Alto. (Air And Space Smithsonian Magazine of September, 2008).

It should be stated that it is not know what type fuel hose clamps were used on the *Keep 19* aircraft. But it is obvious that something very important failed in order to cause such a large fuel leak. Here is a discussion of fuel clamp history, as summarized by Global Security (http//www.GlobalSecurity.org):

> Fuel leaks, occurring in the B-52Fs and preceding B-52Gs, proved difficult to stop. The problem manifested itself from the start. Marman clamps, the flexible fuel couplets interconnecting fuel lines between tanks, broke down on several occasions during the first few weeks of B-52 operation. This caused fuel gushers that obviously created serious flying hazards. Blue Band, a September 1957 project, put new clamps (CF-14s) in all B-52s. Depot assistance field teams did the retrofit well, but Blue Band did not work. The CF-14 aluminum clamps soon showed signs of stress corrosion and were likely to fail after 100 days of service. Highly concerned, the Air Force and Boeing began replacing the aluminum clamps with a Boeing-developed stainless steel strap clamp, the CF-17. Hard Shell, a high-priority retrofit program, put CF-17 clamps in all in-service B-52s. Completed in January 1958, the Hard Shell retrofit was not a fool-proof solution.

Bailout procedures and details came from the USAF flight manual,

"Dash-One," and from personal conversations with B-52 crew members.

"This is an intercepting turn of 60° ... somewhat sharper than similar intercepting turns for civilian aircraft.".... This comment is based on an Air Traffic Controller's Table for final approach course interception. It states a recommended maximum interception angle of 20° if the distance to the approach gate is less than two miles, and 30° if two miles or more. The reason: the sharper the intercept turn, the steeper the banking of the aircraft which puts more stress on the wing.(Machado, p. 84). However, an approach turn of 60° is not at all considered unusual for a Boeing B-52. But with all the other damage to this airplane, this turn proved catastrophic.

"...the beast was rolling over on her back..." from Major Tulloch's narrative. (Appendix B)

"Mattocks and the simulator," and the bail out information came from Adam Mattocks.

Notes to Chapter 3. The Bail Out

Bill Wilson and Dick Rardin's accounts came from J. Sedgewick's article, "Bombs Over Goldsboro" from *This Month in North Carolina History*, UNC Libraries, North Carolina Collection.

Survival kit and life raft information came from personal interview with Staff Sergeant Michael Thomas of the Egress Section of the 371 TRS Training Squadron, Seymour Johnson Air Force Base, Goldsboro, North Carolina.

"....(Major Tulloch) hanging by his seat belt." This information came from his son, Scott Tulloch, in an interview. (December, 2010)

"...The lads were firing their seats and were safely away." This is an excerpt from Major Tulloch's narrative. (Appendix B)

"At base housing Betty Tulloch had been awakened..." came from interviews with Betty Tulloch. (2010, and 2011).

Mattock's escape: From the man himself.

Anne Mattock's story: From the lady herself.

It should be said that Adam Mattocks is the only known man who survived an intentional bail out from the upward hatch of a B-52 without an ejection seat. There was another man, Staff Sergeant Manuel Mieras, who was unintentionally sucked out the upward co-pilot's hatch when his B-52 from Biggs AFB, Texas, was struck by 'friendly fire' of a Sidewinder missile on 7 April 1961. It was accidentally fired by a New Mexico Air National Guard F-100. Sgt Mieras survived but lost a leg in the accident. (*Jet Age Man, p. 123*).

Notes on Chapter 4. The Crash Site.

Personal stories about the crash came from interviews with Billy Reeves, Earl and Mary Lancaster, Rudolph Tyndall, Evan Keel, C. T. Davis, and Morris Cruise, all were eyewitnesses.

"It was eerie as hell...." is a Eugene Price quote from Gary Hanauer's article "The Story Behind the Pentagon's Broken Arrow," (Mother Jones' Magazine, April, 1981.)

Information on the Elroy Fire Department experience came from interviews with historian Evan Keel.

The bomb on Shackelford Road on land owned by William H. Lane, was information from Jes Hales, Mr. Lane's son-in-law and a former B-52 pilot.

Information about the firemen at the scene and the H-43 B helicopter came from interviews with Fred Johnson, a retired fireman from the Nashville (TN) Metro Fire Department. He was an Air Force fireman at Seymour Johnson AFB who worked the crash of *Keep 19*.

"....procedures known as 'Moist Mop" is from *The Day We Lost the H-Bomb,* Barbara Moran (2009) and from *SAC Historical Study #109*, p. 288.

"....His wife's right side 'just burned and burned'" came from interview with Dick Manley, USAF, (Retired). 2011.

"Jack, I've got a real one for you," came from interviews with Dr. Jack B. ReVelle, (2011, 2012, 2013).

"....he played trombone," from The Orange County Register, Dec 27, 2012.

"....highlight was the mess tent at midnight..," came from an interview with Guy Altizer. (2011).

"...We've found the ARM/SAFE switch—and it's on ARM!" came from interviews with Dr. Jack B. ReVelle and Larry Lack.

Information on "General Loper's letter, of 23 Jan, 1961" came from Keeney's book, p. 246.

"X Personnel, and W-7", information came from the Government Document: "Seymour Johnson Air Force Base Accident, Goldsboro, N.C,. W-7-2717, 20 Feb, 1961" by T. T. Scolman and D. R. Smith.

"....the weapon fish-tailed in the earth..." came from ReVelle interviews.

DOD Directive 5230.16, "right to lie," Maggelet and Oskins, *Broken Arrow*.

Information on fire fighting and recovery details came from interviews with Fred Johnson, 2012.

"93,000 cubic yards of dirt was removed" came from brochure of company history, T. A. Loving Company, Goldsboro, NC.

"....many 55 gallon metal drums were buried there..." came from an interview with Rudolph Tyndall, Feb, 2011.

Information on the government's easement of Bomb Site Two came from an interview with C.T. Davis, Feb 8, 2011.

Information on the missing Secondary at Faro and other general information came from Chuck Hansen, who has done extensive research on this and many other nuclear accidents and events. His research papers were donated to the National Security Archive at George Washington University, Washington, DC. He once said that he had been investigated many times by the FBI for possible security violations, but they always concluded that everything he reported had been properly declassified.

Goldsboro or Faro? The location of this Broken Arrow is identified both ways in this work. The Department of Defense used the name Goldsboro based on the easiest recognizable place. Faro is used for the accident site itself when local references are used.

(By the way, it's pronounced Fay-roe, not 'Pharaoh,' an Egyptian ruler.)

Notes on Chapter 5. The Chance of Nuclear Detonation

The Sandia Report is *The History of Nuclear Weapon Safety Devices (Report 98-1184C)*, by David Plummer and William H. Greenwood, of the Sandia National Laboratories, Albuquerque. Obtained through the FOIA by Scott Hardy, 2005.

McNamara's "ran through six or seven steps," and Hansen's "fully loaded pistol," from *The Swords of Armageddon*, by Chuck Hansen. As quoted in the *Greensboro Daily News*, 21 November 1981, p. A1.

McNamara quote on "....failure of two wires to cross...." Keeney's *15 Minutes*, p. 302.

Hansen's quote, "....The parachute-retarded weapon came closest to firing..." came from an e-mail on 21 November, 2000, from Chuck Hansen to Cliff Nelson, UNC Web site creator.

The Investigation

"....electrical solder melting" comment from Plummer and Greenwood. *History Of Nuclear Weapon Safety* (Sandia's NN 922015-99), p. 3.

How Big Were Those Goldsboro Bombs:

Thomas Power's description of damage from "one medium-sized hydrogen bomb," was from his book, *Design for Survival,* written with Albert A. Arnhym,, p. 34.

MK-39, Mod 2. This information is from the nuclear bomb chart found at the Strategic Air Command Web site:

(http://www.strategic-air-command.com/weapons/nuclear_bomb_chart.htm)

"The error of "..each bomb was twenty-four megatons,"is an excerpt from *Kill and Overkill: the Strategy of Annihilation.* (Basic Books, 1962), 127.

"Two hundred sixty times the Hiroshima bomb." Information on how that number was calculated came from the Strategic Air Command Web site, http://www.Strategic-Air-Command.com/weapons/nuclear_bombchart.htm. The Hiroshima *Little Boy* was between 12 and 18 kilotons. At 3.8 megatons, each MK-39 would be the equivalent factor of 211 to 317 Hiroshima bombs depending on which *Little Boy* figure used, or an average of 264.

But that calculation is different from the 1952 Operation Redwing test at Bikini. There, a 3.8 MT device was estimated to equal to...*"roughly two thousand times the size of the Hiroshima bomb."* Keeney, 159.

"...2.4 megatons would exceed the yield of all munitions..." Calculated by Chuck Hansen in *Swords of Armageddon*, based on the US Strategic Bombing Survey (1946), and Bulletin of Atomic Scientists, October 1979.

NOTE related to the 100 megaton Russian bomb, *Tzar Bomba*: There was a plan, scheduled for 1965, called Phase Three of DUSC, Deep Underground Support Center. It called for a hardened facility, 3,500 feet deep for protection against direct hits by 100-megaton weapons, able to accommodate up to 200 people. It was to be located in a deep mine shaft near Cripple Creek, CO, but the project was killed in 1963. (Wainstein, "Study S-467," p. 324). That was one year before the movie *Dr. Strangelove*, with its side story about a fictional 'mine shaft gap.'

What's In The Ground?

"Half life of Plutonium-239 is over 24,000 years…Uranium, four billion years." This information is from the Nuclear Weapons Archive. Also from Moran, p.145, and from Caldicott, p. 61.

NOTE on Declassified information about nuclear weapons is published by the Department of Energy Office of Declassification. Their report "RDD-7," from January 1, 2001, on page 55 of the 108 pages is the following:

"(Certain declassified facts include): t. Special nuclear materials masses: That about 6 kg plutonium is enough hypothetically to make one nuclear explosive device. (93-2)"

Followed by: "NOTE: The average masses of special nuclear materials in the US nuclear weapons or special nuclear materials masses in any specific weapon type remain classified."

In other words, hypothetically we can't tell you how much plutonium is in specific weapons, but here is the minimum it would take to detonate.

It should be again repeated that all previously classified material has gone through the official and sometimes lengthy declassification process.

The size of Secondary came from Dr. Jack ReVell who said he never knew what was in the Secondary, he did not have the need to know, just how to render it safe. But he described this Secondary as about 14" wide, 35" long, and weighing between 200 and 300 pounds.

Bomb Schematic, size, and shape of primary was described by Dr. Jack ReVelle, 2011.

"…Navy Captain "Deke" Parsons, who was in charge of the explosives research…" Deke Parsons would go on to become a Navy Rear Admiral, a member of the Atomic Energy Commission, and Assistant Chief of the Bureau of Ordnance. In between blowing up beer cans and becoming a rear admiral, he had another job: he armed a nuclear bomb on board another flight in 1945. The mission call sign was Dimples Eight Two. The aircraft itself was better known as the *Enola Gay*. From *The Final Storm, A Novel of the War in the Pacific*, by Jeff Shaara, Ballantine Books, p. 386, 442.

"…They finally solved it with the study of hydrodynamics…" is an excerpt from *Dark Sun. The Making of the Hydrogen Bomb*, by Richard Rhodes, 117.

"…MK-39 Secondary has an estimated total weight of at least two hundred pounds…." came from interviews with Dr. Jack ReVelle.

"…value of material in secondary as $237,000." from Luedecke's letter to General Betts, May 17, 1961.

"…Teller found it would take a shock wave…." *Dark Sun: The Making of the Hydrogen Bomb,* by Richard Rhodes, p. 472.

"…the Christy Core was 6.2 kilograms." Ibid.

"…body burden of plutonium was set at 0.65 micrograms." This is an excerpt from Dr. George Voltz, "The Health Risk of Plutonium." (Los Alamos Science, Nov 26, 2000), and a quote from the Chalk River Conferences in Ontario, Canada (1949-1953).

"…(plutonium) as the most dangerous substance on earth, by Glen Seaborg," Caldicott, p. 61.

"….(permissible amount of plutonium) compared to a grain of salt in four cubic yards of soil," is from *The Day We Lost the H-Bomb by Barbara Moran,* 145.

"…22 milligrams if injected, 88 if inhaled," is an excerpt from "The Health Risk of Plutonium," by Dr. George Voelz. (Los Alamos Science, November 26, 2000). All information about the mortality rate and half-life data of Plutonium-239 came from this article.

Materials in Secondary, came from *Broken Arrow, Vol I,* by Maggelet & Oskins, 295-96.

Contents of Thule Secondary scattered, ibid,. 233.

Information about the Thule Monitor end of carrying nuclear weapons aboard alert aircraft. "No publicity is to be given this fact," and General Marshall Garth, memo, January 22, 1968. came from *15 Minutes* by Doug Keeney, 318.

"...I would like to know from him when he went." Ibid, 253.

A note on the Thule Monitor and seat cushions: The end of SAC's airborne alert program came about from the use of seat cushions, several of them, on the Thule Monitor, on January 21, 1968. The third pilot was taking a rest on the lower deck at the *IN* position, the same uncomfortable seat where Major Richards sat on *Keep 19*. The flight was long and cold, making loops around Thule, Greenland. The third pilot piled up three or four cushions, and turned the heat up. At some point he moved, a cushion slipped behind a metal box, made contact with the heater box, and later started to smoke. An on-board fire resulted, which led to the crash of the B-52 G, a Broken Arrow, an international incident over radiation from the crash, and the abrupt end of carrying armed nukes on alert aircraft.

See "Crested Ice, The Thule Accident," *SAC Historical Study # 113*, 23 April, 1969.

Bunker Hill Broken Arrow Secondary, "When it was moved, it ignited again." Ibid, 300.

Plutonium "rides 'on grains of sand": came from Human Health Fact Sheet, August, 2005, Argonne National Laboratory, EVS.

"We are not sure what is under the soil," is an excerpt from G.D Gearina's article. "Area 61," (*The Raleigh News and Observer*, August 11, 2002.)

The Dusenbury quote on "....still an open question as to whether a hazard exists," came from an 2000 e-mail from Dusenbury to Cliff Nelson of ibiblio.org/bomb/full-story.

Notes to Chapter 6. The Cause of the Crash

"... C-130 carrying 452 people ... " is an excerpt from Carl Posey's article "50 Years of Hercules," *Air & Space/Smithsonian Magazine*, Sept 1, 2004.

Wet wing fuel tank information and other wing data, including production dates of G-Model came from the Global Security Web site retrieved from (www.GlobalSecurity.org/wmd/systems/b-52g).

Other information came from the web site, *Boeing B-52G Stratofortress,* by Joe Baugher. This gives the serial number of every G Model, and has excellent reference sources.

Information on the VGH recorder from an interview with Lt. Col. Wilton Strickland, USAF (Ret.), on March 9, 2013.

The comment from Mr. Michael Lombardi, Boeing Historical Research came from an e-mail to author (1 Feb, 2011).

The Weather Factor from Accident Report AF Form 14, and *Inauguration Weather: The Case of Kennedy*, by Jason Samenow, found at: http://voices.washingtonpost.com/capitalweathergang/2009/01/inauguration_weather_the_case.html

The Officer Effectiveness Reports (OERs) of Major Tulloch were provided by Betty Tulloch, who filed her request as Next Of Kin, through the National Military Records Center, St. Louis, Missouri.

Part II. AFTERMATH

Notes on Chapter 7. The Tension of Command

"....If small fires to break out in paint lockers," Keeney, *15 Minutes*, 224.

Information on SIOP-62 came from: *The Creation of SIOP-62*, National Security Archive Electronic Briefing Book No. 130, posted on The National Security Archive, George Washington University at www.gwu.edu The Nuclear Vault, posted July 13, 2004.

"....SIOP written by SAC staff officers selected ...." Nalty, *Winged Shield, Winged Sword*, p.91.

"....Strategic Target Planning staff of 269": from *The Creation of SIOP-62*, National Security Archive Electronic Briefing Book No. 130, p. 191.

A side incident about Polaris nuclear missile submarines from *Study S-467, The Evolution of U.S. Strategic Command and Control and Warning*: In early 1959 General Power asked the Joint Chief of Staff to recommend to the Secretary of Defense that the Navy's new Polaris subs be assigned to SAC "in view of its strategic capabilities." Power also sent a similar letter directly to the Secretary of Defense McElroy. Air Force Headquarters was not impressed. General Power's letter was returned unopened to him, with an attached comment by Air Force Chief of Staff General Thomas D. White that "General Power should readdress his letter to the Secretary of Defense *thru* JCS and should put it in the straight official form in my opinion."

Ike's response to SIOP, from Rosenberg's *The Origin Of Overkill,* p. 104.

"...designed either in retaliation or in a 'preemptive measure.'" from Kaplan, W*izards of Armageddon.*p. 269.

Fred Kaplan and David Rosenberg, both Ph.D. candidates at the time, utilized a brief window of opportunity during the summer of 1981, when some of the secrets of SIOP became available to the public. Provisions had been put in place that would allow reviews of documents that were over twenty years old, and Admiral Arleigh Burke's papers at the US Navy Operational Archives met that time frame and were declassified. He had been the Chief of Naval Operations and played a key roll in creating SIOP-62. Kaplan and Rosenberg had to work fast however, because the Operational Archives were very restrictive on what could be copied using photocopying machines. Kaplan and Rosenberg had to make handwritten notes. A year later, in 1982, the window closed when the Navy reclassified the Burke files. The Defense Department has over-classified and inconsistently released information at various times about SIOP.

SIOP-62 ...."amounting to over nine tons of paperwork..." from *Power's Design for Survival*, p.190.

Information on sorties, POL, and the initiation of airborne alert from *Strategic Air Command Historical Study No. 79, The SAC Alert Program,* 1956-1959.

"Dropkick." From: Steven Schwartz, ed. al. "The Football, U.S. Nuclear Weapons Cost Study Project", in *Atomic Audit: the Costs and Consequences of U.S. Nuclear Weapons Since 1940,* 1998.

"...the blank check from Congress." from Power's *Design for Survival*, p. 162.

Notes on Chapter 8. The Worst Case

Critical Factor Number One: Weapons Systems

Manpower figures came from *Winged Shield, Winged Sword*, p. 76

The deliveries of B-52s is from Eden (ed.) "Boeing B-52 Stratofortress," *Encyclopedia of Modern Military Aircraft*, p. 71.

Weapons doubling in two years, from *Bulletin of Atomic Scientists*, Nov, 1989, p. 53

"ICBMs building by the score..." from Thomas' *Ike's Bluff*, p. 386.

"...693 ICBMs in silos..." Keeney's *15 Minutes,* p. 295.

Ike's calling the weapon numbers, "crazy," etc... Thomas' *Ike's Bluff*, p. 395.

Critical Factor Number Two: State of Communications

McNamara's report to the president that communications were vulnerable, from: *Wainstein, "Study S-467,"* a p. 227-81.

"... EMP not fully known until Starfish Prime in 1962," from *"Nuclear Electromagnetic Pulse,"*, at www.Futurescience.com

NORAD communications break due to fire in telephone junction box, from Keeney, p. 257.

NOTE: The study of EMP continues today, at Sandia Labs, Kirtland AFB, New Mexico. The largest purely wood and glue structure in the world, made with no nails, screws, or metal in any form, large enough to support a B-52, is at Lat 35.029904, Lon 106.557681. Photo available as "Odd Facility Two: The Trestle, http://www.thelivingmoon.com/45jack_files/03files/Kirtland_AFB_Overview.html

The critical need for a bomb detection alarm system was pointed out in the National Security Council's *U.S. Policy on Continental Defense NSC Action No. 1842-d*, dated July 14, 1960.

Information on the bomb detection alarm from *Western Union Technical Brochure,* January, 1963, p. 34.

"SIOP execution as streamlined as possible," from: Wainstein, "*Study S-467,*" p. 283-84.

Information on DEW, SAGE, BMEWS, and the weaknesses of communication systems from *A Historical Study of Strategic Connectivity 1950-1981*, JCS, July, 1983.

Section on "SIOP execution and....spasm war," from Wainstein's, "*Study S-467,*" p. 284.

Critical Factor Number Three: Willingness of the Commanders

"...If we do this overflight right..." is an excerpt from the RAND Report, as quoted by Paul Lahmar, "Stranger Than Strangelove, A General's Foray In the Nuclear Zone."

"I don't care. It's my policy. That's what I'm going to do." from Thomas' *Ike's Bluff,* p. 272, and Kaplan's *Wizzards of Armageddon,* p. 143. Also Rhodes' *Dark Sun,* p. 568.

NOTE: Thomas Power's mission in life: Deterrence. From *Design for Survival,* no specific reference page number, just the entire book. He had submitted the original manuscript to the Department of Defense in April 1959, but found from a notice in the *Army-Navy-Air Force Journal* in August that the Secretary of Defense had "banned" the publication. A few days later, The Secretary of Defense, Neil McElroy, said he had denied final clearance because he considered it inappropriate for an officer in Power's position to publish a book about his area of responsibility while on active duty. General Power retired November 30, 1964 and the book shows two publication dates: 1964 and 1965.

Thomas Power was the last US general without a post-secondary education, as reported by Budiansky, in *Air Power: The Men, Machines, and ideas that Revolutionized War, From Kitty Hawk to Gulf War II.* (p. 366).

"Power, the son of Iris immigrants........" (Hubbell, p. 72-73.)

General Thomas Power died December 10, 1970, and is buried in Arlington National Cemetery.

"Document of Predelegation" is labeled "INSTRUCTIONS FOR THE EXPENDITURE OF NUCLEAR WEAPONS IN ACCORDANCE WITH THE PRESIDENTIAL AUTHORIZATION DATED MAY 22, 1967, NLC MR Case No. 89-341. Declassified April 4, 2001. Retrieved from The National Security Archive at GWU, Nuclear Vault. Found at:

http://www.gwu.edu/~nsarchiv/nukevault/ebb406/docs/Doc%20 5A%20Furtherance%20document%20Oct%201968.pdf

The five authorizing commanders having predelegated authority in 1961 to launch the nuclear force were: The Commander in Chief, Atlantic; The U.S. Commander in Chief, Europe; The Commander in Chief, Pacific; The Commander in Chief, Strategic Air Command; and The Commander in Chief, U. S. Naval Forces.

Instructions For The Expenditure of Nuclear Weapons, p. 23.

Information on McGeorge Bundy's dire warning to JFK about a "commander starting thermonuclear holocaust on his own initiative," from National Security Files, Memoranda NSC Meetings, No. 475. Kennedy Library.

"...The US should strike first...." from the Kennedy Library, National Security Files, Chester V. Clifton Series.

"...The whole idea is to kill the bastards..."is an excerpt from the RAND Report, as reported by William Kaufman of the Boston Globe, 2008.

"....Power as colder, and scarier..." from Evan Thomas, *Ike's Bluff*, 398.

"....Power was mean, cruel..not stable..." Horace Wade, *Dark Sun* Rhodes, 571.

FURTHERANCE... from the National Security Archives Briefing Book No. 406, George Washington University website www.gwu.edu

"Stating in 1961....lockout provision of PALs..." from Hansen's Swords of Armageddon, Vol VIII, p. 44.

The Grave Sites. I saw the name Frank Barnish in a relative's inquiry on a Web page concerning World War II POWs. The Web page was about the Kassel Mission, a little known US Air Corps disaster in World War II. By using an online search for military grave sites, I found that Sergeant Barnish was buried in the National Cemetery in Raleigh, which was visited. I shared all this information with his relatives in Massachusetts, who were most appreciative, especially for the information as to how he died. His cousin, Jerry Barnish, provided photographs.

Frank's gravestone shows him as being a member of the 97th Bomb Wing, which was never assigned to Seymour Johnson as far as I can find. The *Accident Report (AF Form 14)* shows all crew members as being assigned to the 4241st Strategic Wing, Eighth Air Force. The gravestones of the other two casualties show the 4241st. The reason the Ninety-seventh is listed on Frank's stone is unclear.

There were incorrect rumors among the local people at Faro as to how Major Shelton died. One was that he survived the explosion but froze to death in a tree before he was discovered. The tree was three miles due east of the crash site, but over four miles away by road and in a swamp. Another rumor said he died by being impaled on the tree. Another that he 'bled out' at the base of a tree. Those rumors are false. The fact is, his helmet came off when his parachute inflated and he was jerked against the ejection seat, causing instant fatal head injuries. There is no mention on his death certificate about freezing or of injuries from being impaled by a tree. Major Shelton is buried at Fort Sam Houston National Cemetery in San Antonio. He enlisted in 1940, at Fort Sam Houston, on the same grounds, at a place less than a mile from where he is buried.

I could find no national military cemetery record for Major Richards. After searching for a civilian gravesite of Major Eugene Richards from Toocon, Georgia (the way it was spelled in several newspaper accounts), and with no results, I finally realized there is no *Toocon, Georgia*. However, there is a *Toccoa* Georgia. My sister-in-law, Linda, a retired librarian from Kalamazoo, Michigan, always told me, "If you want to find out something, ask a librarian." So I did, and quickly found Major Richards' gravesite in Toccoa, thanks to Michelle Austin of the Toccoa-Stephens County Library and Judy Thomason of the Acree-Davis Funeral Home in Toccoa.

In 2010 we visited the grave sites of the three casualties in Raleigh, San Antonio, and Toccoa. Remembrances were left at each site: a small stone from a North Carolina river, a tiny garland of green pine needles, and a SAC emblem from the SAC museum near Omaha, Nebraska. The stone for the endurance of Nature, the green pine needles for the fragility of life, and the SAC emblem in honor of their service.

Notes to Chapter 9. After Goldsboro

"….ARM/SAFE switch controlled by Radar/Navigator…." is an excerpt from the "Plumber/Greenwood Report" (Sandia Report 98-1184C.

The example of the Mylar capacitor as weak link in a fireset came from *Building the Bombs,* by Charles Loeber, p. 154.

"…Kennedy, shocked by the close call at Goldsboro…ordered PALs." Moran, *The Day We Lost The H-Bomb,* p.147.

"…PALS not used until early in the Kennedy era" Rhodes, p. 568.

"…first PALs as electromechanical locks," from Arming and Fuzing: Techniques & Equipment, found at http://cryptome.org/nuke-fuze.htm retrieved July 2009.

"…Turkish enlisted man with unloaded sidearm," Thomas, *Ike's Bluff*, p. 293.

Two Examples of Mistakes:

October 24, 1962, Volk Field, Wisconsin. "…an interesting event." came from Dobbs, *One Minute To Midnight,* p. 132.

"…..June 3 and 6, 1980. An alarm indicating a massive Soviet missile attack.." is an excerpt from Shaun Gregory's *The Hidden Cost of*

Deterrence: Nuclear Weapons Accidents, (Brassey's UK, London, 1990), 178.

Information on the official summary of the Yuba City Broken Arrow came from *Broken Arrow Vol I,* by Maggelet & Oskins,173, and from *Jet Age Man,* by Earl McGill, 130.

Information on 'go pills' came from:

Go Pills: A War On Drugs?

U.S. pilots stay up taking 'uppers.' Toronto Star, and

Air Force Print News Today.

See Bibliography under *Go,* Walker, and Woodring.

"Whitman's 'jolly pills,'..."*Eisenhower's Heart Attack,* by C.G. Lasby

The use of Dexedrine during Head Start tests. (Keeney, *15 Minutes,* p 218.)

Description of DEFCON:

There are five stages of Defense Readiness Condition, or DEFCON:

DEFCON 5 is the lowest stage, normal peacetime readiness.

DEFCON 4 is the next stage, calling for increased intelligence watch and strengthened security.

DEFCON 3: A very serious event has happened or may happen. This level has been used only three times: The 1962 Cuban Missile Crisis, the 1973 Yom Kippur War, and September 11, 2001.

DEFCON 2: The next step to nuclear war. This step has only been used one time—the Cuban Missile Crisis, the closest the world has ever been to nuclear war. The author heard a comment by a high ranking officer of a B-58 wing at this time. He commented that "his guys were at DEFCON One Point Nine…. sitting in the aircraft, on the ramp, waiting for the 'bust out.'"

DEFCON 1: Maximum force readiness. War is likely. This level has never been implemented. Note that this is not "total nuclear war" as depicted in several movies. DEFCON is a defense condition, not offense.

"Safe Passage," (Keeney, *15 Minutes*, 219).

"…making the Faro site 'safe'…." is an excerpt from the "*1-24-61-Goldsboro, North Carolina Accident #21,*" from the Los Alamos National Laboratory Archives and History Programs, obtained by Paul Dotson, (Declassified report 6/18/04.)

"….and the hole be filled in and forgotten." TWX message dated 4 April, 1961, from Los Alamos Scientific Laboratory to Atomic Energy Commission.

PART III. DEBRIEF

Notes on Chapter 10, Comparisons with Chernobyl and Fukushima

Information on the Chernobyl half-dome came from the article "New Tomb For An Old Disaster," *(Popular Mechanics,* May, 2011)

Information on the Chernobyl roof collapse in 2013 from: BBC News, at http://www.bbc.co.uk/news/world-europe-21449760

"…cost of Chernobyl to be about $235 billion," is from Forbes.com report dated March 17, 2011, based on an article by Mikka Pineda.

"….Browns Ferry….worst nuclear accident until Three Mile Island.." is an excerpt from the article, "The Fire at the Browns Ferry Nuclear Power Station," by David Dinsmore Comey, excerpted from *Not Man Apart.* (Friends of the Earth, 1976).

"…probability of (first) major accident within proscribed intervals…." Memorandum for US Nuclear Regulatory Commissioner Bradford, from David Rubinstein, March 9. 1979.

The Far Future

"….Fukushima Daiichi would mean millions of new cancers…" is an excerpt for the article *"Unsafe At Any Dose,* by Helen Caldicott, MD. (*The New York Times,* May 1, 2011). Used by kind permission of Dr. Caldicott.

In addition to the concerns of cancers from the Fukushima nuclear disaster is one that is more visible: the huge amount of debris now being delivered to the beaches of the west coasts of the United States and Canada. It is estimated to be over twenty million tons, and is both floating and semi-submerged. It is an unprecedented nuclear, biological and chemical (NBC) contamination event. The phrase NBC is also attached to the type of defense clothing associated with Broken Arrows. But war planners never had to contend with a mountain of debris made up of millions of tons of biological waste from everything from pig farms, untreated sludge from septic systems, and tennis shoes. The tennis shoes are still tied, some with human foot bones still inside, all that is left after the six thousand mile journey by way of The Great Gyre, the network of ocean currents. We can now add to the flotsam large numbers of invasive species of various sea creatures, never before seen here, riding along on whatever arrives.

The Death of the Pacific Ocean, by Yoichi Shimatsu, Dec 16, 2011.

Information about Thermo-Lag, and the Davis-Besse nuclear plant came from the article, "Nuclear Agency Beset By Lapses," by Tom Zeller, Jr. (*The New York Times*, May 8, 2011).

Information about the Davis-Besse pressure vessel corrosion came from Helen Caldicott's *Nuclear Power Is Not The Answer,* p. 81.

Miscellaneous Notes:

BOMARC Broken Arrow at McGuire Air Force Base/SAGE:

The command and control system for BOMARC was the biggest and best anti-aircraft defense system in the world—for a very brief period of time. Some critics said it was also the most dangerous to us. SAGE stood for Semi-Automatic Ground Environment. It was designed for defense against swarms of Soviet bombers coming in, hopefully over the Atlantic, where the BOMARCs could reach out 200 miles and safely destroy them before they made landfall. Because once over our cities, the 7 kiloton warhead would probably be as devastating to the cities as BOMARC was supposed to protect. SAGE depended on Soviet bombers staying together in a cluster so one nuclear blast could take out everything in the area. SAGE also has several unique distinctions: it cost more than the Manhattan Project, it was the largest physical computer ever built (and thus probably ever will be built), and became obsolete the same year it became operational, 1963. The computer took up a half acre of floor space, weighed 275 tons, required 150 operators, and had 55,000 vacuum tubes. It had the nickname Clyde, and became obsolete when ICBMs came into being as the primary threat. Source: http://www.globalsecurity.org/wmd/systems/sage.

Seymour Johnson Air Force Base is the only Air Force Base in the world named after a Navy aviator. The man Seymour Johnson was a Goldsboro native who died in a plane crash in 1940, and Seymour Johnson Field was named after him. It was closed after the war and reopened in 1956 as a Tactical Air Command Air Force base. Two years later, the Strategic Air Command came to Seymour Johnson in the form of the 4241st Strategic Wing, the unit of *Keep 19*. In 1963, it was re-designated the 68th Bomb Wing, and utilized B-52 bombers and KC-135 tankers. The SAC Wing was on base for twenty-four years from 1958 to 1982, when the wing was deactivated. The Strategic Air Command was inactivated on 1 June 1992. Today, the base is home of the Fourth Fighter Wing.

NOTE ON REFUELING TECHNIQUES. There were actually three basic inflight refueling techniques, each involving a tanker aircraft flying ahead and above the receiving aircraft. The earliest, and probably most exciting method, developed by Alan Cobham of Great Britain, had the crew of the tanker aircraft shoot a hose from a harpoon-like device across the wing of the trailing aircraft. Once the hose was caught on a hook, it was reeled in and attached to an interior fuel tank. The second method, called the probe and drogue system had the tanker trail out a hose with a cone-shaped receptacle called a drogue. The receiver aircraft, equipped with a nozzle-shaped probe, flew it into the drogue and the fuel flowed into the receiving aircraft's interior fuel tanks. The third method, the flying boom, was devised by Brig. Gen. Clearence S. Irvine (SAC), Brig. Gen. Mark E. Bradley (Air Material Command), and Cliff Leissy (The Boeing Airplane Company). From *Strategic Air Warfare*, Office of Air Force History, 1988.

Captain Taylor Valentine and his EOD team at Seymour Johnson Air Force Base invited Jack ReVelle and me to visit them in their Place Of Business. They were kind enough to give us a tour of the EOD shop on base. To hear these young warriors talk to a man who deactivated two thermonuclear bombs a few miles away and fifty years ago was an amazing event, and thanks to Doc Heidicker, Wing Historian, for setting it up. Those fellows at Seymour Johnson have some really ugly looking toys in their inner sanctum, some collected the hard way. Captain Taylor Valentine is today's counterpart of Lieutenant Jack ReVelle, fifty years later. A photo of this historic event is below. Our sincere thanks to all those young men and women for their service to our country.

EOD Team at Seymour Johnson Air Force Base, Goldsboro, North Carolina, with Dr. Jack ReVelle, 2011.

Photo by author

BIBLIOGRAPHY

"B-52 History" (n.d.). T*he History of the B-52 Stratofortress*. Retrieved from:

http://www.globalsecurity.org/wmd/systems/b-52.htm

Boyne, Walter. *Boeing B-52—A Documentary History*. Washington, D.C.: Smithsonian Institution Press, 1981.

Boyne, Walter. "The Dawn of Discipline," *Air And Space Smithsonian* July, 2009.

Budiansky, Stephen. *Air Power: The Men, Machines, and Ideas That Revolutionized War, from Kitty Hawk to Gulf War II*, New York: Penguin Books, 2004.

Burr, William. "Instructions for the Expenditure of Nuclear Weapons In Accordance with the Presidential Authorization," May 22, 1959. National Security Archive, Washington, DC.

Caldicott, Helen. *Nuclear Power is Not the Answer*. New York: The New Press, 2006.

Caldicott, Helen. "Unsafe At Any Dose." *New York Times* May 1, 2011.

Clifton, C. "Memorandum of Conferences with President Kennedy." *National Security Files, Chester V. Clifton Series. Conferences with the President 3/61-9/61.* National Security Archives, George Washington University

"The Creation of SIOP-62," *National Security Archive Electronic Briefing Book No. 130* (National Security Archive, George Washington University) posted July 13, 2004.

D'Alto, Nick."Oldies and Oddities: Zeppo's Gizmo," *Air and Space Smithsonian,* Sept, 2008.

Dobbs, Michael. *One Minute to Midnight, Kennedy, Khrushchev, and Castro on the Brink of Nuclear War.* New York: Alfred A. Knopf, 2008.

Duke, Derek. *Chasing Loose Nukes, as Told to Fred Dungan.* Riverside, CA: Dungan Books, 2007.

Fine, Kenneth and Steve Herring. "The 50th Anniversary of the Bombs." *Goldsboro News-Argus* 23 Jan. 2011.

Gearino, Dan. "Area 61." *Raleigh News and Observer* August 11, 2002.

Glasston, Samuel and Philip J. Dolan, "The Effects of Nuclear Weapons, 3rd Ed." *U.S. Department of Defense and The Energy Research and Development Administration,* 1977.

Go Pills: A War On Drugs? As retrieved from NBC News.com, December 10, 2012.

Government Document. *OOAMA Airmunitions Letter No. 136-11*

56G, HQ, April 18, 1961. Ogden AMA, USAF, Hill Air Force Base, UT, as found in *"Broken Arrow"* by Maggelet and Oskins, pp. 153-161.

Government Document. *Restricted Data Declassification Decisions 1946 to the Present (RDD-7).* US Department of Energy Office of Declassification. Jan 1, 2001. Found at:

www.fas.org/sgp/othergov/doe/rdd-7.html #148.

Government Document. (Subject Deleted), TWX dated 1961 April 4, from Los Alamos Scientific Laboratory NM. TWX NR S-16. FOIA.

Gregory, Shaun, *The Hidden Cost of Deterrence: Nuclear Weapons Accidents.* Brassey's UK, London: 1990.

Guendulay, J. Manny, "50th Anniversary of B-52 Delivery." *Air Force Print News*, June 30, 2005.

"A Guide To Nuclear Weapons. "(n.d.). as retrieved from: Nuclear Weapons Archive,

http://nuclearweaponarchive.org/

Hanauer, Gary. "The Story Behind the Pentagon's Broken Arrow." *Mother Jones Magazine*, April, 1981.

Hansen, Chuck. *Swords of Armageddon.* CD-ROM. As retrieved from:

http://www.ibiblio.org/bomb

Hardy, Scott. "The Broken Arrow of Camelot: An Analysis of the

1961 B-52 Crash and Loss of the Nuclear Weapon in Faro, North Carolina." MA thesis, Eastern Carolina U, 2005.

Headquarters, Strategic Air Command, "The Strategic Air Command Operations in the Cuban Crisis of 1962." *Historical study no. 90*, Vol 1, FOIA.

———, "Strategic Air Command, the SAC Alert Program 1956, 1959." *Historical study no. 79.*

____, "Strategic Air Command, Alert Operations and the Strategic Air Command, 1957-1991." *Historical Study, 7 Dec 1991.*

Howard, Michael, ed al. *The Laws of War: Constraints of Warfare in the Western World.* New Haven: Yale University Press, 1994.

Hubbell, John G. "Tough Tommy Power—Our Deterrent-in-Chief," May 1964 issue of Reader's Digest.

"Human Health Fact Sheet, Plutonium"*Argonne National Laboratory, EVS.* August, 2005.

Joint Chiefs of Staff. *"A Historical Study of Strategic Connectivity, 1950-1981,"* Joint Chiefs of Staff Special Historical Study, July, 1982.

Kaplan, Fred. *The Wizards of Armageddon.* Stanford:Stanford University Press,1983.

"*The Kassel Mission, 27 September, 1944.*" As retrieved from The Kassel Mission Web site: http://www.kasselmission.com/society.htm

Keeney, D. (Producer), Youman, C. (Director). (2008) *No Easy*

Days: Snakes in the Cockpit [DVD], (Available from Avion Park, Jacksonville, FL)

Keeney, Doug. *15 Minutes: General Curtis LeMay and the Countdown to Nuclear Annihilation.* New York: St. Martin's Press, 2011.

Kohn, Richard H. et al, "Strategic Air Warfare. An interview With Generals Curtis E. LeMay, Leon W. Johnson, David A Burchinal, and Jack J. Catton." *Office of Air Force History,* Washington, D.C. 1988.

Kozak, Warren. *LeMay,* Washington D.C., 2009.

Lasby, Clarence. *Eisenhower's Heart Attack, How Ike Beat Heart Disease and Held on to the Presidency,* Lawrence: University Press of Kansas, 1997.

LeMay, Curtis E. "The Operational Side of Air Offense, B-60725," Remarks to USAF Advisory Board, Patrick Air Force Base, Florida, May 21, 1957. FOIA.

Loeber, Charles. *Building the Bombs: A History of the Nuclear Weapons Complex.* Albuquerque: Sandia National Laboratories, 2002.

Luedeck, A. "Analysis of the Safety Aspects of the [Deleted] Bombs Involved in B-52 Crash Near Goldsboro, North Carolina, SCDR 81-61," *Sandia Corporation,* as attached to letter dated March 27, 1961 to James T. Ramey, Executive Director, JCAE, USAEC. 1961, February. FOIA.

Luedeck, A. letter, "MLC Proposal Regarding Recovery of Atomic

Weapon Component," to Gen. A. W. Betts, Director of Military Application, May 17, 1961,

Machado, Rod. *Rod Machado's Instrument Pilot's Survival Manual.* Long Beach: The Aviation's Speakers Bureau, 1991.

Maggelet, Mike and Jim Oskins. *Broken Arrow Volume II, A Disclosure of Significant US, Soviet, and British Nuclear Weapon Incidents and Accidents, 1945-2009.* Raleigh: Lulu, 2010.

McGill, Earl. *SAC B-47 and B-52 Operations in the Early Cold War.* West Midlands, England: Helion & Company, 2012.

Meisler, H. "The Occurrence and Geochemistry of Salty Groundwater in the Northern Atlantic Coastal Plain." *US Geological Survey Professional Papers 1404-D.* Washington, DC: USCG, 1989 p. 51

Moran, Barbara. *The Day We Lost the H-Bomb.* New York: Random House, 2009.

National Security Files, "'Meetings and Memoranda Series,' NSC No. 475 Kennedy Library," Memorandum From the President's Assistant for National Security Affairs (Bundy) to President Kennedy, January 30, 1961, Washington

Nalty, Bernard. *Winged Shield, Winged Sword, a History of the United States Air Force, Vol II, 1950-1997.* Honolulu: University Press of the Pacific. 2003

Nelson, Cliff, et al. *"Broken Arrow: Goldsboro, NC...The Truth*

Behind North Carolina's Brush With Nuclear Disaster." www.ibibio.org/bomb

"New Tomb for Old Disaster." *Popular Mechanics Magazine.* May, 2011.

Nuclear Bomb Chart. (n.d.) as retrieved from:

http://www.strategic-air-command.com/weapons/nuclear_bomb_chart.htm

Ohmae, Kenichi. "World is Ignoring Most Important Lesson from Fukushima Nuclear Disaster." *Christian Science Monitor* April 5, 2012.

Oskins, Jim and Mike Maggelet. *Broken Arrow: The Declassified History of US Nuclear Weapons Accidents.* Raleigh: Lulu, 2007.

Pineda, Mikka. "Fukushima vs. Three Mile Island vs. Chernobyl." *Forbes.com.* March 17, 2011.

Posey, Carl. "50 Years of Hercules." *Smithsonian Air and Space Magazine* Sept 1, 2004

Plummer, David W., and William H. Greenwood. "The History of Nuclear Weapon Safety Devices." *Sandia National Laboratories, Surety Components and Instrumentation Center* Albuquerque, Oct. 1, 1998.

Power, Thomas, and Albert Arnhym. *Design for Survival.* New York: Coward-McCann, Inc. 1964.

Price, Eugene. "Board of Inquiry to Look into Crash." *Goldsboro News-Argus* January 25, 1961.

Reed, Thomas. *At the Abyss: An Insider's History of the Cold War.* New York: Bresido Press, 2004.

ReVelle, Jack. *"Explosive Ordinance Disposal Report of a Broken Arrow Near Goldsboro, North Carolina."* Wright-Patterson Air Force Base, Ohio. FOIA Mgr, Kirtland AFB, NM.

Rhodes, Richard. *Dark Sun: The Making of the Hydrogen Bomb.* New York: Simon and Schuster, 1995.

Rubinstein, David. "Nuclear Regulatory Commission, Memorandum for: Commissioner Bradford, Subject: Probabilities That The Next Major Accident Occurs Within Proscribed Intervals," March 9, 1979.

Scolman, T.T. and D.R. Smith, "Seymour Johnson Air Force Base Accident, Goldsboro,

N.C. W-7-2717," 20 Feb, 1961. FOIA. Including hand-written "Random Notes on Goldsboro," unsigned, stamped: "U S DOE Archives, RG 326, AEC Collection 1181, Box 1, 1/24/61." FOIA.

Sedgwick, Jessica. "January 1961, Bombs over Goldsboro. This Month in North Carolina History". *UNC Libraries, North Carolina Collection*, January, 1961.

Shaara, Jeff. *The Final Storm, a Novel of the War in the Pacific.* New York: Balentine, 2011.

Sharon, Keith. "When Two Nukes Crashed, He got the Call." and "In 1961, the Future Was in His Hands." *The Orange County Register (CA)* December 12 & 13, 2012.

Shimatsu, Yoichi. *"The Death of the Pacific Ocean, Fukushima Debris Soon to Hit American Shores."* Rense.com. Dec. 16, 2011.

Spear, Ross B. "Official Observer's Report, Air Force Accident, Goldsboro, NC, (Sanitized)", AEC/ALO 1961, Feb 16. FOIA

Simmons, Howard. "Scientist Sees U.S. Mania for A-Stockpilling." The Washington Post, October 21, 1962.

Schwartz, Steven, ed al. "The Football, U.S. Nuclear Weapons Cost Study Project", in *Atomic Audit: the Costs and Consequences of U.S. Nuclear Weapons Since 1940,* 1998. As retrieved from www.brookings.edu/about/projects/archive/nucweapons

Strickland, Wilton. *In the BUFF.* Goldsboro, NC: Strickland, 2003.

Thomas, Evan. *Ike's Bluff, President Eisenhower's Secret Battle to Save the World.* New York: Little, Brown and Company, 2012.

U.S. Nuclear Regulatory Commission, Memorandum for: Commissioner Bradford, From: David Rubinstein, Applied Statistics Branch, Subject: *Probabilities that the next major accident occurs within proscribed intervals,* March 9, 1979, p. 1. Found at:

http://www.greenpeace.org/usa/en/news-and-blogs/news/the-probability-of-a-nuclear-a/

United States Air Force: *"A F Form 14 Section K, History of flight, 24 Jan 61."* FOIA Mgr, Kirtland AFB, NM.

United States Air Force: *"A F Form 14, Report of Aircraft Accident, 24 Jan, 61."* FOIA Mgr, Kirtland AFB, NM.

Voltz, George. "The Health Risk of Plutonium." *Los Alamos Science* Nov 26, 2000

Wainstein, L. (project leader), "Study S-467, The Evolution of U.S. Strategic Command and Control and Warning 1945-1972 (U)," study for the Institute for Defense Analyses International and Social Studies Division,) Arlington, VA, June 1975, as found at:

http://www.gwu.edu/~nsarchiv/nukevault/ebb403/docs/Doc%20 2%20-%20strategic%20command%20and%20control—-%20 evolution%20of.pdf

Walker, W. "*U.S. Pilots Stay Up Taking 'Uppers.'*" *Toronto Star* August 1, 2001.

Western Union Technical Brochure, January, 1963

Woodring, J.C. "Air Force Scientists Battle Aviator Fatigue." *Air Force Print News Today* April 30, 2004.

"World Armaments and Disarmament," *Stockholm International Peace Research Yearbook. (1977),* MIT Press.

Young, D. (1985). USAF Oral History Program, Maxwell AFB, USAF Historical Research Center.

Yancy, Noel. *"Life-Death Story of Flight Told."* *Greensboro Daily News* Jan. 26, 1961.

Zeller, Tom. "Nuclear Agency Beset by Lapses." *New York Times* May 8, 2011

ABOUT THE AUTHOR

Joel Dobson is a former Air Force officer who was in the Strategic Air Command in the 1960s. He is now retired, and lives with his wife Judy, a former nurse, in Greensboro, North Carolina.

Web site: TheGoldsboroBrokenArrow.com

Made in the USA
Middletown, DE
06 June 2015